Law, Norms and Authority

LAW, NORMS AND AUTHORITY

George C. Christie

Duckworth

First published in 1982 by
Gerald Duckworth & Co. Ltd.
The Old Piano Factory
43 Gloucester Crescent, London NW1

ISBN 0 7156 1593 9 (cased)

British Library Cataloguing in Publication Data
Christie, George C.
  Law, norms and authority.
    1. Jurisprudence
    I. Title
    340'.1   K230
    ISBN 0-7156-1593-9

Printed in Great Britain by
Ebenezer Baylis and Son Ltd.
The Trinity Press, Worcester, and London

Contents

Part II: Consistency in Legal Reasoning

Part III: Authority, Legitimacy, and the Law

To the memory of my father
Custis Christie

Preface

The principal recurring issues in legal philosophy are how are legal decisions reached in a manner that is both objective and fair and how does law relate to political authority and the legitimacy of government. The first issue relates to the question of individual justice; the second is part of the great inquiry as to the nature of political justice. The central thesis of this book is that, in the long run, as much harm can be caused to the public's respect for the law by the exaggerated claims of legal philosophers who have idealised the law as by the most fervent critics of the western concept of law. For example, in pursuing the notion of 'right answers', legal philosophers, such as Ronald Dworkin, have assumed a degree of certainty about the law that cannot be supported by evidence obtained from the actual operation of a legal system. This variance between the claims of legal philosophers and actual experience can only eventually lead to public cynicism about law and the western ideal of the rule of law. Similarly exaggerated claims about the relationship of law and authority, particularly as to the dependence of authority upon law, are also made by many of the same legal philosophers. Again, experience does not support these claims. More important, these unsupportable claims distract attention from the very important contributions that law does make to the organisation of social effort.

This book will examine many of the concepts used by legal philosophers to make the claims that they do. These concepts include those of 'rule' and 'norm'; of 'consistency'; and the notion of 'legitimacy' as it relates both to authority in general and legal institutions in particular. Much in this book is critical. It should be kept in mind, however, that the criticism is directed towards those who, in their enthusiasm to defend the law, will only end by undermining its prestige. It should be apparent to any careful reader that the writer has a profound love for the law, his chosen vocation, and for its role in protecting human freedom and making civilised life possible. But, as with anything we love, we show our deepest respect by recognising its limitations and then adjusting the demands we make of it to its capabilities.

I thank my friends W. D. Davies, Mortimer Kadish, Chaim Perelman, George Roberts and E. Phillip Soper for their comments upon my manuscript. George Roberts' encouragement during the writing is particularly appreciated. Finally, I thank June Hubbard for her patience in typing the manuscript and in reading the proofs.

G.C.C.

Part I

The Normative Nature of Law

1. *Introduction*

It has become increasingly common among legal philosophers to consider law as having something to do with norms.[1] Individual laws are said to be norms and a legal system, whatever else may be said about it, is said to consist of a set or sets of norms. Looking at the matter from another point of view, it is said that law is a 'normative' discipline. The use of a terminology based on the word 'norm' and its derivatives has become so pervasive that it has even to a great extent superseded the term 'rule' in the discussions of legal philosophers. This part of the present study will examine the way in which the term 'norm' and its derivatives are used in legal philosophy and why it is that laws are called norms and legal systems are considered to be sets of legal norms. It will be shown that, in any rigorous sense of the term 'norm', there is very little about the law that is normative or appropriately described in the language of norms. A great deal of confusion can be avoided by recognising this fact. Channelling legal philosophy into a study of norms can, for example, have the unfortunate consequence of turning questions about the binding quality of law into logical questions; that is, into questions about the logical structure of normative language. Valuable time and energy are thus diverted away from the difficult but necessary examination of how human beings actually react to the social regulation imposed by a legal order. It will be submitted that, if any features of the law can usefully be

[1] See, e.g., H. Kelsen, *The Pure Theory of Law* (2d ed. M. Knight transl. 1967) (hereafter *Pure Theory*); *General Theory of Law and State* (A. Wedberg transl. 1945) (hereafter *General Theory*); J. Raz, *The Concept of a Legal System* (1970) (hereafter *Concept of a Legal System*); A. Ross, *On Law and Justice* (1958) (hereafter *Law and Justice*). See also R. Sartorius *Individual Conduct and Social Norms*, 53-9 (1975); A. Cullison, 'Logical Analysis of Legal Doctrine: The Normative Structure of Positive Law', 53 *Iowa L. Rev.* 1209 (1968).

described as normative, it is such basic postulates as the requirement
of consistency in judicial decision-making. It is this requirement of
consistency that gives to the law much of its rigour. A model of how
consistency is actually achieved in legal argument will be presented in
Part II of this book. In Part III, we shall explore the interrelationship
between the notion of 'oughtness'—that is usually associated with law
and is often ascribed to the supposed normative nature of law—and
the concepts of authority and legitimacy. In Part IV, after the main
theses have been presented and discussed, some additional
observations are offered on the relationship between law and
authority.

2. *What is a norm?*

A norm is generally said to be a type of directive. It tells people more
than what they must do, under pain of compulsion; it tells them in a
sense what they also 'ought' to do. For this reason, as well as others,
norms are said to be more than 'commands', although they may have
their source in commands. The terminology of norms is also used in
preference to Austin and Bentham's terminology of commands
because the terminology of commands requires one to identify the
'source' of any particular command. The difficulties presented by the
attempts of both these thinkers to trace all law back to the commands
of a sovereign and by their heavy reliance on notions of 'tacit'
commands are well known.[2] It simply is not always possible to trace a
purported rule of law back to a specific commander without taking
enormous liberties in defining what it is to be a commander or to
issue commands. Besides, much of what is considered to be the law
hardly seems much like a command. The statute of wills is a
frequently given example. 'Norm', on the other hand, is a much
more amorphous term which is able to encompass a great deal more
of the law without seeming to require us to fall back on some unusual

---

[2] See H. L. A. Hart, *The Concept of Law* 18-76 (1961) (hereafter *Concept of Law*)
primarily devoted to a criticism of Austin; J. Raz, *Concept of a Legal System* 26-43, 50-9,
74-7. Raz is more critical of Austin than of Bentham. See also J. C. Gray, *The Nature
and Sources of the Law* 85-7 (rev. ed. 1921) (Austin's notion of tacit command); H. L. A.
Hart, 'Bentham on Legal Powers', 81 *Yale L.J.* 799 (1972), especially at 820-2. For
other citations to the criticisms of Austin's theory and for a discussion of Austin and,
to a lesser extent Bentham, see J. Stone, *Legal System and Lawyers' Reasoning* 63-97
(1964).

usages of language. In particular it seems to free us of the immediate necessity, when considering individual laws, of tracing their precise source. The terminology of norms can apparently accommodate, for example, Karl Olivecrona's view of the law as a set of 'Independent Imperatives'.[3]

3. *Why speak of 'norms' rather than of 'rules'?*

(i) *The problem of capturing the 'oughtness' features of law*

The terminology of 'norms' is very similar in usage to the terminology of 'rules'. Indeed, the terms 'rule' and 'norm' are sometimes used interchangeably. Why then should the terminology of norms come now to be preferred by many legal philosophers? Several reasons suggest themselves. First, the term 'rule' has a widely recognised descriptive sense as well as a normative one. For example, the statement, 'The rule is that one drinks red wine with meat', can mean that 'as a rule' (or 'generally') this is what people in fact do. These are the sorts of statements outside observers of a particular society are likely to make to convey the knowledge they have obtained from their observations. In this context, the otherwise inaccurate translation of '*exceptio probat regulam*' as the 'exception *proves* the rule' is not always inapposite. For, not only is it the case that one or even several contrary instances do not falsify a descriptive statement of what is the general practice, but also if one is describing a *general* practice—as opposed to an invariable practice which in practical affairs is a virtual impossibility—there must be exceptions.

The 'rule' about drinking red wine with meat can on the other hand be interpreted as stating what, according to the mores of epicures (or snobs), one *ought* to do. To those forced to associate with such people the 'rule' may thus have a prescriptive sense to the effect that they will be subject to social opprobrium for failing to abide by the rule. For the epicures (or snobs) themselves, however, the 'rule' may have the even stronger prescriptive sense—one might say the 'normative' sense—of stating what they think it is 'right' to do, not because of a fear of critical reactions but because the 'rule' is the 'right' one. Here, where 'rule' is used in a strong prescriptive sense,

---

[3] K. Olivecrona, *Law as Fact* 28-49 (1939); *Law as Fact* 115-34 (2d ed. 1971). Despite the common title these are really two different books. The later work is not even a revised edition, much less a second edition, of the former.

the more accurate translation of the Latin maxim as 'the exception *tests* the rule' seems more appropriate. Because the terminology of norms seems to be appropriate only in strongly prescriptive contexts—whoever heard of an exception *proving* a norm—it has become increasingly common among legal philosophers to use the terminology of norms in place of the ambiguous terminology of rules when they wish to focus on the stronger prescriptive aspects of law; that is, when they wish to focus on the 'internal' aspect of a legal order and how it functions in the minds of actual users of the law.

It is one of the confusing aspects of Joseph Raz's interesting work *The Concept of a Legal System* that he insists on using the terminology of norms, with its overtones of 'ought', but then rather curiously defines what he means by norms in terms that largely ignore the 'oughtness' quality generally associated with the concept of a 'norm'. Building on Hart's and Kelsen's work, Raz conceives of norms as (1) standards of evaluation that also (2) guide behaviour by prescribing certain courses of action. Norms are furthermore (3) created by human acts and (4) accompanied by standard reasons for compliance.[4] In the case of duty-imposing norms, these standard reasons are the reasonably likely critical reactions of others to the fact of non-conformity; in the case of power-conferring norms, the standard reasons are the ability to modify the behaviour of others by exercising the powers in question. In the case of *legal* norms that are of the duty-imposing sort, the 'function of critical reactions is taken over to a considerable extent by organised sanctions'.[5]

Raz admits that orders backed by threats are or can be norms.[6] This is because for him there is no necessary connection between the concept of norm and that of obligation. In the case of duty-imposing rules or norms, obligations only arise when 'the existence of the duty imposing rule depends on persisting and complex patterns of behaviour encompassing a large proportion of the members of the group in which the rule exists, and consisting of critical reactions which are regarded as legitimate by bystanders'.[7] One thus discovers whether a norm exists by looking for certain types of behaviour par- ticularly, in the case of duty-imposing laws, the critical reactions of

[4] *Concept of a Legal System* at 122-7, 147-66.
[5] Id. at 150.
[6] Ibid.
[7] Id. at 149.

others to the non-performance of the act required. Whether one has identified the existence of an obligation depends on the further empirical determination of the quality of this critical reaction. Despite the difficulty of making these empirical determinations, Raz nevertheless assumes that the existence of obligations, as thus defined, in the law 'can be taken for granted'.[8] This is because 'the existence of every law depends on the existence of the legal system to which it belongs, and the existence of legal systems depends on persistent and pervasive patterns of behaviour on the part of a large proportion of the population to which they apply'.[9]

Because of this heavy emphasis on behavioural features, especially the critical reactions of others, in describing what he means by a norm or by an obligation, Raz's discussion insufficiently captures the 'oughtness' quality which many people feel that norms, and particularly law as a species of norms, entail. Certainly, if the binding quality of supposed legal norms as well as the fact of these entities even being norms at all is determined, in the case of duty-imposing norms, by the critical reactions of others, the normative and also the obligatory quality of law would vary from one law to another. No two laws would be norms to the same degree nor would they be obligatory to the same degree.

It is doubtful, however, that Raz would wish to concede this. To avoid such a concession, Raz might thus be forced to abandon the attempt to tie normative terms such as 'norm', and even perhaps 'obligation', so closely to behavioural characteristics. Indeed, in his subsequent work Raz comes close to doing just this.[10] Although he there maintains that normative statements are statements about people's beliefs as to what ought to be done, such statements are not necessarily statements about what people believe they actually ought to do. Rather, they are ultimately statements about people's beliefs as to the membership of such statements in a normative system. In a move that Raz admits is reminiscent of Hans Kelsen's thesis,[11] Raz

[8] Id. at 150.

[9] Ibid. Although the point is not important for our present discussion, one should point out that it is not Raz's view that all laws are norms. On the contrary, he recognises that in a complex legal system there will be laws which are not norms. Cf. note 24, infra.

[10] J. Raz, *Practical Reason and Norms* (1975). In particular see his concluding section, id. at 170-7, entitled 'the normativity of law'.

[11] Id. at 'notes and references,' note 3, p. 189.

asserts that normative statements may or may not describe what people believe they ought to do or even what they do do. The only thing such statements necessarily state is that 'according to [the] law', or to whatever other normative system may be under consideration, this is what one ought to do.[12]

Integrating these views with Raz's earlier insistence on the use of behavioural criteria for recognising the existence of norms is, one supposes, still possible. The content of the purported norm and the possibility of its being a norm could be derived (partly? largely?) from experience but its ultimate normative quality, its actually being a norm, is posited by the speaker by means of a statement expressing the belief that the purported norm is part of a normative system. Whether the same construction is possible with regard to Raz's notion of 'obligation', with its particularly heavy emphasis on the 'critical reactions of others which are considered legitimate by bystanders', is another matter. While obligations are presumably imposed by norms, the fact of there being any such things as obligations would seem to require that the norms which impose them should be capable of generating the requisite critical reaction in others. As already noted, these reactions, as well as the reactions of the bystanders who assess the legitimacy of the initial reactions, will vary in intensity from person to person and often, even with regard to any particular individual, from one obligation to another. At any rate, it would seem that, under Raz's approach, neither an examination of the critical reactions of others nor the logical quality of belonging to a normative system nor even the conjunction of both these features is sufficient to explain and capture fully what Hart and others call the 'internalization' of law. This is the feature which makes it possible to speak of judges and other officials, who are largely immune from the imposition of sanctions and who are only indirectly affected by the critical reactions of others, as being somehow 'bound' by the law. Raz takes it for granted that a legal system is capable of generating these feelings of 'being bound',[13] these feelings of

---

[12] Id. at 176-7.

[13] Raz's 'The Institutional Nature of Law', 38 *Mod. L. Rev.* 489 (1975) on which parts of *Practical Reason and Norms* are based, is premised on the notion, of 'binding determinations' of legal norms and of being 'bound' by the law. This makes it all the more crucial that he should have made an effort to explain what it is, for a norm to be binding and what it is for a person to be 'bound' by the law. In this as in his other later work the notion of being 'bound' by the law seems to be almost a logical quality of law.

being under a 'legal obligation', but does not account for them in his theory of norms or, really, in any other way. And yet, it is precisely in order to account for the fact that law is more than a coercive order (and more than just an abstract logical construction) that many legal philosophers came, like Hart, to prefer the terminology of rules to that of 'commands' and now of norms to that of rules.[14]

(ii) *The problem of adequately identifying the law*

There is another possible reason why legal philosophers, even if only unconsciously, now seem to prefer the terminology of norms to that of rules. If law is not only a set of rules in the prescriptive sense but also a 'rule-directed' discipline, then it must be possible, at least theoretically, to state these rules completely so that one can ascertain from the formulation of the rules themselves the factual situations to which the rules apply.[15] Experienced lawyers would agree, however, that it is counterintuitive to contend that so-called 'rules of law' can be stated completely and that it is still more implausible to maintain that the statement of a rule can indicate completely the situations to which it is applicable. Even the American Law Institute's formulation of the Rule in *Shelley's Case* in the *Restatement of Property*

That is to say in talking about 'binding determinations' his discussion in this piece comes close to suggesting that there is serious social pressure to conform *because* a norm is binding or obligatory rather than the norm being binding because of serious social pressure as he earlier seemed to be suggesting. See also his discussion of mandatory rules and norms as serving as exclusionary reasons in the making of decisions in J. Raz 'Reasons for Action, Decisions and Norms', 84 *Mind* 481 (1975), portions of which have also been incorporated into *Practical Reason and Norms*.

[14] To borrow and adapt de Jouvenel's terminology the normative is concerned with what 'should be' either absolutely or, in the case of the law, in relation to the constitution and the legal structure. B. de Jouvenel, *Sovereignty* 2 (J. Huntington transl. 1957). The same point is made in the writings of a perceptive legal scholar with a very different philosophical approach and background. See K. Llewellyn, 'The Normative, the Legal, and the Law-Jobs: The Problem of Juristic Method', 49 *Yale L.J.* 1355, 1359 (1940), where he stresses the importance of 'normative generalisation,' 'as indicating an expressed judgment of rightness', and eschews 'the statistical sense' of norm where it means 'the normal'. Llewellyn distinguishes the normative aspect of law, which must always be strived for, from the merely 'imperative' aspect of Law.

[15] These questions mentioned in this paragraph are discussed in G. Christie, 'Objectivity in the Law', 78 *Yale L.J.* 1311, 1313-18, 1323-6 (1969) (hereafter *Objectivity*); 'The Model of Principles', 1968 *Duke L.J.* 649 (hereafter *Model of Principles*).

specifically disclaims completeness.[16] Indeed, the difficulty of adequately formulating legal 'rules' is acknowledged as a factor that seriously limits the benefits that might be obtained from applying the techniques of modern logic to legal analysis.[17]

The fact that legal reasoning cannot readily be shown to be a rule-directed activity, in any reasonably rigorous sense, has led to the dispute over the existence of a 'Judicial Discretion' which allows judges a very wide latitude in the decision of cases. As is well known, Ronald Dworkin has denied that judges have any such discretion and has taken H. L. A. Hart to task for suggesting that they do.[18] This controversy has, in turn, led to the dispute over whether, as Dworkin asserts, there exist legal 'principles' to which judges can and must turn when so-called rules of law conflict in some particular applications or do not cover a particular situation.[19] Of course, even if it is helpful to talk about principles in these contexts, there can be a

---

[16] See the *Caveat to Restatement of Property* §312 which, together with §§311 and 313, contains the Restatement's attempt to formulate the 'Rule in Shelley's Case'. The whole question of the completeness of legal rules is discussed in *Model of Principles*. On the incompleteness of even the Rule in Shelley's case see id. at 657.

[17] See L. Allen & M. Caldwell, 'Modern Logic & Judicial Decision Making: A Sketch of One View', 28 *L. & C.P.* 213, 226-34 (1963); A. Cullison, supra note 1 at 1262-8.

[18] See R. Dworkin, 'The Model of Rules', 35 *U. Chi. L. Rev.* 14 (1967) (hereafter *Model of Rules*) in which he elaborated on the thesis previously announced in his 'Judicial Discretion', 60 *J. Phil.* 624 (1963). He has further elaborated his views in 'Social Rules and Legal Theory', 81 *Yale L. J.* 855 (1972) (hereafter *Social Theory*) and 'Hard Cases', 88 *Harv. L. Rev.* 1057 (1975) (hereafter *Hard Cases*). These are among the essays reprinted in *Taking Rights Seriously* (1977) (hereafter *TRS*). Among the principal reactions are R. Satrorius, op. cit. supra note 1, at 181-210; K. Greenawalt, 'Discretion and Judicial Decision: The Elusive Quest for the Fetters that Bind Judges', 75 *Colum. L. Rev.* 359 (1975); G. MacCallum, 'Dworkin on Judicial Discretion', 60 *J. Phil.* 638 (1963). See also G. Christie, *Model of Principles*. For a more recent overview of the controversy and an attempt to assess the degree to which Dworkin has succeeded in his attacks on positivism, see E. P. Soper, 'Legal Theory and the Obligation of a Judge: The Hart/Dworkin Dispute', 75 *Mich. L. Rev.* 473 (1977). Any reference to the literature generated by Dworkin's work must also include the recent 'Symposium on Jurisprudence', 11 *Ga. L. Rev.* 969 et seq., which includes a number of critical evaluations of Dworkin's work, including, id. at 991, *Policy, Rights and Judicial Decision* by K. Greenawalt. The issue also contains a response by Dworkin, 'Seven Critics', id. at 1201. Dworkin has returned to the lists in 'No Right Answer?', 53 *N. Y. U. L. Rev.* 1 (1978) (hereafter *No Right Answer?*). Dworkin's more recent work will be discussed more fully in the text at note 83, infra.

[19] This is one of the principal theses of Dworkin's *Model of Rules*. That Dworkin's own examples did not establish the existence of such legal principles which are distinct from legal rules and that his examples were not in fact cases where there were no applicable rules of law or where the rules so conflicted as to require resort to principles was the major thesis in G. Christie, *Model of Principles*. Dworkin recognises the difficulty of completely stating legal rules and legal principles so as to decide where one ends and the other begins in his more recent *Social Theory*.

conflict between principles as well. Thus, it has been conceded, there will also be a need to weight conflicting or even competing principles if one is to avoid conceding that judges do in fact have discretion in what Dworkin calls the 'strong' sense.[20] If, however, it proves impossible to rank or weight principles—and no one yet has done it—then, if the legal process is conceived of as a system for adjudicating human entitlements, at the very least before deciding difficult cases judges, Dworkin now argues, must be required to 'find a coherent set of principles' that justify, 'in the way that fairness' requires, the decision in the instant case in the light of the 'institutional history' of society's legal structure.[21] These are intriguing arguments, even if they are not wholly convincing explanations of why judges are not as free as they seem. We shall have occasion to look at them more closely in the closing pages of Part I of this book.

It is not, of course, surprising that legal 'rules' are unable to fulfil the stringent requirements that would be necessary if the legal decision-making could be viewed as a 'rule-directed' activity. If so-called legal rules were complete and self-applying, their application by the courts would be largely a deductive process, which it clearly is not.[22] The terminology of 'norms', however, seems to provide a means whereby legal philosophers can still maintain both that laws are prescriptive entities and that, in theory, it is possible to describe a legal system by providing a complete statement of all the norms of that system. Legal reasoning can thus be a 'norm-directed' discipline even if it is not what might be called 'rule-directed'. This feature of the theory of norms comes out clearly in Joseph Raz's work. Although Raz, at least in his *The Concept of a Legal System*, differed from Kelsen and even from Ross, in divorcing the notion of norm from that of obligation, his notion of norms has always shared the logical features usually associated with norms. He thus shares with Kelsen the view that a theory of norms not only must but can identify the norms that constitute a legal system. For example, Raz thinks that it is meaningful to talk of a complete description of a legal system. A complete description of a legal system at any given instant—what Raz calls a 'momentary legal system'—consists of a set

---

[20] See R. Dworkin, *Model of Rules* at 25-7, 35-6 (*TRS* at 24-7, 34-7).

[21] R. Dworkin, *Hard Cases* at 1098-9 (*TRS* at 120-1).

[22] These matters are discussed in G. Christie, *Objectivity* at 1314-18.

of normative statements in which '(1) every one of the statements in it describe (part of) the same momentary system as all the others and (2) every normative statement which describes (part of) the same momentary system is entailed by that set'.[23] No one may have ever achieved this feat but it is postulated as being theoretically possible and, presumably, worth trying to do. How is it possible for 'norms' to fulfil this unifying function? Raz suggests it is because 'norms' are for the legal philosopher what 'propositions' are for philosophers of language.[24] Both 'norms' and 'propositions' are abstract entities. They are different from, and are not necessarily captured by, any particular linguistic formulation. Words may fail us in our efforts to state or describe them. Indeed, the conventional argot of philosophers is that one attempts to describe the 'meaning' of a proposition. Presumably, one tries to do the same with legal norms. In this way, one may recognise his inability to capture the completeness of a norm in any particular verbal formulation and yet continue to maintain that a legal system can in fact be described by means of a complete statement of all the norms comprising that system. This, then, would be another reason for preferring the terminology of norms to that of rules which seems to confine us, more than the terminology of norms, to some unique and authoritative verbal formulation.[25]

[23] *Concepts of a Legal System* at 189.

[24] This can be seen in a number of places in his work. For example, in elaborating on the implications of Austin's theory he states that 'a command is an abstract entity, i.e., is not identical either with the act of issuing a command or with the words used in that act, just as a proposition is not identical either with its assertion or the words used in asserting it'. *Concept of a Legal System* at 12. Again, in the course of his treatment of what it is to describe a momentary legal system, Raz most certainly seems to apply the conceptual framework with which he reconstitutes Bentham's doctrine of the structure of law. That is, Raz accepts that: 'Laws will continue to be regarded as non-linguistic abstract entities. A law will be said to have a structure corresponding to the structure of a normative statement which completely describes it, and it alone' (id. at 55) Cf. id. at 178: 'The fact, if it is a fact, that legislators do not often use right terms in enacting laws is no reason why jurists in describing these laws should not use right terms.' By 'right terms' Raz means, right, duty, etc. What Bentham called laws, Raz usually calls legal norms but sometimes he reverts back to the simpler 'laws'. Raz, when he is speaking most strictly reserves the term 'legal norm' for a law directing the behaviour of human beings by imposing duties or conferring powers' (id. at 75). For completeness' sake it should be pointed out that Raz recognises the existence of laws, such as those that create rights, which are part of a legal system but which do not impose duties or confer powers but which are internally related to the latter; i.e. to laws that are norms. Id. at 168-86. For present purposes this refinement is not important.

[25] It is obviously not my present purpose to give, even if I could, a definitive exegesis of the notion of rules and that of norms and of the relationship between them. Certainly that the term 'rule' has more purely descriptive senses than that of 'norm' is generally accepted. Nor, of course, am I denying that rules of law are often treated as a type of

4. *Problems created for legal theory by the use of the terminology of norms*

(i) *The relationship between validity and efficacy*

Law exists in the 'real world'. It has a context and must ultimately be discussed in that context. Most legal philosophers have recognised this, and the contemporary legal philosophers who view law as a set of norms are no exception. Indeed, it may be said that they are particularly aware that law must be discussed in its factual context, and quite rightly so. This concern is nowhere shown more clearly than in their discussions of the notion of 'efficacy' and the relationship between that notion and the notion of validity. While norms cannot be said to be true or false, they must meet a comparable logical requirement, namely that of 'validity'.[26] An 'invalid' norm is not in fact a norm, at least not in any context in which it is not valid. It is this notion of validity which supplies the link between the modal logic that characterises the legal ought and the ordinary indicative logic that characterises the writings of scholars and other observers of the legal scene. Thus, although norms themselves can be neither true nor false, statements about norms, such as a scholar's statement that a particular norm is or is not valid, are capable of being true or false.

What makes a norm valid is a complex question to which many different answers have been given. Validity may, for example, depend on content or on source or on method of creation or on some combination of these factors. But most contemporary legal philosophers—whatever the other criteria of validity they have imposed—have also insisted on some sort of efficacy as well before they are prepared to recognise the validity of a purported norm. A norm is said to be efficacious when it is in fact applied when circumstances arise which make that norm applicable. A legal system is said to be efficacious when the norms of which it consists (or some sufficiently high percentage of them) are efficacious, that is that they

---

norm. I have conceded that the terms are often used interchangeably. On the general subject of norms and rules, an influential theoretical discussion is contained in G. Von Wright, *Norm and Action* 1-16 (1963).

[26] For a general discussion of the notion of 'validity', see S. Munzer, *Legal Validity* (1972). See also, G. Christie, 'The Notion of Validity in Modern Jurisprudence', 48 *Minn. L. Rev.* 1049 (1964). At the time this article was written, I thought that it would be useful to consider the law as consisting of sets of norms, a position which I have long since abandoned.

are in fact applied when circumstances arise which make those norms applicable.

The precise relationship between efficacy and validity has, however, been a difficult one to describe. Most writers seem prepared to accept that a legal system is only valid when it is efficacious and that it is efficacious only when the norms of which it consists (or some sufficiently high percentage of them) are themselves efficacious. The difficulty is in deciding what is the relationship between the efficacy of an individual norm and its validity. The two limiting positions are; (1) There is no necessary connection between the efficacy of any particular individual norm and its validity. All that the validity of a particular norm requires is that it should belong to a valid legal system, that is one which is valid because some (high) percentage of its norms are in fact efficacious. (2) No individual norm is valid unless it is itself also efficacious. This latter position is implicit—if not indeed explicit—among the various realists, whatever their other differences.[27] Kelsen, on the other hand, at one time, came quite close to embracing the former position. In his *General Theory of Law and State,* Kelsen in fact several times stated that an individual norm does not cease to be valid merely because it is inefficacious.[28] At the same time, however, he somewhat undercut this position by his explicit recognition that no legal system can avoid the application of desuetude.[29] That is, he accepted the civil law doctrine that when, over a long period of time, the courts do not and probably will not apply a norm, in circumstances calling for its application, the norm in question loses its validity. In his later work Kelsen abandoned his

[27] This position is clearly articulated in A. Ross, *Law and Justice* 29-51.

[28] *General Theory* at 119, 122. H. L. A. Hart comes close to accepting Kelsen's position, at least with respect to a current as opposed to past legal system such as Roman Law. *Concept of Law* 100-01. That is, Hart, like most English and American lawyers, does not believe there is any necessary connection between the efficacy of a purported rule of law and its validity.

[29] *General Theory* at 119-20. The doctrine has never really been accepted in common law countries. Poe v. Ullman, 367 U.S. 497 (1961), which refused to consider the constitutionality of Connecticut's never enforced birth control legislation in the context of a declaratory judgment action, raised the possibility that the Court might recognise the doctrine. See A. Bonfield, 'The Abrogation of Penal Statutes by Non-Enforcement', 49 *Ia. L. Rev* 389, 423-40 (1964). Any such expectations were destroyed when the Court struck down these statutes on the merits in Griswold v. Connecticut, 381 U.S. 479 (1965) when an attempt was made finally to enforce the statutes. There was no suggestion that desuetude might be involved despite almost ninety years of failure to enforce.

attempt totally to divorce the validity of individual norms from their efficacy. He came to recognise that, even apart from the extreme case represented by desuetude, there always is some relationship between the validity of any norm and its effectiveness.[30]

Most writers have, of course, agreed that there is some necessary relationship between the validity of a norm and its efficacy. In this regard it has become important to focus on the nature of the group among whom a norm is not efficacious. That a norm is largely ignored by ordinary citizens does not seem to affect critically its validity. Similarly, at least in the English-speaking world, the fact that police, prosecuting authorities, and other similar officials ignore a particular norm again does not seem to preclude its being valid, whatever the realists might have maintained. But it is another matter when the courts themselves ignore a particular norm. Here, as Kelsen recognises,[31] there seems to be some hard-to-state relationship between efficacy and validity. Of course, if one could be sure that courts would never apply a particular norm one would have some confidence in asserting that such a norm is no longer valid, if it ever was. But what about the less extreme situation which is the only one that in practice ever arises?

(ii) *Difficulties created by the need to establish the relationship between efficacy and validity*

The problems which arise from tying the notion of efficacy to that of legal norm are of two kinds. First, it is often difficult, if not impossible, to arrive at a sufficient consensus as to what are the applicable legal norms—or what exactly is their meaning—to permit one to state with certainty that any given set of circumstances are indeed those that call for the application of those norms.[32] This step is necessary in order to provide a means of deciding definitively whether or not the application of, or the failure to apply, the norms in question demonstrates that these norms are or are not efficacious. When nothing vital is at stake it is very easy to state the law in a way that makes it seem much more certain than it really is and nothing is lost by this. But, if enough is at stake—usually money, but not

---

[30] *Pure Theory* at 211-13.

[31] I am referring particularly to Kelsen's later view cited in note 30 supra.

[32] See the discussion at pp. 7-10, supra.

always—it is another matter. Then, each word counts and every nuance of meaning is important. It is fashionable in judicial opinions glibly to state the so-called 'common-law rule' in an oversimplified way in order to contrast the clarity of that rule with the uncertainty of the modern law with which the court is then wrestling. It is sometimes a useful rhetorical device, but it is nothing more than that. Justice White, for example, 'restated' the 'common-law rules' of libel in *Gertz v. Robert Welch, Inc.*[33] in a way that any scholar would maintain was clearly inaccurate as well as clearly oversimplified.[34] It would, of course, have been pointless to embark on the lengthy exegesis that a more accurate statement of the complexity of the law on that subject requires. If he had, however, the contrast between the supposed clarity of the common law and the difficulty of tracing out the scope of the modern law generated by *New York Times Co. v. Sullivan,*[35] would not have been so evident. One notes how when, in 1959, the question of the burden of persuasion at common law in an action for trespass to person actually became an issue in a pending action in the English courts, it turned out that the common-law rule was not so clear after all.[36]

The difficulty in extracting from legal materials sufficiently precise

[33] 418 U.S. 323 (1974).

[34] Id. at 369, 371-5. Indeed, he accepted the American Law Institute's 1965 and 1966 proposed restatement of the law in this area, *Restatement (Second) of Torts* §§ 558-623 (Tent. Draft No. 11, 1965 and Tent. Draft No. 12, 1966) at a time when the Institute had already withdrawn many of the most important changes made in this 'restatement' and returned to a position more in line with that taken in the original *Restatement of Torts* in 1938. See *Restatement (Second) of Torts* § 569 (Tent. Draft No. 20, 1974).

[35] 376 U.S. 254 (1964).

[36] Fowler v. Lanning, [1959] 1 Q.B. 426, 1 All E.R. 290, 2 W.L.R. 241. It had been asserted as dogma that once an injury directly caused by the defendant had been shown, the burden of persuasion on the issue of fault was on the defendant. Diplock, J., as he then was, found that this was not so. In the more recent Miliangos v. George Frank (Textiles) Ltd., [1976] A.C. 443 (1975). Lord Wilberforce and Lord Simon, of Glaisdale, were particularly categoric in stating that a judgment of an English court could only be expressed in sterling. Lord Simon felt the rule could even be traced to the Year Books. Lord Cross of Chelsea, on the other hand, asserted, with a persuasive review of the authorities, that the 'rule' was not clearly established, and in his judgment wrongly so, until the *Havana Railways* case. In re United Railways of Havana and Regla Warehouses Ltd., [1961] A.C. 1007, *Miliangos* overruled *Havana Railways*, Lord Simon dissenting, on the issue of the time at which the value of a sum due in foreign money was to be converted to English money, substituting the date enforcement of the judgment was authorised for the date of the breach of the obligation to pay.

statements of legal norms (or of their meanings) to enable one adequately to test the relationship between their validity and efficacy cannot, of course, be eased by concentrating upon what courts do rather than what they say. For, if one ignores the internal element of the law and concentrates on the external behaviour of decision-makers and other users of law, one almost always finds the evidence somewhat ambiguous. On the other hand, if one tries to refine one's notion of what the law is by referring not only to what these users of law do but also to what they actually believe the law to be, one is confronted with the hazardous task of ascertaining what these people do in fact believe; and sometimes even the further problem that what they believe may well be at variance with what they do.

The second major difficulty in tying the notion of efficacy to that of valid legal norms is that, even if the experts are prepared to agree on one precise statement of the norm—or to agree on its 'meaning'—the fact remains that very few, if any, purported norms are *always* applied whenever a factual situation arises which makes the norm applicable. As we noted earlier, the fact that a purported norm is largely ignored by the citizenry at large, or even by prosecutors and other similar officials, is not of itself fatal to the claim that the norm in question is in fact still valid. But the situation is more difficult when the so-called norm is ignored by the courts. How can a purported norm actually be a norm if it is not applied by the courts when factual circumstances arise which would appear to make the norm applicable?

One way, of course, of handling this disparity between prior legal theory and the subsequent actions of the courts is to say that one had originally formulated the norm in question incorrectly or that one had stated the norm incompletely by failing to mention the exceptions. Or, one might claim that he had indeed correctly formulated the norm in question, but that there was a conflicting norm which took precedence in those particular factual circumstances. If this conflicting norm is the same 'kind' of norm as the one originally in question, recognition of its existence amounts to a narrower reformulation of the original norm. But sometimes this conflicting norm is said to be a norm of a different kind, a second order norm often called a 'principle' or a 'standard' which is not always applicable. The 'model of principles' is an intriguing one because it permits one to account for the apparent inconsistency and incompleteness in a legal system without being forced to admit that judges and other decision-makers have a great deal of freedom in the actual decision of cases. At the same time, as we have already noted, no one has been able to put forth an adequate theory of these second-order norms which would enable one to explain to others when these norms override the ordinary or first-order norms. That judges and others appeal to principle is indisputable. That one can state when judges will or should so appeal (and to which principle) is another matter. No one certainly has thus far been able to do so. Notions such that the principles used must be part of a 'coherent set' and that to justify a decision adequately they must meet the requirements of 'fairness' and of due regard for the 'institutional history' of a society's legal structure, to which we adverted earlier,[37] are intriguing and un-questionably useful. They remind us, for example, of how important consistency is in legal reasoning. They are not, however, adequate to the needs of legal theory.

Finally, there are situations in which scholars will not wish to reformulate the original norm in the face of a judicial decision failing to apply that norm under circumstances calling for its application, but yet are not prepared to explain this discrepancy by resorting to any principle or any other conflicting norm which took precedence in that situation. When this occurs we are left again with our original question. 'How can something be a norm if it is not applied by the courts when it is supposed to be applied?' Or, to put it another way, how can that purported norm be a valid norm of the legal system to which it is said to belong?

The usual way in which scholars have attempted to surmount this difficulty—and it is the way chosen both by Kelsen and by Raz, his critic—is to insist that a scholar's statement of the norm is only a descriptive statement of the content of the norm.[38] Whether that description is in point of fact the statement of a norm depends on how it is considered by the users of the norm—meaning by 'users', pre-sumably, more than judges or other officials, but also all those who modify their conduct because of the existence of a purported norm. Thus, according to Kelsen, if these people consider a purported norm as more than a prescription of what they *must* do, that is if they consider it as also a prescription of what they *ought* to do, then the

---

[37] See text at note 21, supra.

[38] H. Kelsen, *General Theory* at 70-81. J. Raz, *Concept of a Legal System* at 44-50; cf. note 24 supra.

purported norm is indeed a norm.[39] For Raz, of course, as we have already seen, a duty-imposing norm is, in the first instance, merely a directive that is backed up by standard reasons for compliance in the form of the likely critical reactions of others.[40] In a mature legal system these are usually organised sanctions. Thus far, however, we are still in the realm of 'must'. By calling it a norm we may be asserting that the directive is part of a normative system, but this is merely to state a logical conclusion and a logical relationship. We still have not, from a behavioural point of view, necessarily left the realm of 'must'. To enter into Kelsen's universe of ought, under Raz's analysis, we would need something like Raz's further concept of obligation, which depends on the particular quality of the critical reactions of others 'which are regarded as legitimate by bystanders'.[41]

The crucial point to be drawn from these analytical approaches is that a scholar's statement about what is a norm—or in Raz's terminology, a norm which people are under a legal obligation to obey—is to a very large extent a statement about what people believe. It is, in point of fact, a statement about what people believe they ought to do. The fact that they do not actually behave in a certain way does not necessarily mean that they do not think they ought to behave that way. Thus a scholar who is confronted with an instance in which a purported norm was not applied where it would seem to have been applicable, and who is not prepared, in order to account for this phenomenon, to reformulate the norm or to recognise some conflicting norm that takes precedence in those circumstances, can none the less continue to maintain that he has accurately described a valid norm. This, he can maintain, is what people believe they ought to do, even if they do not on occasion do it. If, however, the failure to apply the norm becomes sufficiently widespread then the norm in question might be said to cease being valid owing to its lack of efficacy. In making this latter determination, what judges do will be more important than what other people do. When a sufficiently large number of its purported norms cease to be efficacious, then it may be said that the legal system to which these norms belong also ceases to be valid owing to its lack of efficacy. Thus there is a point at which the

---

[39] See H. Kelsen, *Pure Theory* at 44-7; cf. id. at 202-5

[40] See the discussion at p. 4, supra, and the citations there given to Raz's work.

[41] Ibid. For the words in quotation, see J. Raz, *Concept of a Legal System* at 149.

discrepancy between what people supposedly believe and what they do becomes crucial. But, short of this point, one can continue to maintain that people believe one thing even when in point of fact they are doing something entirely antithetical to this supposed belief. In this way, scholars can accommodate the fact that the norms they talk about as being valid norms of a legal system are not always applied.

(iii) *A more general discussion of the question of the efficacy of legal norms: the problem of consistency between practice and belief*

How convincing are these devices of scholars to preserve the integrity of their legal theories and to make possible scholarly talk about legal norms? The model of principles is at least logically capable of bearing the burden placed upon it, if only it could be elaborated adequately, a subject about which enough has been said already. What about the leeway presented us by the theory of norms that allows us, up to a point, to continue to maintain that a particular norm is valid even if it is not applied when it should be and the scholar can supply no satisfactory explanation of why it is not? On the favourable side of the balance it might be said that the device recognises that there are several dimensions of 'ought'. What people *legally* ought to do does not exhaust the realm of ought. There are other normative orders besides the legal one. Most people certainly recognise the existence of a moral dimension to their lives and, therefore, when confronted with alternative courses of action, what they believe they legally ought to do is not the only thing they must consider. What they believe they morally ought to do may in some cases be equally, if not more, important. When this is the case, a person's failure to follow a legal norm does not necessarily mean that he does not recognise it as being applicable or legally binding.

Whether or not a person can feel himself simultaneously emotionally committed to overlapping normative orders is a question I do not wish to discuss. Kelsen equivocated somewhat on this point.[42] I shall assume that he can. I shall also reject a possible

---

[42] *General Theory* at 15-24, 373-6; *Pure Theory* at 59-69. See also Kelsen's essay, 'Natural Law Doctrine and Legal Positivism', reprinted as an appendix to *General Theory* at 391-446. Kelsen always maintained that law and morality are different techniques of social organisation. What differentiates law and morality is that 'law is a coercive order, that is, a normative order that attempts to bring about a certain behaviour by

implication of H. L. A. Hart's work[43]—which Rawls comes close to accepting[44]—that at least 'officials', in a basically just society, are incapable of such joint allegiance. That position can be considered as a statement of linguistic usage; namely, that to be an official of a normative system is to consider the norms of that system as primary when one is acting in his official capacity. Or it can be considered a metanormative principle to the effect that, when acting as an official, let us assume of a 'nearly just' political society of the type that Rawls is talking about, one must apply the applicable norms of that system (or resign, or cease to *act* as an official of that society or cease to *be* an official of that society?). I shall assume, rather, that even officials acting in their official capacity can experience these conflicting normative obligations so that scholars can rightly maintain that, even if such a person does not in fact act in a certain way, that person may nevertheless accept that *legally* he *ought* so to act. He may, in other words, despite his contrary actions, continue to accept the validity of the norm in question and of the legal system to which it belongs.

To concede this point, however, is not to resolve the difficulty but

---

attaching to the opposite behaviour a socially organised coercive act, whereas morals is a social order without such sanctions'. *General Theory* at 62. In his earlier work Kelsen assumed that, while all sorts of moral orders were possible and had indeed been recognised by men, there was only one possible *objective* moral order. This, of course, was the assumption made by the traditional natural law school. Kelsen rejected the idea of a natural law and with it the notion of an objective moral order. Furthermore, he assumed that an individual who did accept the natural law tradition would always accept the primacy of the natural law. Likewise, he assumed that individuals who shared his point of view would accept the primacy of the human legal order, if they were prepared to accept the validity of any general system of social order at all. They might fail to comply with some of its norms because of their individual emotive reactions but these could not be called conflicting imperatives. In the second edition of *The Pure Theory*, however, Kelsen, in the portions cited above, clearly admits that if one rejects the concept of a single absolute system of morals and accepts instead the relativity of morals, then the legal order, as a normative order, that is as an order of *ought* propositions, is by that very fact a type of moral order. Under this view a conflict between law and morality is no longer a conflict between the norms of two epistemologically distinct and non-comparable social orders but a conflict between the norms of two different moral orders, that is between two social orders of the same basic type. While one who accepts the validity of one of these orders will still refuse to obey the conflicting norms of the other order, the analytical separation of law and morality has nevertheless been compromised by this shift in Kelsen's thought. Moreover, the possibility of an individual's being confronted with conflicting norms issued by the various moral orders to which he may feel committed now does seem to arise.

[43] *Concept of law* at 107-14.

[44] J. Rawls, *A Theory of Justice* 111-14, 342-4 (1971).

to pose it in a more acute form. Assuming that rational men can be said to accept as valid and binding norms which they sometimes do not apply in circumstances when these norms are, according to their terms, applicable, how much inconsistency between belief and action is possible? It has been said by the philosopher Bernard Williams,[45] for example, that one of the differences between the deontic logic of ethical discourse and the indicative or alethic logic of the scientist is that the universal propositions of ethical discourse are not necessarily disproved or shaken by the counter-example. People can continue to feel committed to these universal propositions, even if they sometimes disregard them in practice. This is shown by the remorse and regret people sometimes experience after they have so behaved. People are often morally weak or inexcusably ignorant or, as we shall discuss later on, even irrational on occasion. The point is further made that, even though most conflicts in the application of ethical norms can be resolved by redefining those norms more narrowly and precisely, some such conflicts cannot be so resolved. One can and often does, as a rational man, recognise norms which conflict in some particular applications. Furthermore, these conflicts can exist under circumstances where there is no evident higher norm which permits one to resolve the conflict in purely logical terms. One who is required to act is forced to resolve the conflict by *ad hoc* methods. He shows his allegiance to the norm which he did not apply by feeling regret—but, in this case, not remorse—at not being able to act in accordance with the norm.

If this is so in ethics, why is it not so in the law? Judges and other officials are sometimes faced with the same conflicts, whether between two legal norms or between legal norms and those of some other normative order to which they feel emotionally committed, and these conflicts must be resolved in the same way. Undoubtedly they are capable of feeling, and often do experience, the same feelings of regret, helplessness, even remorse. Judges, too, therefore, may be said to be constant in their acceptance of the legal norms, even when in some circumstances they behave in a manner inconsistent with those norms. The difficulty with this position is obvious. It is like the

[45] B. Williams, 'Consistency in Ethics', *Proceedings of the Aristotelian Society,* Supp. Vol. 40, 1 (1966). On the same general subject, see also R. Trigg, 'Moral Conflict', 80 *Mind* 41 (1971). The problem is also discussed in R. Hare, *Freedom and Reason* (1963) (especially in ch. 4 'Ought and Can' and ch. 5 'Backsliding'); E. Lemmon, 'Moral Dilemmas', 71 *Phil. Rev.* 139 (1962).

difficulties presented by the appeal to principles to explain judges' deviations from the supposed primary norms of law. Either the *ad hoc* methods of resolving particular conflicts between particular norms can be generalised, in which case they are no longer *ad hoc*, and the conflict between the norms no longer exists because we now have a means for ranking our obligations,[46] or one is forced to recognise that, in the really difficult legal cases, which are often politically and socially difficult cases as well, the rule of law is nothing more than rule by judges—a rule, and this may be the point of the model of principles, which is hopefully in accordance with the judiciary's best judgment, about, the moral, political, and social needs of society.[47] But, if this is so, is law really a set of binding norms and is the judicial process the application of these norms to practical situations? Indeed, is it not then fatuous to assume either the possibility or even the desirability of a 'complete description of a legal system' which supposedly consists of a set of norms that, taken together, completely describe it?

Despite these difficulties, a further consideration that might be placed on the favourable side of the balance is that, when scholars insist that they can continue to describe a particular purported norm in a certain way, even in the face of contrary judicial behaviour, they are simply recognising that people do not always behave rationally. The fact that people's actions sometimes contradict their supposed beliefs does not mean that they do not have these beliefs. Of course, there are limits to the extent to which we are prepared to recognise irrationality as a phenomenon of normal human beings. When the discrepancy between belief and action becomes too great we shall refuse to accept the sincerity of a man's belief or consider him as mad or, perhaps, claim that he does not understand how to use ordinary language. In such a case we would say that, for him, the norm is not a valid norm. When the non-observance is sufficiently widespread, the

---

[46] This is the approach adopted by E. Lemmon, supra note 45.

[47] Cf. T. Kearns, 'Rules, Principles, and the Law', 18 *Nat. L.F.* 114 (1973). Lawyers, of course, not only accept that judges and other officials do have discretion in the 'strong' sense of that term; they also insist that such discretion is inevitable and indeed necessary. See K. Davis, *Discretionary Justice* (1969). The problem is how to structure discretion so as to prevent its abuse. The assumption that law is a closed system that contains within it, provided that enough study is devoted to the task, the solution to all problems which require decision does permeate some religious communities. See S. Schechter, *Aspects of Rabbinic Theology* 134-7 (new ed. 1961).

norm may be said to lose its validity as a norm of a social order owing
to its lack of efficacy. The fact, however, that the scholarly approach
we have been discussing can thus take into account, up to a point, the
irrational component of human behaviour, without abandoning the
central thesis—that a legal system is a normative system consisting of
sets of individual norms—would thus seem to be an argument in its
favour.

There are, however, some difficulties which must be considered.
Granted that people often do behave irrationally, the usual instances
we have in mind are those in which people act unthinkingly, those in
which, when we point out the discrepancy between action and belief,
the actor says: 'Well, I suppose I did behave irrationally, but there it
is, I'm only human.' The implication is that, if the actor had
recognised the discrepancy between his beliefs and his actions, he
would not have acted as he did and that in the future, if he is aware of
what he is doing, he will act in accordance with his belief about what
he ought to do. In terms of our previous discussion, we might expect
the speaker to evidence feelings not only of regret but even of remorse
for his actions. Naturally, he could also accommodate the discrepancy
between action and belief by abandoning his belief but, under the
hypothesis now being explored, we are assuring a constancy in belief.
We would be very, very puzzled, however, if, at the moment of
action, the person in question declared: 'I accept the validity of the
legal order; I recognise that this is what I legally ought to do; I am not
aware of any moral reason not to fulfil my legal obligation; *but* I just
won't do it even though physically I am able to.' To those who
accept, in however attenuated a form, Aristotle's statement that 'man
is a rational animal' this would be simply too much. There would be
no point in engaging in legal theory if human beings were that
irrational. However much we might be prepared to excuse
inconsistency in the face of irreconcilable conflicts between two norms
recognised by the speaker, this latter type of inconsistency is beyond
the pale.

The thesis under consideration which permits a scholar or other
observer to describe the legal order as a set of *norms*, even if the
behaviour of individual users does not always accord with these
supposed norms, thus depends on a very weak link, the beliefs of the
individual users of these norms. If they do not behave in the manner
prescribed by the norm then the scholar must, in order to preserve the

logical structure of his system, either change his statements of the norms or assert that the users are not thinking properly or that, unfortunately, these users do not really know the norms of the system under which they are operating. If he refuses to adopt any of these courses to explain the discrepancy between belief and action, he must embark on an extended and ultimately inconclusive discussion of the notion of consistency in normative discourse. Moreover, even if the users behave in the manner in which, according to the norms described by a scholar, they ought to, it is not at all clear that these users' notions of what the norms are always coincides with that of the scholar. Finally, even if their behaviour coincides with that prescribed by the scholars and even if these users accept the scholar's statements as to what the norms are, a scholar or other outside observer can never be sure that the user accepts the scholar's norms as norms in the same way as does the scholar. Assuming that norms are directions as to what an official ought to do—even if he does not do it—do these norms bear the same relationship to considerations of morality or of expediency or even of personal advantage in the mind of the official as they do in the mind of the scholar?

The idea of a norm, the basic building block of the concepts of law and a legal system is thus a very ethereal one. One can, of course, confine the term 'norm' solely to a logical context. In that case it merely tells one that a particular statement is part of a larger set of statements; that a particular normative statement, if you will, is part of a normative system. To do so, however, leaves largely untouched the question of how the so-called norms of the system are experienced by the people purportedly subject to some particular normative system. One can understand why most realists attempted to define law solely in behavioural terms. The insights of the realists should not be rejected merely because there are logical difficulties with a predictive theory of law. The most often mentioned criticism, of course, is that decision-makers are not involved in predicting what they are going to do or even in predicting what others will do, but in deciding what to do.[48] While lower court judges are partly concerned with pre-

---

[48] See H. L. A. Hart, 'Scandinavian Realism', 1959 *Camb.L.J.* 233. None the less, it should be noted that in some situations, such as a federal diversity case where the federal courts are required to apply state law, the federal judges are required to guess what the state courts would do and their statements of what state law is are no more than that. The same problem arises in all courts when conflict-of-law principles point to the law of some other jurisdiction.

dicting the reactions of appellate courts, this is not the whole of what they are doing. And, of course, while the judges of final appellate courts are obliged to some extent to take into consideration the reactions of legislatures and of the public at large, this is a very small part of the decision-making process of these tribunals. Law can thus not usefully be considered as a set of predictions of official behaviour.

A second criticism of predictive theories is that they are unbelievably complex.[49] There are an infinite number of predictions of varying degrees of probability about the behaviour of officials that can be made by an infinite number of observers and none of these predictions is any more authoritative than any of the others. Even if we could identify a sub-class of observers called experts—are these expert observers to be defined as those whose predictions we predict will be correct?—the fact remains that the experts are often wrong in their assessment of legal outcomes. And what about the situations which even the so-called experts admit are so fluid that any predictions they make are of a low order of probability. Are the low-order-of-probability predictions law too?

A third point which can be raised against the realist view, that what we call law is a set of predictions about what courts will do in fact, is that a complete description of people's behaviour must take account of what people believe they ought to do. Ross has attempted to expand the predictive theory of law to do just that by defining the law as predictions of what judges will do *because* they feel legally 'bound' to.[50] Unfortunately, the inclusion by Ross of this element of psychic compulsion in his definition of law is more in the nature of an hypothesis made by the observer in order to make possible a coherent explanation of the phenomena which he observes than an observable matter of fact. This is because Ross believes that a national legal system is an 'externally given, inter-subjective phenomenon, and not merely . . . a subjective opinion . . .'[51] He consequently lays his major emphasis on observation of the behaviour of judges.[52] Thus, for Ross and the other realists, actions speak louder than mere words. They wanted to concentrate on what judges did because, to some extent quite rightly, they suspected that much of what judges said was

[49] See G. Christie, supra note 49, at 1068-74, particularly 1071-4.
[50] A. Ross, *Law and Justice* 29-74.
[51] Id. at 72.
[52] Id. at 16-18, 43-4, 70-4.

rationalisation constructed after they made up their minds how they would decide the case before them.[53]

Finally, many realists were inconsistent in assuming that they knew who the officials were—using non-predictive theories of law in the process—rather than recognising that, under a behavioural approach to law, who is an official must be determined by examining the behaviour of the persons said to recognise them as officials and the reasons why this recognition is forthcoming.[54] This inconsistency comes out particularly clearly in the work of Karl Llewellyn, who defined law in terms of the interaction of official and lay behaviour.[55] Although he recognised that it might be possible to define who is an official in behavioural terms by describing the various roles played by people in society,[56] he never actually tried to establish who were judges and other officials by exploring in depth any such behavioural model. Llewellyn assumed that he knew who the judges and the other officials were and he did so on the basis of the old doctrinal examination of the law that he was so intent on criticising as inadequate.[57] One imagines that Llewellyn did not take the trouble to establish who were officials by behavioural means because of the difficulty of

[53] The most extreme expression of this view is contained in J. Hutcheson, Jr., 'The Judgment Intuitive: The Functions of the "Hunch" in Judicial Decision', 14 *Cornell L.Q.* 274 (1929), where it is argued that the judge's opinion is almost always sheer rationalisation. Jerome Frank came close to adopting Hutcheson's extreme views on this point in, *Law and the Modern Mind* C. XII (1930). Ross shows some sympathy for the extreme view in *Law and Justice* at 43-4. All the realists, however, suspected to some extent that judicial opinions were merely rationalisations.

[54] Although their criticisms are much more wide-ranging, this point seems to underlie the critiques of the realist position of both Kelsen and Kantorowicz. See H. Kantorowicz, *The Definition of Law* 18-19 (A. Campbell, ed. 1958); H. Kelsen, *General Theory* at 175-8.

[55] K. Llewellyn, 'A Realistic Jurisprudence: The Next Step', 30 *Colum.L.Rev.* 431, 456-7 (1930).

[56] Id. at 457. See also note 57 infra.

[57] This failing characterises even Llewellyn's most important statement of the methodology of the behavioural study of legal phenomena. K. Llewellyn, 'The Normative, the Legal, and the Law-Jobs: The Problem of Juristic Method', 49 *Yale L.J.* 1355 (1940). In this paper he discusses the principal analytical tools he uses, namely the focusing on 'Law-Ways', on 'Law-Stuff', and on the 'Law-Jobs', and on how these bear on 'the adjustment of the trouble case' (id. at 1375). It is his notion of 'law-stuff'—which includes 'rules of law, legal institutions of any kind, the presence and activity of lawyers, judges, jailors, law libraries and their use, courts, "habits" of obedience, a federal system . . .' (id. at 1358)—which it seems particularly impossible under his method of approach to reduce to purely behavioural phenomena but which rather seems to depend upon the traditional non-behavioural analytical framework.

separating out, through an examination of role models and other behavioural tests, important union, religious, and professional leaders, whom we normally do not consider as being officials of the state, from people like judges and Internal Revenue personnel whom we do consider as officials.[58]

Nevertheless, while accepting all these criticisms of legal realism, it is still the case that scholars who have defined law in terms of 'norms' have been much too glib in dismissing the work of the realists with its heavy emphasis on actual behaviour. The theories of the scholars who have defined law in terms of 'norm', like those of the more perceptive realists such as Ross, ultimately depend on something that is fundamentally unknowable, namely what people believe. Indeed, by rejecting the primacy of overt behaviour insisted upon by all the realists, these scholars are even more dependent on what the users of the law believe are the norms governing their actions. This dependence upon beliefs is not even avoided by Raz who, unlike Kelsen, makes the existence of a norm depend on the behavioural reactions of people. For, according to Raz, a norm, even if it is not always the conscious **creation** of a human will, as Kelsen **maintained**,[59] must operate as a norm among the members of the social group to whom the supposed norm purportedly applies. That is, in some way it must be recognised by the members of the social group as being a norm. After all, in the case of legal norms which Raz recognises as being capable of imposing legal obligations, it is **people's** feeling that a 'critical reaction' to deviations from the purported norm is *'legitimate'* that is crucial in identifying the presence of the obligation and presumably also the norm that imposes it.[60] Thus, although for Raz the identification of a norm requires resort to behavioural

---

[58] How to handle this problem presented an embarrassment to one of the precursors of American legal realism, John Chipman Gray, who was forced to fall back on the amorphous and not satisfactorily defined concept of 'the real rulers' of a society. See J.C. Gray, *The Nature and Sources of the Law* 67-9, 121-5 (2d ed. 1921).

[59] For Raz's criticism of Kelsen on this point, see *Concept of a Legal System* at 64-9, 125. Raz recognises, however, that even if a norm can be created without any conscious intention to create a norm, the creation of a norm does require the existence of a higher norm 'investing an act with the character of a norm-creating act' (id. at 68). Raz recognises that the existence of 'original legal norms' presents 'special problems' (ibid.) and the conclusion seems inescapable that even under his views of things these original legal norms must have some relationship to acts of human will.

[60] Id. at 148-9 (emphasis supplied).

evidence—in particular regularity of conduct[61]—complete identification of the content of a purported legal norm that imposes obligations, as well as of the fact that it does indeed function as that kind of norm, requires a resort to human beliefs.

Some of these problems would, of course, be obviated if scholars who insist upon defining the law in terms of norms redefined their norms every time the courts acted in a manner inconsistent with the norms as previously defined. Naturally, however, scholars are reluctant to do this. Such a move would be tantamount to accepting the fundamental insight of the hard-core realists that overt behaviour is primary over belief, for these scholars would immediately be confronted by the need to explain the significance of judicial behaviour inconsistent with their own previous statements of the norms. Does this inconsistent behaviour show that the scholars were mistaken in their previous statement of the norm? Or does it show that the norm has changed? These are certainly very difficult questions to decide. It should be clear now that an insistence that the law consists of norms, which at first glance appears to be self-evident, masks a great many difficulties which can only be ignored at the cost of making legal theory a word game with little relationship to the phenomena it purports to explain. Defining the difficulties away, as is done in the presuppositions of those who use normative terminology in describing the law, simply will not do.

5. *How is the law normative?*

Max Weber distinguishes a legal order from other mechanisms, including custom, for resolving disputes within a group by the presence in the legal order of an enforcement staff; i.e., by the presence of a burcaucratic organisation which decides when it will intervene and apply the coercive power of the group on behalf of a party to a dispute.[62] A legal order, like other social orders, is moreover characterised by the fact that conduct under it—in the case of the legal order, at the very least the conduct of the enforcement

---

[61] Id. at 148.

[62] M. Weber, *Law in Economy and Society* 5 (M. Rheinstein, ed.; transl. E. Shils and M. Rheinstein, 1954) (hereafter *Law in Economy and Society*). This work is an English translation of portions of Weber's *Wirtschaft und Gesellschaft* (2d ed. 1925).

staff—is 'oriented towards determinable maxims' because, among
other reasons, 'it is in some appreciable way regarded by the actor as
in some way obligatory or exemplary for him'.[63] Most observers
would, of course, agree that legal activity is 'oriented towards
determinable maxims'. The difficulty, under Weber's definition,
concerns the question of what it is for these maxims to be
'regarded . . . as in some way obligatory or exemplary' and how this
notion is to be applied in concrete situations.

Certainly, as a matter of ordinary language, Weber's definitions
are compatible with the view that the maxims or norms of the legal
order are not very binding at all, that they are little more than the
topoi or commonplace seats of argument recognised by students of
informal argumentation since the days of Aristotle.[64] And, regardless
of whether Weber would have agreed to this interpretation of his
definitions, it may not be very far from the truth.

It is worth noting that Ross comes close to enunciating a similar theory
of norms. He tried to accommodate the normative aspects of law to a
predictive theory of law by treating statements about valid law (or valid
legal norms) as predictions that a judge will behave in a certain way
because he feels bound to do so. To take into account the fact that
even a realist might not always want to abandon his descriptive statements of the legal norms of a system any time judges behaved in a
contrary manner, Ross reformulated his theory in a narrower form.
A statement by a scholar as to what are the valid legal norms of a legal
system is a prediction that, when the appropriate circumstances arise,
the norm in question 'will form an integral part of the reasoning
underlying the judgment' rendered in the case.[65] Ross wished to accommodate his theory to the fact that not only might the facts be such
as to bring into operation superseding legal norms but also that 'the
ideas which the judge holds as to what is valid law do not constitute
the only factor by which he is motivated'.[66] Thus a scholar confronted with seemingly unexplainable (or irrational or inconsistent)
behaviour is not necessarily always obliged to reformulate his doc-

---

[63] Id. at 3-4, 11-16.

[64] For a brief review of the literature, see G. Christie, *Objectivity*, at 1323-6.

[65] A. Ross, *On Law and Justice* at 42.

[66] Id. at 43. Relying on the work of Jerome Frank, Ross also stressed how subjective
can be the judge's assessment of the facts that are in dispute in a case. Ibid.

trinal statements. But what is it for a supposed norm to form an 'integral part' of the judge's reasoning processes? Moreover, in order to do so, must it have the same verbal form and intentional meaning for observer-predictor and judge-decider? One can avoid these problems by treating the norms as maxims, in which case it is also easier to see how they could form an 'integral part of the reasoning underlying' a decision, even if that decision were contrary to one's expectations formulated on the basis of those maxims. But then would these maxims be 'norms'?

The basic difficulty which legal philosophers have unsuccessfully tried to ignore by conceptualising law as a set of norms is that one of the major assumptions of contemporary legal philosophy is false. This assumption is that not only is legal reasoning more rigorous than other kinds of informal argumentation—which may perhaps be true—but it is also sufficiently more rigorous to justify the conclusion that it is *qualitatively* different from other forms of informal argumentation. This qualitative difference between legal reasoning and other forms of informal argumentation is sometimes expressed by considering law as a form of what Perelman has called 'quasi-logical reasoning'.[67] Perelman himself, however, uses the term 'quasi-logical argument' because legal reasoning is sometimes cast in the form of a deductive chain; he has no illusions about legal reasoning being a type of formal logic. Indeed, since no sophisticated observer believes that legal reasoning is essentially deductive in nature—that is why it is a type of informal argumentation—how is it possible to explain this supposed qualitative difference between legal reasoning and other forms of informal argumentation? Why, in other words, should one expect legal reasoning to be any more 'quasi-logical' than other types of informal reasoning? It is here that legal philosophers have fallen back on the notion of norms which, unlike the maxims of common sense, are 'binding' on judges and other participants in legal activities. What makes the model of norms plausible is that, if one could state a legal proposition in sufficient detail with particular reference to a specific situation, it does seem possible to state with comparative certainty what the decision of a court would be should that situation

---

[67] C. Perelman & L. Olbrechts-Tyteca, *The New Rhetoric, A Treatise on Argumentation* 218-20 (J. Wilkinson and P. Weaver transl. 1969).

arise; and some decisions of courts are in fact highly predictable.[68]

But are such complex and detailed statements, assuming it were possible to formulate them, norms? The predictability of result such verbal formulations make possible could be accounted for by a notion of consistency among cases rather than by any 'normative' or emotion-generating quality of the formulation in question. Moreover such reformulations would be too prolix and specific to accord much with common-sense notions of what a norm is. Indeed, Raz makes it a major part of his criticism of Kelsen's restatement of Austin's theory that Kelsen's norms are so very cumbersome and prolix.[69] Raz maintains, and I think correctly, that the notion of a norm in ordinary language is of something reasonably concise and general.[70] I would further suggest that, in ordinary language, it is something that is capable of being the focus of an emotional response from people. The doctrinal statements of most scholars are of course capable of meeting these requirements. The problem, as we have seen, is that it is difficult to see how these general statements actually operate as norms rather than merely as maxims in the course of legal reasoning. One can, of course, try to have the best of both worlds by first stating the norms in terms that are concise and capable of being considered as norms, and of being the focus of the requisite emotional response, and then treating these concise statements as a shorthand for the true norm which is much more complex and detailed. In this way, one can transfer the potential for focusing an emotional response to the complex, prolix, and fairly specific statement which, by itself, seems incapable of fostering this effect in anyone. Unconsciously, this is what many legal theories in point of fact do.

It cannot be stressed too strongly, however, that the theory of norms fails in its purpose of explaining why legal reasoning is qualitatively different from most other forms of informal argumentation. It is not only that the resulting norms would have to be so complex and specific that it would be hard to believe anyone could consider these statements as 'binding'. Even if one were to assume that people

---

[68] Under these circumstances, legal reasoning would approach closely the deductive model. For a discussion of the place of deduction in legal reasoning see the references in note 12 supra.

[69] J. Raz, *Concept of a Legal System* at 114-20.

[70] Id. at 142-7. Raz also criticises Bentham's formulations which, if preferable in some ways to Kelsen's, are still too repetitive and complex. Id. at 146-7.

are capable of treating these cumbersome statements as norms, to make it profitable to define law as a set of such norms would require both judges and scholars to formulate and agree on the formulation of such norms *before* the decision of concrete cases. But if the law consists of such detailed and specific formulations whose application to a case can be considered 'compelled', it is hard to conceive of a norm's actually being formulated before the decision of the cases from which the norm was extracted. Nevertheless, unless this kind of inter-personal agreement on the norms were capable of formulation *before* these cases were decided it would be difficult to consider most legal decisions as the application of binding norms, unless of course one were prepared to say that prior agreement on the norms is unnecessary. All that would be necessary, under this view, is that the users of the law consider the law as being a set of norms. The fact that each user's notion of the norms is to some extent idiosyncratic would be irrelevant. Judging then would be similar to what many people think doing right is. What is important is that each man should do what he considers right. To say that law is rule-directed or norm-directed is to say that each user of the law acts in accordance with what he conceives to be the rule or the norm and no more. Perhaps this is all that many people mean when they say that law consists of norms.[71] Is this, however, in fact what most people do when they use the law, namely make use of what they are prepared to admit may be only their individual notions of what norms are? This is a difficult question, to which we shall return at the end of Part I. For the moment, however, it does seem plausible to assume that many people would be reluctant to abandon the notion that norms are generally accepted and that this is one of the reasons, if not the principal reason, that they are norms. In short, most people seem committed to the view that there is such a thing as a correct and incorrect formulation of a norm and that the individual user of a norm is not the sole or even the final arbiter of correctness. Unless this is so, there is no point in legal philosophers talking about law as a set of norms. They should try some other approach.

---

[71] Professor Dworkin at one time came close to espousing this view. See R. Dworkin, 'Judicial Discretion', 60 *J. Phil.* 624 (1963); cf. G. MacCallum, 'Dworkin on Judicial Discretion', id. at 638. Dworkin suggested that, even if it is impossible to achieve an agreement as to what would be the correct decision in a difficult case, for each judge nevertheless there is a right decision and it is the judge's duty to arrive at that decision.

6. *The importance of consistency in the law*

One must recognise that legal reasoning is not basically different in kind from other types of informal argumentation. What it shares with the more rigorous forms of informal argumentation is a strong insistence on consistency. Law may also be unusual among the various sorts of informal argumentation in having highly developed techniques for achieving consistency. More will be said about this in Part II. For the time being I wish to focus on the important role of consistency in legal reasoning. If anything about the law may be said to be normative, it is this requirement of consistency in its application. There is also considerable agreement among judges and other officials that they are bound to apply the constitution and validly enacted statutes. If one wished to, one could call the verbal statement of these assumptions the 'basic legal norms'. They really are more particular expressions of the fundamental normative judgment—quasi-ethical, perhaps even quasi-religious in character—that judges are bound by the 'law', whatever it might be, and are to apply it regardless of personal predilections. In short, they are an expression of the ideal that men should live under the rule of law and not under the personal rule of other men. These feelings, together with a commitment to consistency, are the very core of anything that can be called law or a legal system. The notion that law must therefore also consist of particular norms which we must somehow strive to discover and then apply is, of course, a natural response to these very basic feelings even if, as it turns out, it is not a supportable one.

Consistency, of course, is not unique to legal reasoning. It is a fundamental requirement of rationality and of all purposeful behaviour. One recalls how Hume, after first stating that it is a feature of human nature that people prefer short-term to long-term advantages, struggles to explain how human progress is at all possible. He suggests that it is by establishing a class of leaders and loading them with privileges. One thereby creates a group of people who find it in their short-term interest to strive for the long-term interests of the populace.[72] This is obviously unsatisfactory. How are the leaders able to perceive the long-term interests of the nation?

[72] D. Hume, *A Treatise of Human Nature*, Bk. III, Pt. II, § VII (534-9) (L. Selby-Bigge, ed. 1888) (hereafter *Treatise*); cf. id. at Bk. III, Pt. II, § IX (552).

What happens if the truly long-term interests of the nation are against the short-term interests of the leaders who, after all, have only a limited life expectancy and may be expected to display a robust desire to remain in power? I would suggest that if one wants quick answers to what makes human progress at all possible it is because we are trapped by our own rhetoric. It is human nature to pontificate. Talk, of course, is easy when no significant practical interests are at stake. Sooner or later, however, we are confronted with factual situations which test our pontifications. If we never apply our pontifications to actual events, our statements are soon classed as empty rhetoric devoid of content and not meant to be taken seriously. Daily pledges of allegiance and the normal run of sermons often degenerate into this empty ritualistic form. But once we start to apply our pontifications to the facts of life we become trapped by a combination of what we have done and what we have said in the past. To put the matter in Humean terms, for some of us and on occasion even for most of us, the short-term interest in not appearing ridiculous by behaving inconsistently forces us, however reluctantly, to practise what we preach, that is, to behave consistently.[73]

I would suggest that the ending of slavery and now of segregation and the inferior status of women are instances where exactly this has happened. If we claim that all human beings are created equal and purport to act on that basis in dealing with certain groups of people, sooner or later the requirement of consistency will force us to behave accordingly in our dealings with other groups of people. Otherwise, we will have to admit openly that we are either irrational or, what on a moral level is an analogous notion, insincere. Whether, in the course of our initial actions towards some group of people, we enunciated the principle of the equality of all human beings because we felt it was a binding moral norm or because it was the socially

---

[73] These questions are pursued at greater length in my paper, 'Rhetoric, Consistency, and Human Progress, Legal or Otherwise', that was the basis of the 1976 Pope John XXIII Lecture delivered at the Catholic University of America in March 1976. 26 *Cath. U. L. Rev.* 73 (1976). Hume, of course, recognised that 'men are rightly addicted to general rules' and that without pausing to reflect they 'often carry . . . [their] maxims beyond those reasons, which first induced . . . [them] to establish them'. *Treatise* at Book III, Pt. II, § IX (551). This is a somewhat different, although important, point. Men can and do, in their unreflective moments, pursue a spurious or 'foolish' consistency. I am considering the case where men have reflected and now realise that their immediate interest conflicts with the maxims they have enunciated on the occasion of their prior actions.

expedient thing to do is really not crucial. Cynics and opportunists have been trapped in their own rhetoric as much as so-called idealists who feel that their conduct is directed by norms that they accept as binding. The process of legal decision-making consists in permitting the parties to present argument as to what is and what is not consistent with the existing body of the law,[74] and these arguments are supposed to, and indeed often do, decisively influence the decision-makers. Whatever other factors may influence their decision-making, it is beyond dispute that they are motivated by a desire to appear to be consistent. It is the purpose of scholarly criticism to ensure that decision-makers strive hard to keep up this appearance.

All of this having been said, one is immediately met with the observation that few, if any, people would agree that the process of applying the law is wholly consistent. How does one account for this variance? I would try to do so in two ways. First, how seriously we are able to take a requirement of consistency and apply it to our various activities depends on a combination of how seriously we take the activity in question and upon the means available to us to achieve consistency. It is common ground that law is a serious activity.[75] The ritual and solemnity surrounding judicial activity is designed to emphasise this in case the importance of what transpires in courts were not enough to make it clear. In the law, moreover, there are highly stylised means of achieving consistency. To illustrate what I mean, a model of how consistency is achieved in the law is set out in Part II. It is the availability of more sophisticated machinery for achieving consistency rather than the fact that law supposedly consists of norms that accounts for the more rigorous standards of consistency in legal argument. But, as is also shown in Part II, there are limits to the degree of consistency that is unobtainable. This, then, is one reason why one can never hope to be able to convince sceptical observers that the law is completely consistent.

The other reason complete consistency is unobtainable and possibly—here I am sceptical—undesirable, is that there are two

[74] In Part II of this book, I submit that the existing body of the law is most usefully considered as a set of past authoritatively determined cases. Statutes are treated as the set of the paradigm cases covered by a statute together with the prior judicial decisions, cases, if any, interpreting a statute. See pp. 57-61, infra.

[75] The seriousness of legal activity is well stated by H. L. A. Hart, *Concept of Law* at 84-6.

kinds of rationality running through the legal process. Using Weber's terminology, we may call them *formal* rationality and *substantive* rationality.[76] Consistency is more a requirement of formal rationality although, of course, without some degree of consistency substantive rationality, even human communication itself would be unachievable. Indeed, formal rationality may be defined as the type of rationality in which consistency is the *sine qua non*. In formal logic, for example, consistency is the ultimate goal. Without it there is no 'logic'. Therefore, even if total consistency were obtainable, which it is not, we might be unwilling to obtain it at the cost of sacrificing the other values which we group together under the rubric of 'substantive rationality'. If the end does not always justify the means, it may perhaps sometimes be more important than the means. At any rate, since legal reasoning utilises ordinary language and since there are inherent limitations to the degree of consistency obtainable in any system of argument that uses ordinary language—because the meaning of the terms used in ordinary language is never precisely defined and is always subject to modification—complete formal rationality in any meaningful sense is not even a theoretical possibility in legal argument.

If the normative quality of law is associated with the requirement of consistency, and if consistency itself is a requirement of all rational argument, although legal argument may have available techniques of achieving consistency that are generally not available to other forms of informal argumentation, how do we account for the quality of 'oughtness' which surrounds the conclusions of legal argument and which seems lacking in other forms of informal argumentation? This does indeed seem to be a qualitative difference between legal reasoning and other forms of reasoning, particularly non-formal ones. The difference can partly be explained by the seriousness of the matters affected by legal argument and by the overwhelming power, at least in the modern state, which can be mobilised to enforce legal decisions,[77] but these factors do not seem to be enough to account entirely for this qualitative difference in the notions of oughtness surrounding our concept of law and the conclusions of legal

[76] This distinction underlies much of Weber's writing. For an extended treatment of the distinction, see M. Weber, *Law in Economy and Society* at 224-55.

[77] This is a point emphasised by the Scandinavian legal realists, particularly Hagerstrom and Olivecrona, whose work will be discussed in Part IV of this book.

reasoning. A more complete account would have to bring in notions of authority and legitimacy. These are questions to which we shall turn in Part III. What we have maintained in this portion of the book is that this quality of the law is not adequately explained by postulating that law consists of a set or sets of binding norms which state what judges and other users of the law ought to do.

7. *The binding nature of law*

(i) *General observations*

It has been suggested that if anything about the law could be said to be truly normative—that is felt to be binding by a large number of people living in a political society—it is certain basic and widely shared commitments. These include the acceptance by most people (and by most judges and officials themselves) that judges and other officials are bound to apply the constitution and validly enacted statutes. There is also, finally, a fundamental commitment to consistency in the application of the law. Is there anything more to the binding nature of law when law is looked at from the societal point of view? There is no question that, even when people cannot agree as to exactly what the law on a particular question is, they still talk about legal obligations despite the fact that they are unable to agree on the exact content of those obligations. I have suggested that in order to account for these feelings—which the various theories of norms have tried to account for but in point of fact have been unable so to do—we must broaden our inquiry and examine concepts like authority and legitimacy which are crucial components of any examination of an on-going legal system. As has been previously noted, this is an inquiry that will be pursued in Part III. Is there anything else to be said on the subject of the binding nature of law before we embark on that extended inquiry?

Certainly, when judges talk about rules of law, or legal norms, that impose legal obligations or duties, the judges are often making claims that such entities do in fact exist and that they have in fact correctly identified them. The same may often be said about similar statements about legal rules or norms made by lawyers. Furthermore, these claims about the existence of norms and the obligations they impose

may indeed often be more than claims that such normative statements are part of a particular normative system. It will be recalled
that this is how Raz ultimately resolves the problem of 'the
normativity of law'.[78] For him, to declare that some statement
describes a legal norm is to express a belief about a logical relationship, namely that the norm in question is part of some normative
system. For many lawyers and judges, however, the claim that some
verbal formulation states a legal rule or norm often is in fact a claim
about the psychically binding nature of the purported rules or norms.
Raz, of course, would be prepared to admit this could be so. But the
people making these claims would often also be prepared to assert,
contra Raz, that it is this feature of psychic compulsion and this feature
alone that accounts for the normativity of law. In other words, for
these people the normativity of law is not primarily a logical quality.

Admittedly, when stress is laid on the quality of actually being
bound it is impossible to determine exactly what the norms imposing
these binding obligations are. The reactions of people differ and
moreover these people might not all understand the norm in precisely
the same way. When this psychic feature of so-called norms is stressed
as accounting for the normativity of law, what is a norm becomes a
fairly individualised thing. The most each speaker can assert is that
some particular norm that he identifies creates the appropriate
feelings of being 'psychically bound' in himself and he believes that
they produce the same effects in others. Raz's conclusion that
normative statements are logical statements about the membership of
a purported norm in a normative system may have been partially
reached in order to avoid this extreme individualisation of what so-
called norms are. Nevertheless, his conclusion, which has entailed the
sacrifice of many features of what for many people is the essence of
the normativity of law, is itself subject to the problems of extreme
individualisation. That is, a speaker's statement that some verbal
formulation is a norm is merely an expression of the speaker's own
belief that the purported norm is a member of a normative system.
The evidence from which he reaches that belief is rarely so clear as to
produce the exact same belief in all other informed observers however
disinterested they might be. In the last analysis to view statements
about legal norms as statements expressing beliefs as to the membership of a normative system may be no more than a recognition of the

[78] See text accompanying note 12, supra.

truism that each person has to organise his experience in a way that gives it a certain minimal logical coherence.

These are all problems to which we adverted earlier when we argued that it is not very helpful to think of a legal system as a collection of objectively ascertained legal rules or norms.[79] And yet, despite the logical problems, there is no question that the model of a legal system as a set of binding norms which psychically operate on large numbers of people continues to seem attractive. One method perhaps of avoiding the logical problem is Ronald Dworkin's original suggestion that, even if it is true that there is no objective test which can conclusively determine in many cases whether a judge reached the right decision; i.e., the decision which the valid norms of the legal system compelled him to reach, nevertheless for each individual judge there is one right answer.[80] It is the individual judge's duty to search for this right answer. Does this mean anything more than that a judge should be honest and try his best? And try his best to do what? To reach the right decision, of course. But what is the right decision? It is the decision that is right for him. But what is the decision that is the right one for any judge? Are we back to the 'judicial hunch'? Are good judges therefore what Judge Hutcheson would call 'good hunchers'?[81] How does a person know he has come up with the right decision or, if you will, the right hunch? Is it something he feels in his bones? Is it something that can generate the same emotional reaction in others? One recalls that Karl Llewellyn's notion of the 'law of the singing reason' came close to making this sort of claim as to how one knows one has arrived at the correct legal conclusion.[82] Clearly all this will not save the theory of norms. One cannot maintain that the law

[79] See text at pp. 7-10, supra.

[80] This is a thesis which underlies most of Dworkin's writing. It was first articulated in his 'Judicial Discretion', 60 *J.Phil.* 624 (1963) and to some extent, was still being pursued in his 'Hard Cases', 88 *Harv.L.Rev.* 1057 (1975) (*TRS* at 81). Cf. note 18, supra and text. See also the text at note 71, supra. As we shall see shortly, however, Dworkin has over time come more and more to insist that there is in fact one objectively correct right answer even though he still concedes it may not be possible conclusively to establish what the right answer is to the satisfaction of all objective observers.

[81] See J. Hutcheson, 'The Judgment Intuitive: The Function of the "Hunch" in Judicial Decision', 14 *Cornell L.Q.* 274 (1929).

[82] K. Llewellyn, *The Common Law Tradition: Deciding Appeals* 183 (1960). Cf. id. at 222-3.

consists of sets of norms because people feel that it does. A coherent theory of law as a set of norms demands more than that.

Over the course of time Dworkin has tried to put some flesh into his contention that there are 'right answers' even in 'hard cases'. Initially, as we have seen, he asserted that when the existing rules of law did not cover a case or where the existing rules of law were in conflict, resort could be had to principles to discover what the right decision was.[83] He recognised, however, that a number of principles could point in competing directions and might even directly conflict. Thus a means for weighting principles must be discovered but thus far neither he nor anyone else has produced that weighted list of principles. Taking a slightly different tack, Dworkin then asserted that, in difficult cases, it is the task of the judge 'to find a coherent set of principles' that will justify 'in the way that fairness requires' the decision in the instant case in the light of the 'institutional history' of society's legal structure.[84] Pursuing this suggestion further he has now, in his most recent work, claimed that in an advanced and complex society with a long legal tradition, such as the United States or Great Britain, it will only be in relatively rare cases that one set of principles, and the decision they justify, will not provide a better fit with society's basic legal structure than a competing set of principles pointing to a different or even contrary decision.[85] Dworkin does not support this assertion; he assumes that it is obviously true. He assumes that there is some notion of 'normative consistency' that

---

[83] See pp. 8-9, supra and accompanying footnote references.

[84] *Hard Cases* at 1098-9 (*TRS* at 120-1). Where the case concerns the interpretation of a statute the inquiry is pitched in terms of 'which interpretation of the different interpretations admitted by the abstract meaning of the [statutory] term [is under consideration], best advances the set of principles and policies that provides the best political justification for the statute at the time it was passed.' *No Right Answer?* at 13. See also *Hard Cases* at 1086-7 (*TRS* at 108-10). While criticising Dworkin's distinction between direct judicial resort to policies, which according to Dworkin is legitimate, and judicial resort to principle, which according to Dworkin is legitimate, Professor Greenawalt illustrates the lack of warrant for any claim that resort to these institutional principles narrows the range of judicial decision-making as much as Dworkin claims it does. K. Greenawalt, 'Policy, Rights, and Judicial Decision', 11 *Ga. L. Rev.* 991 (1977). I will not pursue the question further as to whether Dworkin's approach channels the task of statutory interpretation sufficiently to permit meaningful talk of the right answer in the interpretation of statutes. I refer the reader to cases like Standard Oil Co. v. United States, 337 U.S. 293 (1949).

[85] *No Right Answer?* at 20.

can be relied upon to support his position.[86] Furthermore, when one
of these rare cases arises, that is when no one set of principles is
accepted by most of the participants in the legal enterprise as
dispositive of the hard case in question, recourse should be had,
Dworkin now asserts, to what he calls 'moral facts'.[87] These, in some
way, proceed from moral and political theory and ultimately produce
moral rights. Thus, in the hard cases, when legal theory cannot
produce the right answer, the right answer may still be found by
asking what moral rights are at stake. Dworkin claims that it will be
an 'extremely rare' case, if any such cases 'exist at all', that there will
be any 'no-right-answer' cases in the United States and Great
Britain.[88]

The difficulties with this last point are obvious. It assumes
ultimately that there are almost always 'right answers' to moral
questions because otherwise, under his theory, there cannot always
be right answers to legal questions. Many people would, of course,
not accept this view of the decidability of moral questions.[89]
Furthermore, the use of such terminology as 'moral rights' lends a
spurious sense of concreteness to his discussion. The sense of
concreteness is spurious because, although the notion of a right seems
to be specific enough at least if we could articulate the moral theory
that generates the right, in point of fact whatever the theory—legal or
moral—the notion of right is meaningless without the correlative
notion of duty. Take the so-called 'right to marry and found a family'
that is contained in the Universal Declaration of Human Rights.[90]
Does this right entail merely a duty upon the state not to interfere
with an individual's personal decision to marry and have children or
does it mean that the state has a duty to provide each person a mate or
that some other individual has a duty to marry him? Dworkin in his
writings often discusses a 'presumed absolute right to be treated as an

---

[86] Id. at 28-9. In Part II of this book, in which we will discuss the notion of
consistency in the law, it will be seen that the notion of normative consistency in the
law is a very difficult one indeed and that, if normative consistency is a requirement
for the existence of consistency in legal reasoning, consistency in legal reasoning may
be unattainable.

[87] Id. at 30-2.

[88] Id. at 31-2.

[89] This is one of the points stressed by K. Greenawalt, supra note 84, at 1037-53.

[90] Art. 16, par. 1.

equal, that is with equal concern and respect'.[91] Suppose we all agree that there is such a moral right. What follows from that? What positive acts can we demand from other people or the state? Again, take the right of free speech that is guaranteed by the First Amendment of the United States Constitution. Does it entail a right not to have other people physically prevent one from speaking? How about inter- ference with speech by other people making so much noise that the speaker cannot be heard? Suppose no one wants to come and listen to the speaker. Can he insist that other people must come and listen to him or give him time on the radio or space in a newspaper? The notion of a right by itself answers none of these questions. It is for this reason that under Hohfeld's scheme of jural relations it is meaningless to talk about a person having a right *to do* anything.[92] All a person has are rights that other people do some specific thing, such as pay him $1,000 or not hit him, etc., and without knowing what these specific things are that others must do or not do the notion of a right is largely an empty one. Hohfeld's strictures on the notion of legal rights are just as relevant to the notion of moral rights. Thus, even if one could agree on what are the so-called moral rights accepted in a particular society, recourse to such rights is only helpful to resolve disputes if they are fleshed out into a statement of what duties on the part of other people they entail. Dworkin has not done this and thus cannot legitimately rely on the notion of moral rights to support his claim that there still are right answers in those difficult legal cases in which legal materials do not provide the right answer.

(ii) *Concluding preliminary remarks on the notion of the binding nature of law*

We have previously had occasion to refer to Ross's attempt to accommodate the normative aspects of law to the realist view that the law consists of sets of predictions of the future behaviour of judges.[93]

---

[91] See e.g. *No Right Answer?* at 31.

[92] This is the point of Hohfeld's criticism of John Chipman Gray's discussion of a 'right to eat shrimp salad'. J. C. Gray, *The Nature and Sources of the Law* 19 (2d ed. 1921). See W. Hohfeld, *Fundamental Legal Conceptions* 40-1 (1919) (responding to the first edition of *The Nature and Sources of the Law*, which is differently paginated). In Hohfeld's scheme what Gray and others called rights to do something are merely privileges. A privilege to do something is simply the absence of a duty not to do something.

[93] See the discussion in the first part of Section 5, supra, and also the discussion in Section 4, supra at 23-7.

A statement purporting to state a valid norm is a prediction that, when a set of facts arises to which the norm is applicable, the norm in question 'will form an integral part of the reasoning underlying the judgment' rendered in that case.[94] For Ross, the major source of these predictions, as well as the major source of confirming them, will be the observable behaviour of judges. We have already had occasion to review the major criticisms of realism and these need not be repeated here.[95] For present purposes it is enough to note again that H. L. A. Hart, who views the law as a set of rules, has made the valid criticism that a judge is not concerned with predicting his own behaviour.[96] A judge is concerned, rather, with deciding a case in accordance with the law that he considers binding upon him in the case before him. Therefore, statements as to what are the legal rules or norms binding upon judges cannot be shorthand statements of predictions of the behaviour of judges. Thus far the criticism is well taken.

But it is a mistake summarily to dismiss Ross's work; for I believe he has come close to an important insight. When a person states a supposed rule or norm of law, I would assert that such a person is expressing his present belief that the requirements of consistency in the application of law and a commitment to the fundamental postulates of a legal system, such as the primacy of the constitution and of the validly enacted statutes of that system, will require a judge to decide cases as if the purported norm were binding upon him. If the person making the statement as to what is a valid norm is a judge he is doing one or both of two things: he is stating his present belief that the requirements of consistency and the fundamental postulates of the legal system require him to decide the case before him in accordance with the purported norm he has enunciated and/or he is stating his present belief as to what these same factors will require a future judge to consider as binding in a future case. The questions, on the other hand, that the theory of norms has tried to answer, namely the question of what is a legal system and even the question of what is the law of that system, are all empirical questions that cannot be decided definitively by logical analysis.

I consider that the above analysis brings into view just about all the sense that really can be made of statements concerning 'valid legal

[94] A. Ross, *Law and Justice* at 42.

[95] See pp. 23-6, supra.

[96] See H. L. A. Hart, 'Scandinavian Realism', 1975 *Camb. L. J.* 233.

norms'. It is, moreover, probably this minimal meaning of statements about legal norms that explains why legal philosophers are reluctant to give up the assumption that there are such things as valid and binding norms of law and accounts for the widely shared feeling that judges really are searching for right answers; answers that are right not only in the sense of being just but, more importantly, right because they are the correct answers.

As I have noted several times, the whole question of the existence and, particularly, of the acceptance of a legal system is tied up with the questions of authority and legitimacy that will be explored in Part III. First, in Part II, however, I will consider how the requirement of consistency operates in legal reasoning.

Part II

Consistency in Legal Reasoning

1. *Introduction*

The discussion in Part I proceeded on the basis not only that the theory that law consists of set of norms is unsupportable but also that a theory of norms is not necessary in order to account for either the comparatively greater rigour of legal argumentation or the fact that judges and other participants in the legal process feel 'bound' by the law. Much of the work that the theory of norms is unable to perform, despite its promises to the contrary, can be accomplished and explained if we recognise the importance of consistency in legal reasoning and examine the means by which legal argument achieves consistency. The model to be presented below is an explication of how consistency is achieved in legal argument.[1] It approaches the problem by asking what it is we are saying when we assert that the validity of legal reasoning is to be judged by objective rather than subjective criteria. For surely, if there is anything to the assertion that consistency plays a major role in legal reasoning, there must be objective criteria for ascertaining whether any particular process of legal reasoning has in point of fact met the requirement of consistency. What is meant by objectivity in legal reasoning will appear sufficiently as the discussion proceeds.[2] It may nevertheless be helpful at this point to stress that, if a system of decision-making is to be called a legal system, it must make it possible for people who

---

[1] The model of reasoning to be presented below is adapted, with some deletions, changes, and additions, from that presented in G. Christie, 'Objectivity in the Law', 78 *Yale L.J.* 1311 (1969).

[2] Because the discussion contained in this book is directed towards general philosophical notions rather than precise legal issues many of the legal questions presented as illustrations are not pursued as fully as they would be in a law review article. Those interested in more extended discussion of some of these legal issues, and for more detailed citations of authority are referred to *Objectivity in the Law*, supra.

disagree strongly over the merits of a decision to agree nevertheless that the case was properly decided, or, if this is impossible, at least to agree that the decision was adequately justified. Although it is generally accepted that the law does in fact meet this requirement, scholars have been unable to show how and why it is met or even to prove that it is met at all. Part II of this book will attempt to explain this inability by examining the conditions which judicial decision-making must fulfil in order to meet the minimal standard of objectivity. It should in addition be noted that, in the parlance of contemporary philosophy, the proposed model is an explication of the concept of legal reasoning. As an explication, the model is prescriptive because, in exploring the concept, it attempts to stipulate what legal reasoning would have to be in order to meet the demands of objectivity made upon it. Yet it is also descriptive because it is partially based on what actually occurs in the legal process.[3]

2. Traditional theories of legal reasoning

Because identifiable 'norms', 'rules', 'principles' and 'standards' do not exist, any theory of legal reasoning that requires them is necessarily incomplete. If one asks himself what so-called rules of law are, he will be obliged to conclude that they are constructs formed by scholars writing books and articles, by lawyers litigating cases, and by judges preparing to decide cases. As such they serve a very useful purpose. They are first of all, a helpful mnemonic device for classi-fying large numbers of cases. They provide a concise shorthand for referring to matters which, at any particular moment, are not in issue.[4] As general statements of our expectations and preferences,

---

[3] On the subject of explication, see Hempel, 'Fundamentals of Concept Formation in Empirical Science', 2 *International Encyclopedia of Unified Science No. 7* 11-12 (1952).

[4] See L. Fuller & R. Braucher, *Basic Contract Law* 327-8 (1964). For other sources recognising the purely instrumental nature of legal 'rules', see Cook, 'Scientific Method and the Law', 13 *A.B.A.J.* 303 (1927); Corbin, 'Sixty-eight Years at Law', 13 *U.Kan.L.Rev.* 183 (1964). The point was put very well by a noted contemporary philo-sopher: 'Principles and laws may serve us well. They can help us to bring to bear on what is now in question what is *not* now in question. They help us to connect one thing with another and another. But at the bar of reason, always the final appeal is to cases' (emphasis supplied). Wisdom, 'A Feature of Wittgenstein's Technique', in J. Wisdom, *Paradox and Discovery* 90, 102 (1965). The same point has been made by the Supreme Court. '[T]he error made by the Court of Appeals was precisely its reliance

they also provide a means of predicting the outcomes of future cases and arguing about the desirability of those outcomes. Yet the position that rules are the actual content of the law, rather than a means of understanding it, is untenable because there are any number of so-called rules which logically can be constructed out of any given number of cases, and there is no authoritative statement of which is correct. Under traditional theory, not even a court's express attempt to state the correct rule is authoritative; it is only evidence of what the rule is, and sometimes not even the best evidence.

If we took seriously the attempts of even the most prestigious courts to state correct rules of law, we would be forced to conclude that half the decided cases in England and America were decided improperly.[5] Indeed, these attempts at generalisation have left us with the unsolvable problem of distinguishing between the supposed *holding* of a case, often expressed as a rule or rules of law, and what is merely *dictum*. The English have taken this distinction more seriously than the Americans, although they have often concentrated on formulating the rule of a particular case rather than the rule of a series of cases. They have nevertheless found even the search for the *ratio decidendi* of individual cases to be the pursuit of a chimaera. The best minds in the profession joined in the search but have disagreed even as to what was being sought.[6] Attempting to base their search on some notion of the

---

on formulas extracted from their contexts rather than on pragmatic analysis.' Provident Tradesmen's Bank & Trust Co. v. Patterson, 390 U.S. 102, 119, n.16 (1968) (Justice Harlan).

[5] See, e.g. Le Lievre v. Gould, 1893 1 Q.B. 491 (C.A.), in which Lord Esher was compelled to retreat from the principles delimiting the nature of liability for negligence that he had enunciated in Heaven v. Pender, 11 Q.B.D. 503, 509 (C.A. 1883). Compare Lord Atkin's famous statement concerning the extent of liability for negligence, in Donoghue v. Stevenson, [1932] A.C. 562, 589 (Scot.), with Commn'r for Railways v. Quinlan, [1964], A.C. 1054 (P.C.), especially id. at 1070.

[6] Compare Goodhart, 'Determining the Ratio Decidendi of a Case', 40 *Yale L.J.* 161 (1930), reprinted in A. Goodhart, *Essays in Jurisprudence and Common-Law* (1931), with Gooderson, 'Ratio Decidendi and Rules of Law', 30 *Can.B.Rev.* 892 (1952); cf. G. Williams, *Learning the Law* 71-7 (7th ed. 1963). See Goodhart, 'The Ratio Decidendi of a Case', 22 *Mod.L.Rev.* 117 (1959). For a general review of the subject see J. Stone, *Legal System and Lawyer's Reasoning* 267-80 (1964). See also K. Llewellyn, *The Bramble Bush* (1960); Simpson, 'The Ratio Decidendi of a Case and the Doctrine of Binding Precedent', in *Oxford Essays in Jurisprudence* 148 (A. Guest ed. 1961). For an interesting review of the subject by a philosopher, see Sartorius, 'The Doctrine of Precedent and the Problem of Relevance', 53 *Archiv fur Rechts— Und Socialphilosophie* 343 (1967). For a rejection of the view that there is only one *ratio decidendi* in a case and a reinterpretation of *ratio decidendi* as an hypothesis whose verification is supplied by an examination of

relevant facts of a case, they found that selecting the relevant facts was no easier than determining the rule of law itself.[7] Here again, a court's statement that certain facts were relevant to its decision was not conclusive,[8] and the difficulties of the search were compounded by the possibility that later courts might say that the bar misunderstood the *ratio decidendi* of any particular case. *Hedley Byrne & Co.* v. *Heller & Partners, Ltd.*[9] revealed that the Court of Appeal and most of the bar had been operating for seventy-five years under a mistaken view of the *ratio decidendi* of *Derry* v. *Peek.*[10] A concept of such mythical

---

hypothetical cases, see R. Stone, 'Logic and the Law: The Precedence of Precedents', 51 *Minn.L.Rev.* 655, 659 n.21, 661 n.24 (1967).

[7] The failure of the attempt to buttress the theory on some notion of the 'relevant' or 'material' 'facts' is discussed in detail in J. Stone, *Legal System and Lawyer's Reasoning* 267-74 (1964).

[8] Attempts to treat a particularly succinct and sensible judicial statement as a statute, so that future development of the rule would be an interpretation of that statement, have ended in failure. Cf. the treatment of Indermaur v. Dames, L.R. 1 C.P. 274 (1866) in London Graving Dock Ltd. v. Horton [1951] A.C. 737. Lord MacDermott declared: 'The matter cannot, of course, be settled merely by treating the ipsissima verba of Willes, J., as though they were part of an Act of Parliament and applying the rules of interpretation appropriate thereto' (id. at 761). See also Lord Porter's speech, id. at 744, Lord Normand's speech, id. at 751, and the House of Lords' treatment of the 'rule of construction derived from Shelmer's Case', Gilb. 200 (1725), concerning the meaning of the word 'money' in a will, in Perrin v. Morgan [1943] A.C. 399, 405.

[9] [1964] A.C. 465 (1963). The case stated that liability for negligent misrepresentation could lie even in the absence of the special relationships of attorney-client, trustee-beneficiary, etc., and that Derry v. Peek, infra note 10, merely held that an allegation of outright fraud had been inadequately proved rather than that an action for negligent misrepresentation would not lie on the facts of that case.

[10] [1889] A.C. 337. Among those who seem to have been confused was Lord Devlin, a member of the panel that decided *Hedley Byrne*. See P. Devlin, *Law and Morals* 15 (1961). In *Hedley Byrne*, the House of Lords declared that there was no warrant for this misunderstanding after Lord Shaw's speech in Nocton v. Ashburton, [1914] A.C. 932, 965. *Nocton* came twenty-five years after *Derry* itself and twenty-one years after the *ratio decidendi* of *Derry* was misunderstood in Le Lievre v. Gould, [1893] 1 Q.B. 491. Whether many eyes were opened in 1914 is another matter, however. The Court of Appeal felt bound to follow *Le Lievre* in Candler v. Crane, Christmas & Co., [1951] 2 K.B. 164. Even Denning, L.J., who dissented in *Candler*, was unaware of the true state of affairs, for he thought that while *Derry* did rule on the question of liability for negligent misrepresentation, it had merely held that on its own peculiar facts an action would not lie. [1951] 2 K.B. at 177. In *Law and Morals* Lord Devlin himself seems to have thought that *Nocton* was only a limited exception to the general rule denying liability for negligent misrepresentation absent a contractual duty of truthfulness. Moreover, in his speech in *Hedley Byrne*, Lord Devlin indicates that the misunderstanding of *Derry* was general in the profession. [1964] A.C. at 528. This general misunderstanding, as well as his own earlier feelings on the issue, may account for

proportions does little to bolster attempts to establish the objectivity of legal reasoning by reference to the binding nature of legal precedent as expressed in rules.[11]

In America, the most generally accepted theory of the nature of legal reasoning is that of Edward Levi. Levi hypothesised that the law consists of rules, however imprecise, derived from previously-decided cases and existing statutes.[12] When new cases arise, the courts must declare a rule which encompasses the relevant statutes, the unoverruled past cases, and the new case. If the courts cannot state such a rule, then some or all of the past cases must be overruled until it is possible to subsume the new case and the remaining prior cases under a single rule. The present case will then be decided in accordance with this rule. The process is repeated as new cases arise. Levi characterised his method of legal reasoning as a 'moving classi-fication system'.[13] It has often been described as a process of synthesis

---

Lord Devlin's hesitation in indicating when such liability would arise. [1964] A.C. at 523, 532. The question whether the information was directly communicated to the person who relied upon it assumed an importance in Lord Devlin's mind which it did not seem to have when he wrote *Law and Morals*. See [1964] A.C. at 533. It is in-disputable that the contemporary understanding of the profession was that, in the absence of privity of contract or some special relationship, such as attorney/client or trustee/beneficiary, Derry v. Peek established that no action lies for merely negligent misrepresentation. See 34 *Solicitor's Journal* 140 (1889).

[11] As we have seen, it is sometimes asserted that the notion of rule is necessary to account for the 'binding' nature of law. See H. L. A. Hart, *The Concept of Law* 77-96 (1961). For one who accepts it, a rule is a good reason for acting in the way the rule directs, over and above prudential reasons which might exist. Such a person adopts what Hart calls an 'internal' point of view, as opposed to the 'external' point of view of a person who obeys a rule only because of fear of sanctions. Leaving aside the facts that rules cannot be specified precisely and that most people are unaware of most of the so-called legal rules which bind them, there still seem to be few people in society who can be said to accept *all* of its rules as binding independently of fear of sanctions. 'Internal' factors may often play a small part in determining obedience to laws governing the sale of liquor, sexual behaviour, taxation, and traffic. As we have repeatedly maintained in this book, to ask why law is binding is to ask more than a logical question.

[12] See E. Levi, *An Introduction to Legal Reasoning* (1948) (hereafter cited as *Introduction to Legal Reasoning*). See also E. Levi, 'The Nature of Judicial Reasoning', 32 *U. Chi. L. Rev.* 395, 398-403 (1965) (hereafter cited as *Nature of Legal Reasoning*).

[13] Id. 398, 406. See also *Introduction to Legal Reasoning* at 1-3. Levi distinguished between cases and statutes on the ground that the words of a statute are fixed authoritatively, although he admits that there 'may be some ambiguity in the words used' (id. at 28; cf. id. at 30). He refers primarily to vagueness rather than ambiguity in the strict sense. All words are to some extent vague; not all of them are ambiguous. See G. Christie, 'Vagueness and Legal Language', 48 *Minn. L. Rev.* 885 (1964). Thus

and resynthesis.[14]

The late Professor Karl Llewellyn, who used a similar model of the judicial process, described in greater detail the techniques courts use in operating this moving classification system.[15] If, for example, a court wishes to follow precedent, it could say that 'the rule is too firmly established to disturb',[16] thereby also affirming that the present case was within the scope of the rule obtained from prior cases. If it wished to avoid overruling previous cases, a court could say that each case of the type before it 'must be dealt with on its own facts',[17] thus restricting the scope of the rule for which the prior cases stood. To extend the reach of an earlier case, a court could lift some general language from a prior case and put it into rule form without regard to the limitations imposed by the facts of that case.[18] In short, the decision-making techniques that Llewellyn catalogued are means by which the courts, in the process of synthesis and resynthesis, can openly or covertly reformulate the rule for which the prior cases stand.

The difficulties with this model are immediately apparent. First, the theory must recognise that subsequent courts are always free to reformulate the rule of law for which prior cases stand. Furthermore, as Levi[19] and Llewellyn[20] both admit, there are no objective criteria for deciding what is the correct rule of law to be found in any prior case or cases. The latter is the more serious problem. If the theory is to describe an objective decision-making procedure, it requires the existence of objectively discernible rules of law which serve as the starting points of legal reasoning. In point of fact, however, there are logically any number of rules of law to be derived from any case or

---

the 'moving classification system' applies to statutes as well as cases, subject to Levi's proviso that in interpreting statutes a rigorous notion of stare decisis must be observed. *An Introduction to Legal Reasoning.*

[14] It seems to me that this terminology is the most usual. Cf. N. Dowling, E. Patterson & R. Powell, *Materials for Legal Method* 155-215 (1946).

[15] K. Llewellyn, *The Common Law Tradition: Deciding Appeals* 77-91 (1960) (hereafter cited as *Common Law Tradition*). See also K. Llewellyn, *The Bramble Bush* 56-69 (1960) (hereafter cited as *Bramble Bush*).

[16] *Common Law Tradition* at 77.

[17] Id. at 84.

[18] Id. at 79.

[19] *Introduction to Legal Reasoning* at 1-4.

[20] See *Common Law Tradition* at 62-3.

series of cases. In addition, because statements in prior judicial opinions are themselves not rules of law but only evidence from which the correct rules may be ascertained, the theory must acknowledge that there can never be, even momentarily, an authoritative statement of a correct rule of law. Yet under the theory, rules of law are the essential raw material of legal reasoning.

Levi apparently recognised the difficulty of establishing correct or true rules of law. He construed Professor Wechsler's call for 'neutral principles' as a plea for extending the synthesis of existing cases to include as many similar hypotheticals as one can realistically imagine, and then rejected the plea as unwise.[21] He feared that, in attempting to increase the rationality of judicial decisions, Professor Wechsler asked too much of the courts. Levi suggested that Wechsler's request might even be dangerous, because, in attempting to find a rule of law to cover this extended range of hypotheticals, the courts may be led to decide future cases prematurely and to foreclose the consideration of important distinctions.

Professor Llewellyn was also aware of the difficulty of formulating a correct rule of law from a case or series of cases. He expressed this difficulty in terms of the 'minimum' and 'maximum' values of precedent, or in other words, the narrow and broad interpretations of case.[22] However, Llewellyn was never able to establish criteria for deriving these minimum and maximum values, or for determining whether a particular precedent should be given minimum, maximum, or some intermediate value in a particular case. Thus Llewellyn was forced to look beyond the mechanics of legal reasoning

---

[21] *Nature of Legal Reasoning* at 403-5. Part of Levi's objection to extending the synthesis to as many hypothetical cases as possible seems to result from his assumption that the ultimate basis of analogy is the 'similarity' between the cases under consideration. See *Introduction to Legal Reasoning* at 7, 9. It is submitted that epistemologically this assumption is incorrect. There are an infinite number of differences and similarities among any group of cases. A large number of similarities among the cases does not make the cases similar if there are significant differences as well. Thus the usefulness of analogy can be increased by dealing with differences rather than similarities, for when a significant difference is found the inappropriateness of the analogy will have been shown conclusively. The situation is not unlike questions about the truth of scientific hypotheses. For example, statements like 'all swans are white' can only be disproved; they can never be proved conclusively. See K. Popper, *The Logic of Scientific Discovery* 27-31 (1959). This epistemological point of view is reflected in the model of legal reasoning to be presented below.

[22] *Bramble Bush* at 69. Cf. Merryman, 'The Authority of Authority', 6 *Stan. L. Rev.* 613 (1954).

to support his thesis that the judicial activism of the past thirty years had not destroyed the predictability of judicial decision-making. He found this predictability in the fact that, in addition to generally accepted techniques for handling precedents, there were also 'correct results' to cases. Certain results, moreover, were so important that courts would occasionally be obliged to reach them regardless of what the accepted means of arranging precedents would permit.[23] In most situations, technique and result were interrelated. Capable practitioners and judges were aware of a 'Law of Fitness and Flavor' which enabled those who understood it to know what results justified what techniques.[24] Llewellyn posited finally a 'Law of the Singing Reason' which was fulfilled when 'a rule which wears both a right situation-reason and a clear scope-criterion on its face yields regularity, reckonability, and justice all together'.[25] In short, the law was predictable because it was a craft with known techniques, whose practitioners had long apprenticeships and whose goals were those of common sense. Since the decision-makers, the judges, were visible, the astute attorney was able to observe the responses of judges and thus to assemble the package of result and technique that was best for a particular court.

No one can deprecate the value of Llewellyn's insights into the nature of the judicial process, but it is more important for our purposes that his herculean attempt to demonstrate the predictability of judicial decision-making by means of the traditional model was forced to revert to a sense of craft and the notion of skill. The occasional contention that there is a correct decision for every case, even if it cannot be shown what that decision is,[26] seems no more than an extension of Llewellyn's view of the legal process as a skilled craft and of the lawyer as a skilled craftsman or even an artist. While a description of law as art may satisfy lawyers reminiscing at their clubs, it would be disquieting if this were the only answer that could be made to laymen who claim that law is not an objective process.

---

[23] *Common Law Tradition* at 219-22.

[24] Id. at 222-3.

[25] Id. at 183.

[26] That this surprising view—that for any judge there is only one correct decision, even if others cannot ascertain what it is—should be expressed by men of great ability is evidence of the felt need for objectivity in the law and of the inability of traditional models to meet this need. See the discussion of Dworkin's assertions in this regard in Part I, supra, section 7 of this book.

The profession must provide a better rationale than this or prepare to abandon its pretensions. It was out of dissatisfaction with legal theories of this type, with their focus on unknowable entities and their invitations to sophistry, that the legal realists emphasised the study of what the courts in fact were doing. The realist reaction was stimulated by traditional theories which insisted upon the existence of particular 'rules of law' even after the courts had decided cases in a manner irreconcilable with their existence.[27] Unfortunately, as we have already discussed in Part I, there are also serious inadequacies in the realistic approach.

3. *Law and argumentation*

Despite the many disappointments that have been experienced in the attempt to find criteria which establish the objectivity of judicial decision-making, the quest for these criteria has been resuscitated as part of the modern revival of the study of argumentation. The man most prominently associated with this revival is the Belgian philosopher, Chaim Perelman.[28] Perelman studies the techniques of practical reasoning and argument discussed by Aristotle in the *Topics* and the *Rhetoric*, applying and extending them to the problems of modern argumentation. Aristotle divided practical reasoning into two basic categories.[29] The first, dialectical reasoning, consists of reasoning deductively from premises that are only probable or that

---

[27] This is theoretically possible under the Blackstonian view that judicial decisions are only 'evidence' of what the law actually is, and that 'it sometimes may happen that the judge may *mistake* the law'. *1 W. Blackstone, Commentaries* *71. If a theory distinguishing judicial decisions from law is to be comprehensible, however, law must be defined as the prediction of the long-range trend of judicial decisions. Otherwise, to maintain a particular decision was not law would be tantamount to asserting that the critic had some special vision of truth which others lacked.

[28] Perelman's major work is the two-volume *Traité de l'Argumentation* (1958) which he co-authored with Mme. L. Olbrechts-Tyteca. This work has been translated into English. C. Perelman, *The New Rhetoric, A Treatise on Argumentation* (J. Wilkinson & P. Weaver transls. 1969) (hereafter cited as *Treatise*). Where pages in the *Treatise* are cited, parallel citations to the French edition will appear in brackets. Some of the papers reprinted in C. Perelman, *The Idea of Justice and the Problem of Argument* (Petrie transl. 1963) (hereafter cited as *Idea of Justice*) are similar to chapters in the *Treatise*.

[29] Cf. *Rhetoric* Bk. I, chs 1-2, 1354a-1356b25, in 11 *The Works of Aristotle Translated into English* (W. Ross ed. 1928) (hereafter cited as *Aristotle*); *Anal. Post* Bk. I, ch. 1, 71a1-10, in 1 *Aristotle*.

are generally but not universally considered true.[30] Because the premises used in dialectical reasoning are not necessarily true, the conclusions, though deduced correctly from these premises, will also not necessarily be true. Aristotle called the premises of dialectical reasoning *topoi* and in the *Topics* supplied a great number of examples of them.[31] *Topoi* are typically commonplace statements such as, 'what is desired for its own sake is more desirable than what is desired only for its effect',[32] or, 'of two things not otherwise distinguishable, that which produces the more beneficial effects is the more desirable'.[33] The *topoi* are not dissimilar in function from many maxims of the law, particularly those of statutory interpretation.[34] Like legal maxims, *topoi* can frequently be marshalled in support of contradictory conclusions.

Aristotle's second broad category of practical reasoning was rhetorical argument, which is concerned with persuasion and thus, should the discussion pertain to possible courses of action, with motivating the listener to act in a certain way.[35] Rhetoric employs a variety of tools. The astute orator will not only use dialectical reasoning but will also appeal to the presuppositions and the prejudices of his audience. He will know how to enhance his own prestige in order to dispose his audience to accept his views and how to destroy the prestige of his opponents in order to undermine the effects of their arguments.

Perelman was concerned with both dialectical and rhetorical

---

[30] *Topics* Bk. III, ch. 1, 100a-30ff., in 1 *Aristotle*; *Topics* Bk. I, ch. 10, 104a5ff., in 1 *Aristotle*.

[31] See especially Books II-VIII of the *Topics*. Aristotle sometimes called the syllogisms formed from the *topoi* enthymemes (*Anal. Pr.* Bk. II, ch. 27, 70a10, in 1 *Aristotle*), although he elsewhere restricts the term to the description of syllogisms which appear in the process of rhetorical reasoning. *Rhetoric* Bk. I, ch. 2, 1356bl-20. But cf. *Rhetoric* Bk. I, ch. 1, 12, 1255al-10.

[32] *Topics* Bk. III, ch. 1, 116a27-31.

[33] *Topics* Bk. III, ch. 2, 117a5-15.

[34] For a listing of typical maxims of statutory construction and a demonstration of the fact that different maxims can be marshalled in favour of contradictory decisions, see Llewellyn, 'Remarks on the Theory of Appellate Decision and the Rules or Canons about how Statutes are to be Construed', 3 *Vand. L. Rev.* 395 (1950). Much of this article is reproduced as Appendix C to *Common Law Tradition* at 521. For the broader 'maxims of equity', see J. Pomeroy, *Equity* 363 (1941).

[35] For a discussion of the scope and purpose of Aristotle's conception of rhetoric, see *Rhetoric* Bk. I, ch. 2 (1355b25ff.). See also id. Bk. I, ch. 1 (1354aff.).

argument.[36] He noted, of course, that the commonplace statements which can serve as premises in practical reasoning will vary with one's society and audience.[37] He pointed out contemporary examples of the commonplace arguments found in Aristotle and other ancient writers.[38] Perelman's major emphasis, however, was rhetorical argument—on persuading people to accept the conclusions and to act in accordance with the wishes of the orator.[39] In the main, his discussion was an expansion of Aristotle's method of analysis. His stressed that, in the last analysis, the test of a good argument is whether it succeeds with the audience to which it is addressed.[40]

Perelman concluded from his study of argumentation that the major problems of legal reasoning concern the 'interpretation' of legal rules. Interpretation occurs (a) when there is a conflict between two existing rules,[41] (b) when it is claimed that an otherwise applicable rule is not valid,[42] or (c) when there is no applicable rule on the subject but the judge is legally obliged to decide the case.[43] He did not, however, attempt to provide more enlightenment on these problems of interpretation than to remind us of the obvious point that the normal techniques of argumentation will apply. Not surprisingly, Perelman concluded that analogical reasoning plays a relatively

---

[36] *Treatise* at 1-9 [1-12]; cf. *Idea of Justice* at 134-42.

[37] *Treatise* §§2-9, 21, 26, 27. Perelman observes, however, that there are general groupings into which commonplace statements of varying content can be placed. The categories which he notes are quality, quantity, order, existence, essence, and person. Id. at 85 [114]. See also id. at §§22-4.

[38] Id. at §§21-4.

[39] Id. at 1-9 [1-12]. Perelman's conclusions regarding the techniques of rhetorical argument do not differ significantly from those of Aristotle. See id. at 5-8 [6-10]. See also id. at §§ 1-12.

[40] See id. at §§ 1-10.

[41] Id. at 196-7 [264-5], 200 [269], 414-15 [554-5], Cf. id. at 59 (78-9), where Perelman notes that there may be a conflict in the interpretation of a particular rule similar to the conflict between two rules.

[42] Id. at 59 [78-9].

[43] Id. at 59-60 [78-9], 131 [176]. Perelman discusses this situation in substantially the same manner in *The Idea of Justice* 100-1. The judge is 'legally obliged to decide the case' under some European codes which put the judge 'under an obligation to give judgment under pain of denial of justice'. Another legal problem discussed in both the *Treatise* and *The Idea of Justice* is the use of presumptions of fact as starting points of legal argument. *Treatise* 102-4 [136-40]; *The Idea of Justice* 102-8.

minor role in level argument, because what many people call analogical reasoning Perelman believes to be only the presentation of examples or instances of general rules.[44] He did not discuss at any length the application of law to concrete factual situations, since he assumed that such application is a rule-directed activity and therefore easier than 'interpreting' or establishing the existence of rules of law.[45]

In some of his other work, Perelman develops his emphasis on what he calls the 'quasi-logical' nature of legal argument. He sees the legal system as giving concrete expression to one of the more fundamental components of our sense of justice, the concept of equality.[46] The function of the legal process is to insure equality according to legal entitlement.[47] The quasi-logical nature of Perelman's conception of legal argument is emphasised when he declares that equality in this sense is the logical consequence of following legal rules. He recognises, however, that the rigour of this logic is tempered by our notion of 'equity'.[48] It ensures that we do not treat with excessive inequality persons who, apart from the rule of law then being applied, are generally considered as being essentially the same.[49] Perelman has not been content, however, to focus only on the application of law. He is interested in the broader and less formal aspects of 'justice'. He rightly believes that the rules of law themselves must be susceptible to impersonal criticism as well. The tool we use in this type of criticism is our notion of the 'arbitrary'.[50] A rule of law will be arbitrary if it cannot be deduced from a more general rule, which may be another legal rule or a moral rule. Eventually, however, we will reach the fundamental moral values of our society. We cannot go behind these by any process of quasi-logical reasoning that is so central to Perelman's notion of justice, particularly in a legal setting. We must

[44] *Treatise* 373-4 [502-3].

[45] Perelman discusses the application of legal rules as a subcategory of interpretation. If there is doubt about the applicability of a rule, it must first be made more precise so that its applicability or inapplicability becomes self-evident. *Treatise* 241 [325], 351[472], 354-5 (477), 356-7 (479-80).

[46] *Idea of Justice* 15-26. See also *Treatise* at § 52.

[47] *Idea of Justice* at 24-6.

[48] See id. at 29-36.

[49] See id. at 32.

[50] See id. at 45-50, 56-7.

either accept these fundamental values or argue about them with whatever rhetorical tools we possess; we cannot deduce them.[51] These again are interesting insights whose validity most people would be prepared to accept, with perhaps the *caveat* that, in a modern legal system, the most that one can hope to show is that its subsidiary 'rules' will not be inconsistent with society's generally accepted fundamental values. It is too stringent a requirement to insist that these subsidiary rules must be logically derived from these fundamental social values. These fundamental values are much too general and, what is more important, much too incomplete to account for the vast number of legal rules generated by a complex and heterogeneous society.

Even with these additions, however, we are still left with the problem of what Perelman calls the interpretation of legal rules that arises whenever legal materials need to be applied to concrete fact situations. Perelman is certainly aware of the problem, and, in some of his more recent work, has devoted considerable energy to the problem of what continental scholars call *'lacunae'* or gaps in the law.[52] Nevertheless, however, although Perelman's work on argumentation and its uses as a means of persuasion is interesting and perceptive, the reasons for the supposed objectivity of judicial decision-making as reflected in its drive for consistency, will not be found there.

The assumption that legal conclusions are controlled by rules underlies much of the other contemporary philosophical discussion about the nature of non-formal argumentation.[53] The fallacy of this assumption is particularly well illustrated by the conclusions of

[51] At one time, Perelman took the position that values were arbitrary. See id. at 57. But since the publication of his *Treatise*, he has resiled from that position. See *Idea of Justice* at 57, n.1, a note added to the English translation.

[52] *Le Problème des Lacunes en Droit* (C. Perelman ed. 1968). Perelman's contribution was, 'Le problème des lacunes en droit, essai de synthese', id. at 537. In continental jurisprudence, *lacunae* or 'gaps' which judges may properly fill in the process of applying the law, are distinguished from *creux* or 'cavities' which courts may not fill because it would entail the assumption of a legislative role. Perelman has also edited *Les antinomies en droit* (1965) and *Etudes de logique juridique*, Volume 1 (1966); Volume II (1967). His most recent work in English is *Justice, Law, and Argument, Essays on Moral and Legal Reasoning* (1980).

[53] See e.g., S. Toulmin, *The Place of Reason in Ethics* (1950). Toulmin asserts that, just as rules are institutionalised 'good reasons' for conclusions in legal arguments, similar good reasons can be found in ethical arguments. The use of the legal analogy pervades Toulmin's *The Uses of Argument* (1958). In *The Logic of Choice* (1968), Professor G. Gottlieb discusses the problem of legal decision-making to support his thesis that

Professor Julius Stone who actually tried to apply Pereleman's work to legal analysis.[54] Stone was unable to say more than that leading cases serve the function of Perelman's commonplace seats of argument, or Aristotle's *topoi*.[55] This observation is not especially valuable, as Stone himself acknowledged.[56] The basic and difficult question is how legal *topoi* are used and how it can be said that particular legal decisions are correctly derived from these starting points. If there are no means of answering these questions, it would be hard to say that there is anything objective in legal reasoning; one would be led to conclude that legal reasoning, far from being a more rigorous form of argument, suffers from all the defects of ordinary argument. Thus contemporary legal and philosophical writing on the nature of argumentation has not helped significantly to confirm our intuition that judicial decision-making is objective, that it somehow has higher standards of consistency than ordinary informal argumentation. If anything, an examination of this literature makes us start to doubt our instincts. Perhaps our trouble has been that we have been proceeding upon a wrong assumption as to the nature of legal reasoning. We must therefore begin again and ask ourselves what we mean by legal reasoning.

4. *Preliminaries to a fresh approach to the problem of objectivity in legal reasoning*

(i) *Reference points for a theory of legal reasoning*

We start from the premise that if judicial decision-making is objective it must have objectively discernible reference points. It has been suggested that rules of law provide such reference points and that they

---

choice in the law is 'guided' by rules. Like Toulmin, Gottlieb builds on Gilbert Ryle's notion that rules are 'inference tickets' [*see* G. Ryle, 'if', 'so', and 'Cause', in *Philosophical Analysis* 323 (M. Black ed. 1950)] concluding that rules 'guide' legal decision-making by leading from the 'material facts' to a decision of the case. G. Gottlieb, supra this note, 32-49. What facts are material is to be determined by (i) the applicable rule, (ii) maxims and rules of interpretation, (iii) moral rules and principles, (iv) economic and social considerations, and (v) the consequences of the proposed decision. If this is how rules of law guide decisions, then the control they exercise does not justify a claim that judicial decision-making is an objective process. Moreover it is often the purpose of law to exclude from consideration social and economic facts like race, sex, and wealth because they are deemed immaterial.

[54] J. Stone, *Legal System and Lawyer's Reasoning*, supra note 6, at 325-7. See also J. Stone, *Social Dimensions of Law and Justice* 768-81 (1966).

[55] J. Stone, *Legal System and Lawyer's Reasonings*, supra note 6, at 334-5.

[56] Id. at 335.

may even be considered the premises of legal reasoning. Yet the lack
of an authoritative form for the so-called rules of the common-law,
together with their incompleteness, makes them inadequate for this
role, however useful they might be for other purposes.[57] If one is
seeking something that he can call 'the law', if he is seeking the fixed
reference points of legal reasoning, all he will find are those marks on
paper called statutes and cases. Although the authoritative style in
which statutes are stated seems to differentiate them from cases, I
shall disregard the distinction for present purposes because I wish to
make clear that only the uninterpreted statute is unambiguously law,
just as only the uninterpreted case is law. There is no transcendental
world of 'meaning' in which we can take refuge when debating the
meaning of a particular case or statute.[58] Whether adequate or
inadequate, vague or precise, the words must speak for themselves
however little they may tell us. Legislative history and the climate of
the time may assist in interpreting a statute and in predicting the
outcome of a case, but they provide nothing specific enough to be
incorporated into a definition of the law. If we wish to identify something as the law then it is a statute which is the law and not a statute
plus its legislative history. Similarly, in so far as they are part of the
law, cases themselves are the law and not cases plus the *ratio decidendi*,
'rule', or 'rule of law' that one might wish to superimpose on them.

The importance of insisting that only the raw form of a statute is
definite enough to be called 'the law' and the great danger inherent in
attempts to hypostatise one's interpretation of statutory provisions
into a 'rule of law' are graphically shown by an example from the life
of Justice Holmes. Holmes was an ardent supporter of the result in
Hepburn v. *Griswold*,[59] which struck down a congressional attempt to
make paper money legal tender. Soon after that decision, Holmes
wrote a letter to the American Law Review defending the result of the
case. He argued:

---

[57] As already noted, it is often desirable to summarise legal knowledge or to express
our conclusions about a particular legal question. Labelling such summaries rules is
not harmful so long as one does not endow them with an authoritativeness which
neither legal theory nor reality permits them to bear.

[58] The Constitution does not differ in this respect from ordinary statutes and case law.
Even if, as is often contended, the provisions of the Constitution have a fixed meaning,
the reformulation of that meaning into directly applicable terminology must remain
unauthoritative.

[59] 75 U.S. (8 Wall.) 603 (1870).

It is hard to understand, when a power *is* expressly given, which does not come up to a required height, how this express power can be enlarged as an incident to some other express power. The power to 'coin money' means, I take it . . . (1) to strike off metallic medals (coin), and (2) to make those medals legal tender (money). I cannot therefore, see how the right to make paper legal tender can be claimed for Congress when the Constitution virtually contains the words 'Congress shall have power to make metals legal tender'. It is to be remembered that those who deny the power have only to maintain that it is not granted by implication. They are not called on to find a constitutional prohibition.[60]

Nevertheless, shortly after the letter was published a differently-constituted Court overruled *Hepburn* v. *Griswold* despite the vigorous dissent of Justice Fields, who adopted Holmes' argument.[61]

The fallacy in Holmes' argument was pointed out several years later by James Bradley Thayer,[62] who found Holmes' reasoning 'obviously defective'.[63] Thayer correctly pointed out that Holmes' error lay in the syllogism on which he based his argument. Holmes' initial premise that Article I, Section 8, of the Constitution empowers Congress 'to coin money' was unexceptionable. However, his restatement of this provision as a grant of power 'to strike off metallic medals (coins) and to make those medals legal tender (money),' imputed to the Constitution an explicitness which it lacked. If Holmes had taken the constitutional text as he found it, his argument would have had to take a different form, which Thayer stated as follows: '(a) Congress has an express power to coin money; (b) in that is implied a power to make it a legal tender; and (c) this implied power excludes an implied power to make anything else a legal tender'.[64] As Thayer himself concluded, 'That argument is not a strong one.'[65]

---

[60] 4 *Amer. L. Rev.* 768 (1870). The letter is signed 'H'., and is ascribed to Holmes by Howe in the second volume of his biography of Justice Holmes. M. Howe, *Justice Oliver Wendell Holmes: The Proving Years* 52 (1963).

[61] Knox v. Lee and Parker v. Davis, Legal Tender Cases, 79 U.S. (12 Wall.) 457 (1871).

[62] Thayer, 'Legal Tender', 1 *Harv. L. Rev.* 73 (1887).

[63] Id. at 83.

[64] Id. at 84.

[65] Id. Apparently, Holmes eventually acknowledged his error. See M. Howe, supra note 60, at 55. Howe intimates that Holmes may have come to believe that syllogistic reasoning should not play a dominant role in the resolution of constitutional issues. However, it is not Holmes' reliance on syllogistic reasoning that accounts for his error, but rather his substitution of an abstraction of his own creation for the words of the Constitution.

Of course, even if we agree that objectively discernible reference points are desirable, the question remains whether even statutes and cases can fulfil that purpose. I would answer that as an empirical fact they can. Experienced legal observers can agree among themselves as to whether a particular identifiable object is a statute or a case, even when these terms are taken in a broad sense to include constitutional provisions (as in the Holmes example), administrative regulations and decisions, and local ordinances. This much understanding is sufficient for purposes of the following discussion.

The contention that the only identifiable things which can accurately be called law are statutes and cases is not, of course, a novel one. Joseph Bingham presented the argument persuasively over fifty years ago.[66] Bingham shrewdly pointed out a contradiction in the traditional requirement that courts must find general rules under which new cases can be subsumed before any such cases can be decided.[67] On the one hand, courts were instructed to decide only the case before them and not to decide moot questions or to give advisory opinions; on the other hand, the requirement that they base decisions on general rules in fact compelled them to determine what would be the proper decision in cases not before them. Bingham was met, however, with Morris Cohen's contention that his views were 'old nonsense'.[68] Cohen argued that, if the law consisted only of statutes and cases, there was no way of explaining how the courts proceeded from decided cases to the decision of new ones.[69] It is true that Bingham's inability to answer this question was a serious shortcoming of his work.[70] Yet Bingham's point was that the traditional view of law as a collection of rules did not satisfactorily explain how to proceed from decided cases to new cases either, and,

---

[66] Bingham, 'What is the Law?, 11 *Mich. L. Rev.* 1, 1-25, 109-21 (1912). In Erie R. R. v. Tompkins, 304 U.S. 64 (1938), the Supreme Court rejected the view that the common law could have any foundation other than state statutes and state court decisions. Bingham, however, was making the more fundamental point that the law of a state was not only *found* in the statutes and decisions; it *was* the statutes and decisions.

[67] Bingham, 'Legal Philosophy and the Law', 9 *Ill. L. Rev.* 98, 112 (1914).

[68] Cohen, 'Justice Holmes and the Nature of Law', 31 *Colum. L. Rev.* 352, 361 (1931).

[69] Id. at 362-3.

[70] Kocourek raised this point in a review of Bingham's 'What is the Law?', supra note 66, although he was not as unsympathetic to Bingham's views as was Cohen. Kocourek, 'Review' 8 *Ill. L. Rev.* 138 (1913).

indeed, that it obscured the process.[71] My purpose in what follows is to remedy this shortcoming in Bingham's work.

(ii) *Necessary assumptions*

We have shown that the reference points of judicial reasoning, the statutes and the cases, can be ascertained in an objectively valid manner. Our problem is to examine whether it is possible to contend that judicial decision-making, based as it is on the statutes and the cases, is an objective process. In considering this problem, it will be necessary to make an assumption about the social objectives of the judicial process. It will be assumed that the primary social purpose of the judicial process is deciding disputes in a manner that will, upon reflection, permit the loser as well as the winner to feel that he has been fairly treated.[72] As Professor Fuller has contended, this goal requires that courts grant the parties the right to present proofs and reasoned arguments to them *and* that the courts squarely meet the proofs and reasoned arguments addressed to them by the parties.[73]

In performing these tasks, the courts will not and should not be oblivious to what they deem are the demands of justice or of social policy. All men, including judges and lawyers, are goal-oriented and can be expected to utilise all available means, including the legal system, to achieve their goals. Nevertheless, the furtherance of social and moral ends or the achievement of other goals through the judicial process should be secondary to its function of deciding fairly disputes between the parties who invoke it. Under this view, therefore, the courts are in a position somewhat similar to that of the managers of a game who wish to make the conditions of play such that the losers as well as the winners will wish to continue to play. The fairness of the judicial process should not be sacrificed even in the name of other

[71] Bingham, supra note 67, at 102-3.

[72] Whether any particular loser in the judicial forum will feel this way is another question. We are concerned with the optimum conditions for making it possible for losers to feel this way.

[73] L. Fuller, 'The Forms and Limits of Adjudication 26', December 29, 1959 (paper delivered in Chicago before the Association of American Law Schools). An abbreviated version of this paper was delivered at the 1960 meeting of the American Society of International Law. Fuller, 'Adjudication and the Rule of Law', 54 *Proceedings of the Am. Soc'y of Int'l Law* 1 (1960). Fuller's paper has recently been posthumously reprinted, in a somewhat expanded form, in 92 *Harv.L.Rev.* 353 (1978). See also Fuller, 'Collective Bargaining and the Arbitrator', 1963 *Wis.L.Rev.* 3.

social or moral goals, and the courts will therefore at times be unable
to pursue social or moral goals because of the requirement that the
judicial process be fair.

Almost everyone would agree that the fair decision of disputes
between the parties before the courts is an important function of the
judicial process, but it is crucial to note that courts and commentators
have not always been willing to treat it as the central social function of
judicial decision-making. As will subsequently be made clear,
however, if fairness to the parties in the resolution of their disputes is
not accepted as the primary social function of the judicial process, it
will be impossible to maintain that the process is objective. Moreover,
one could think of better ways to resolve basic social and political
disputes than the judicial process. Its stylised procedures, its restricted
fact-finding processes, and the limited number of parties present in
any case, make it particularly ill-suited to the resolution of such
disputes. Perhaps in more primitive times, when the courts policed
the morals of the community through the construction of common-
law crimes, the courts were obliged to play this role because more
adequate machinery did not exist. Today, however, the justification
for such a role is considerably weakened. Indeed, if the resolution of
the great issues of the day is the most important function of the
judicial process, it is not surprising that the courts are unable to
propound neutral principles; under these circumstances, the only way
in which the courts could satisfy the demand for neutral principles
and reasoned decisions would be to provide a comprehensive and
publicly acceptable theory of government and economic organisation.
This is surely an impossible task.

Even courts that would make fairness the chief goal of the judicial
process may fail to achieve it for at least two reasons. Occasionally,
the courts, under the pressures of the calendar, decide cases either on
issues not raised by the parties or on points only cursorily briefed and
argued. A particularly glaring example of this failing was the
Supreme Court's decision in *United States* v. *E.I. du Pont de Nemours &
Co.*,[74] in which the Government attacked du Pont's holding of 23 per
cent of all General Motors common stock. The case was tried and
argued almost exclusively under Sections 1 and 2 of the Sherman Act
because the parties had no indication that any other statutory

[74] 353 U.S. 586 (1957).

provisions mentioned in the complaint were relevant. In the Supreme Court, on the Government's appeal from the dismissal of the complaint, only a few pages at the end of the briefs and the minutes of oral argument were devoted to Clayton Act cases. Indeed, counsel for du Pont made no reference to the Clayton Act until Justice Douglas raised the question at the end of counsel's argument. The Court nevertheless decided the case under Section 7 of the Clayton Act by drastically reinterpreting that provision. Whether such reinterpretation was justified is not the point at issue. Rather, the point is that however certain the Court was that its decision was correct, at the very least the parties were entitled to rearrangement and perhas even to a remand.

The second eroding factor is the subtle transformation of the role of the amicus curiae from disinterested friend of the Court or spokesman for the public interest in the person of the Attorney General to vociferous spokesman for private interests.[75] Under such a broad view of his role an amicus may well attempt to take control of litigation. Professor Mermin has shown in his studies of the fate of the Wisconsin Development Authority that the Wisconsin Supreme Court twice ruled on the constitutionality of the Authority on points raised for the first time by an amicus curiae, despite the high quality of legal counsel employed by both parties to the dispute.[76]

An example on the federal level was the manoeuvring which surrounded the *Rosenberg*[77] case at its last stages. After the case had seemingly run its course, counsel for one Edelman, a man having no connection with the litigation, filed a petition for a writ of habeas corpus based on a ground which the 'able and zealous' attorneys for the Rosenbergs had fully considered and had rejected earlier in the litigation. Because the Rosenbergs were under sentence of death, the Supreme Court reluctantly decided to hear arguments on the issue. Unless carefully regulated, the granting of an expanded role to the amicus curiae, even in the name of the public interest, can partially compromise the integrity of the judicial process.

---

[75] See Krislov, 'The Amicus Curiae Brief: From Friendship to Advocacy', 72 *Yale L.J.* 694 (1963).

[76] S. Mermin, *Jurisprudence and Statecraft* (1963); Mermin, 'Concerning the Ways of Courts: Reflections Induced by the Wisconsin "Internal Improvement" and "Public Purpose" Case', 1963 *Wis.L.Rev.* 192.

[77] Rosenberg v. United States, 346 U.S. 273 (1953).

These methods by which control of litigation can be taken away from the parties are significant because the model of legal argument that is about to be constructed demands at least that Professor Fuller's minimal requirements of fairness be fulfilled. While Professor Fuller's requirements are not by themselves a sufficient guarantee either of fairness or of objectivity, the model will not work unless the parties to a lawsuit are permitted to present proofs and arguments to the court and unless the court responds to those proofs and arguments.

5. *A fresh approach*

(i) *General*

Our task, then, is to ascertain whether there are any reasonably objective means for determining how to proceed from the objectively-given reference points of the judicial process—the statutes and the decided cases—to the decision of new cases. In terms of the social function that we have posited for the legal system, only such a claim of objectivity will make it possible for the losers in the judicial forum to feel that they have been fairly treated. As we have noted, fairness requires that a party before a judicial tribunal be permitted to present proofs and arguments and that the tribunal's decision meet these proofs and arguments. Beyond this minimum, we are obliged to provide criteria which, if we are speaking in terms of 'fairness', will permit us to say that the proofs and arguments of the parties have been *adequately* met and which, if we are speaking in terms of 'objectivity', will permit us to say that a case has been *properly* decided. Without such criteria, a disappointed litigant cannot be criticised if he refuses to acknowledge the objective character of the judicial process and if he claims that the court's statements about his arguments are only window-dressing and that his participation in the process was merely a charade.

In order to avoid confusion, it is important to make clear at the outset what we shall be saying when we declare that a case has been properly decided. It is too stringent a requirement to impose upon a theory of legal argument to insist that, before we can claim that a case was properly decided, we must show that the case would not have been decided in any other way. It is impossible in many instances to establish objectively that there is only one correct decision to a case. The model to be presented will claim, however, that it is possible to establish objectively whether a decision was incorrectly decided, and therefore whether a case was correctly decided in the sense of not being incorrectly decided, a property which several possible decisions of a case can sometimes share. In the model, the terms 'properly' and 'improperly' decided will refer to cases 'correctly' and 'incorrectly' decided in the sense just indicated. If we can supply criteria for making such claims, we will have shown that it is possible to construct a model of legal argument which permits the conclusion that judicial decision-making is an objective process. Criticism of judicial decisions can then also have an objective foundation. In providing such criteria and in constructing this model we shall at the same time be explaining what it is for a court *adequately* to respond to the proofs and arguments addressed to it by the parties.

(ii) *The model*

We wish to propose the following model for legal argument. First, legal reasoning differs from most other types of practical reasoning in that its reference points are objectively given in the form of marks on paper called statutes and cases. Legal reasoning is thus spared the argument over premises that characterise ethical disputes. Secondly, no new case can be decided differently from any of the decided cases unless it is 'significantly different' from all such cases. A similar requirement applies in the use and interpretation of statutes,[78] whether or not they have already been interpreted by prior cases. The model requires that anyone who wishes to use a statute in the course of legal reasoning gives what he believes to be the paradigm case or cases covered by the statute. 'Presenting a paradigm case' does not mean divining the 'true meaning' of the statute—the model makes no such demand—but only presenting a case as to which it is asserted that, whatever else *may also* be covered by the statute, this case *is*. The party must then argue that the instant case is or is not significantly different from *any* such paradigm case. Thus, a party who asserts that a statute requiring motor vehicles to pay a road tax is applicable to go-karts or to farm tractors must state what he claims to be the

[78] In the discussion that follows, the term 'statutes' will include constitutional provisions, administrative regulations and local ordinances.

paradigm case covered by the statute. In this instance, the paradigm case would presumably be the family motor car, although of course the bus or long-haul truck might equally be paradigm cases under the statute.[79] If a party were unable to supply any such paradigm cases, he would be forced to conclude that the statute was unintelligible.[80] Cases also could be unintelligible, in the sense that people might be unable to reach even minimal agreement as to their factual circumstances (e.g., whether the plaintiff was run over by defendant's automobile) or even as to their results (e.g., whether the plaintiff received judgment for $10,000). Unintelligible cases, however, are much less dangerous than unintelligible statutes because they are more likely to be ignored.

When a case is brought before a court, any of the parties may assert that the case is like a prior case or is governed by a particular statute. Where the interpretation of a statute is at issue, a party will be obliged, as has been explained above, to supply a paradigm case, unless the statute has already been the subject of judicial decision and the party is content to use the prior decision as a paradigm case. In default of supplying such a paradigm, a party will be subject to the use of paradigm cases supplied by the other party or by the court. Under the model, no criterion of relevancy is imposed upon the cases that a party claims are applicable. Naturally, the model will work better if the parties behave in good faith, but the model does not require any prior screening of cases and statutes. If one casts his net

[79] The example is suggested by Burns v. Currell, [1963] 2 Q.B. 433. Materials relating to legislative history will be helpful in establishing paradigm cases. Undoubtedly, a concern with making the lawsuit as far as possible a contest between contending parties led Justice Jackson to condemn the American practice of using legislative aids because '[a] side from a few offices in the larger cities the materials of legislative history are not available to the lawyer who can afford neither the cost of acquisition, the cost of housing, or the cost of repeatedly examining the whole congressional history'. Schwegmann Bros. v. Calvert Distillers Corp., 341 U.S. 384, 396 (1951) (concurring opinion). While one may share Justice Jackson's concern for the small town attorney, one cannot ignore the growing urbanisation of American society and the increased use of complex legislation to meet social problems. Fairness seems to dictate broadening the distribution of legislative materials, not restricting their use.

[80] Because an unintelligible statute provides no basis on which one can regulate his conduct, ideally one would hope that a totally vague statute would be declared void for vagueness. Unfortunately, the void-for-vagueness cases show an 'almost habitual lack of informing reasoning', and the void-for-vagueness test is often a way of deciding cases without articulating basic differences of policy between courts and legislatures. 'Note, The Void-for-Vagueness Doctrine in the Supreme Court', 109 *U.Pa.L.Rev.* 67, 70-1 (1960). Cf. Christie, 'Vagueness and Legal Language', 48 *Minn.L.Rev.* 885 (1964).

wide enough there are some likenesses between any two cases decided within the same legal system, and it is fruitless to argue about how many such likenesses are necessary before one can be said to control the decision of another.

When the parties have cited the statutes and cases that they claim control the instant case and the court has supplied to the parties its own list of statutes and cases, the case will be ready for decision. Naturally, in presenting the statutes and cases which they deem controlling, the parties will also be presenting arguments to the court as to why the case should be decided in their favour. These arguments will have a bearing upon the court's decision for reasons that will appear obvious once the mechanics of the judicial decision-making process are described in greater detail. Under the model, the court is free to decide the case in a manner different from that of the decided cases and from the paradigm cases under statutes only if it can point to a significant difference between the instant case and each of the decided cases and paradigm cases.

In deciding the case before it, the court may also refer to hypothetical cases posed by the parties or by the court itself. The consideration of hypothetical cases is an important adjunct to the method of reasoning now being presented, for hypothetical cases are of material assistance in establishing the relation of the instant case to the prior cases and to the paradigm cases. To be pertinent, a hypothetical case must be one not significantly different from the instant case. A court which has constructed or which is referred to such a hypothetical case must then determine whether the hypothetical case is itself significantly different from the prior cases and the pertinent paradigm cases. For the court to decide the instant case in a particular way, not only the instant case but also all pertinent hypothetical cases must be significantly different from the prior cases and the paradigm cases pointing to a contrary result. Only then can it be said that the instant case is truly significantly different from these cases and not just apparently significantly different.

The use of hypothetical cases thus broadens the scope of a court's inquiry and helps it to deal with the body of law which it is administering. Hypothetical cases, for example, help a judge to appreciate the reach of his decision by indicating the extent to which, in deciding the instant case, he is committing himself to decide future cases in a particular way. Similarly, hypothetical cases are a bridge between the instant case and previously decided cases whose relevance to the instant case the judge has not initially appreciated. In this way, hypothetical cases broaden his understanding of existing legal materials and help him to comprehend more fully their restraining influence on the choices available to him in the instant case. At the same time, the model requires that hypothetical cases themselves pass the significant difference test and thereby prevents their use from degenerating into a ludicrous and improper *reductio ad absurdum*, the so-called 'parade of horrors' which law students are quite properly told to avoid.

The key to the basically analogical model of legal reasoning that is being described here is the concept of a significant difference. Under the traditionally-accepted model of legal reasoning discussed earlier, two cases are considered similar if they illustrate the same general rule and significantly different if they illustrate conflicting or inconsistent rules. This is not a particularly helpful test because there are any number of rules, many conflicting and inconsistent, for which two cases can stand. Depending upon which rule is accepted as 'correct', it is possible, under the traditional model, to distinguish on its facts any case from any other case or cases. The traditional model thus provides an objective test of judicial decision-making only if there is some way of choosing, in terms sufficiently concrete to be useful, the 'true' or 'correct' rule for which a case or group of cases stands. Unfortunately, experience has clearly confirmed that there is not. Under the proposed model, on the other hand, the significant differences between cases that will justify differences in result will lie in the factual circumstances of the cases rather than in the rules or principles which they supposedly illustrate. It should be clear that this criterion is, as a logical matter, an easier one to meet. It is logically more stringent to insist that, before any two instances can be classed as similar, one must construct a general rule or definition such that all other instances which one might wish to characterise as similar will fall within it, than it is to provide that any two cases will be considered similar if, according to whatever criterion of similarity is imposed, they are within a certain degree of proximity.[81] The advantage of the model is that it is easier to decide whether a group of cases are

---

[81] See Lucas, 'The Lesbian Rule', 30 *Phil.* 195, 204-13 (1955); cf. Mayo, 'Rule-making and Rule-breaking', 15 *Analysis* 16 (1954) see also Shwayder, 'Moral Rules and Moral Maxims', 67 *Ethics* 269 (1957).

significantly different from one another according to any given factual criterion than to decide the 'proper' rule or rules under which all these cases should be grouped. The only question is whether we can realistically come close to fulfilling even this easier logical requirement, and, even if we can, whether we will thereby be able to show that judicial decision-making is an objective process.

The nub of our theory, then, is that it reduces disputes about the propriety of judicial decisions to disputes about the significant factual differences among cases. Naturally, in proposing which of the infinite observable factual differences among cases should be examined, the litigants and the judge will be influenced by their personal values and goals, as well as by the particular results they desire in the instant case and the empirical data at their disposal. While the judicial process is not rule-controlled, it is, in the last analysis, an arena for purposive activity ultimately founded on the human preferences and values often grouped together under the rubric 'policy'.[82] The model, however, takes note of the fact that policies are often vague and amorphous and may also be limitless in number and conflicting. In order to achieve an objective decision-making procedure, it therefore recognises policies only as they are filtered through the facts of the previously-decided cases and of the paradigm cases under statutes. This is the point of the significant difference test. The model, furthermore, tries to focus disputes about significant factual differences among cases, in the realm of decidables, rather than in the realm of undecidables as is the case with disputes about the 'true' rule or principle for which cases stand.

This focusing can be illustrated at several levels of argument. At the simplest level, in attempting to determine what are *in fact* significant differences among cases, there will be some differences among cases which common sense will tell us are not significant. For example, if the only difference between two cases is that in the first the plaintiff had black hair and in the second he has red hair, common sense tells us that this difference is so insignificant as to be even

---

[82] Recognising the importance of value judgments in the decisional process (that may, with perfect propriety, be called rules or 'rule-like') does not mean that we have now recognised that legal reasoning is rule-controlled. The absence of an authoritative form of statement for the expression of such value judgments and the fact that no particular value judgment is dispositive in legal reasoning precludes the assertion that the recognition of the importance of values is an admission that legal reasoning is rule-controlled.

irrelevant. Of course, a party is always free to contend that this factual difference is significant, but, unless he can give some additional reasons, the court will not accept his contention.[83] Beyond these easy cases, there will be points of difference between cases that the decided cases and the paradigm cases under statutes have already shown not to be significant or not even to be relevant. This illustrates the proposition that law can be viewed as a calculus, which builds on its established theorems, embodied in statutes and decided cases, using its characteristic methods of transformation and standards of consistency.[84] If a Caucasian man has recovered a judgment against the manufacturer of ginger beer for negligently permitting a snail to get into the bottle, it is not a significant difference, in our system of law, that in the next ginger beer case the plaintiff is a woman or a Negro man. In other words, whatever the personal scheme of values of the parties, the empirically-given statutes and decided cases (which reflect the values of our society) have refused to recognise factual differences of this type as relevant in these situations.[85] Accordingly, such factual differences are not significant under our model, for under it courts will examine only those factual differences among cases whose relevance has not already been rejected in the statutes and the decided cases. Naturally, a party is always free to assert that differences in skin colour alone are significant factual differences. However, the universal rejection of this assertion by the statutes and the unoverruled decided cases, all of which must be distinguished under the model, will preclude acceptance of the assertion. The statutes and decided cases will also restrict the possible significant differences between cases even when the relevance of certain types of

[83] Under the more traditional theory of legal argument, while one might intuitively know that such differences are insignificant, he would still be obliged to undertake the additional and often unnecessary inquiry of determining whether the cases in question stand for a rule expressed in terms of all men, all human beings, all adults or all U.S. citizens.

[84] For a discussion of the calculus-like nature of law and the points at which law resembles mathematics and logic, see Stone de Montpensier, 'The Compleat Wrangler', 50 *Minn. L. Rev.* 1001 (1966); R. Stone, 'Affinities and Antimonies in Jurisprudence', 1964 *Camb. L.J.* 266, 280-5; cf. R. Stone, 'Ratiocination Not Rationalisation', 74 *Mind* 463 (1965).

[85] If there were empirical evidence that Negroes were more, or less, susceptible to the chemicals contained in the ginger beer bottle than Caucasians, a difference in race might be a significant difference between the cases, but then the cases would not be ones where there was *merely* a difference in race.

facts, in a given set of circumstances, has to some extent been recognised. Thus in deciding whether a particular factual difference is significant, a judge will find his freedom to conclude that the difference is significant restricted by the existence of prior cases which cannot be distinguished from the instant cases and in which arguments asserting the significance of the distinction under consideration were rejected, because he will be obliged to take into consideration the nature of such arguments and the circumstances in which they were made.[86]

Next, there will be differences which scientific evidence will help show to be either totally irrelevant to the instant case, or, if the differences have some connection with the case, factually insignificant. For example, in one case of intentional homicide the victim may have died immediately from gunshot wounds; in another quite properly carrying the same penalty, the victim may have lived for hours after being shot and then succumbed despite the best efforts of competent physicians. Scientific evidence here demonstrates that the time factor is irrelevant. The importance of scientific evidence will not, of course, be limited to such clear cases. In a suit to enjoin the operation of an airport as a nuisance, for example, the total yearly traffic of the airport will be of more practical importance, in distinguishing among the cases, than the assertion that 'the public interest requires airports'; and the decibel level of sound created by the planes will be more important than the maxims *sic utere tuo* or *cujus est solum, ejus est usque ad coelum.*

The model of judicial decision-making being presented will promote every effort to reduce disputes about significant differences to disputes over measurable differences, or to disputes about matters susceptible to scientific examination. Of course, there will remain a class of cases involving factual differences whose significance, despite all available scientific evidence, is still disputable. Here, the advocate has leeway in argument, and a tribunal has leeway in decision. Nevertheless, regardless of what the tribunal may think of the justice of the claim and regardless of its view of social policy, in order to decide any

---

[86] Suppose a party argued that the number of persons injured by the defendant's conduct constituted a significant difference between the instant case and a prior case. If, in another case not significantly different from the instant case, a court had rejected the argument that the difference was significant because multiple lawsuits would burden the courts, that case would be relevant. The party would have to supply an additional factual distinction to support his claimed significant difference.

two cases differently it must come up with at least a plausible significant factual difference between them. By 'plausible' is meant a difference which is accepted as such by the vast majority of observers. The parallel to scientific reasoning is apparent. What makes a scientific conclusion or hypothesis plausible is that its justification conforms to certain widely accepted standards for evaluating empirical evidence. In this approach to legal reasoning, a conclusion is accepted as plausible not because of any intrinsic characteristics, but because its justification conforms to certain accepted standards for evaluating empirically given legal materials. In law as in science, we proceed by using a previously agreed upon method of arriving at conclusions on the basis of the evidence available.[87]

It is submitted that this model of legal argument, because it controls the decisions of courts[88] and protects the participation of the parties in the resolution of their disputes, will permit the assertion that judicial decision-making is objective and fair. This is something that the traditional model of legal reasoning does not permit. The supposed conflict between logic and experience in the law arises only when the decision-makers focus on the construction of ersatz general rules to which experience must somehow be made to conform.

(iii) *The model and recent judicial decisions*

In order briefly to illustrate the model of legal reasoning that has been constructed and to document its promise of reducing legal disputes to

---

[87] The fact that a court has convincingly shown that its decision in a particular case was not controlled by the statutes and the prior cases, and thus that it is free to follow admittedly distinguishable cases or to strike out in new directions, does not guarantee that people will *like* the decision which the court reaches. This will depend on the court's skill in justifying its decision.

[88] Because of its rigorous attention to particulars, some major contemporary philosophers have found the law a fruitful source of illustrations in their examination of *non-deductive reasoning. See, e.g., 'A Plea foe Excuses' in J. Austin, Philosophical Papers* 123, 135-6 (1961); Wisdom, 'The Logic of God' in J. Wisdom, *Paradox and Discovery* I (1965); Wisdom, 'Gods', in J. Wisdom, *Philosophy and Psycho-Analysis* 149,152-9 (1957); Wisdom, 'Philosophy, Metaphysics, and Psycho-Analysis', in id. at 248; cf. Bambrough, 'Principia Metaphysica'. 39 *Phil.* 97 (1964). Wisdom's famous metaphor, in *Gods*, characterising reasons in non-deductive reasoning as 'legs of a chair' rather than 'links of a chain' is often cited by legal philosophers in conjunction with their discussions of Perelman's work on argumentation. See J. Stone, *Legal System and Lawyer's Reasonings* 327 (1964); Weiler, 'Two Models of Judicial Decision-Making', 46 *Can. Bar Rev* 406, 431, n.65. It must be kept in mind, however, that, unlike

arguments over observables, it may be helpful to use the model as a critical tool for examining several comparatively recent decisions of the Supreme Court. In the course of this examination, an indication will be given of what would have been proper decisions in cases which were not properly decided in terms of the model. Although some of the cases involved questions of constitutional interpretation, all of them were purportedly decided in the traditional judicial manner; none were cases in which the Court acknowledged exercising any basic legislative or political function entrusted to it by the Constitution.

In *Gibson* v. *Florida Legislative Investigation Committee,*[89] the Florida courts had adjudged the petitioner in contempt of the Florida Legislative Investigation Committee. The Investigation Committee was a duly-constituted committee of the Florida State Legislature and had summoned Gibson, the President of the Miami Branch of the N.A.A.C.P., to appear and to bring with him the membership lists of his chapter. Gibson appeared but did not bring the lists. When asked if certain persons previously identified as Communists or members of Communist front organisations were members of his branch, he testified that he could not associate these persons with the N.A.A.C.P. and that the N.A.A.C.P. had taken action to exclude subversives from its ranks. Fourteen people who had been identified in previous testimony before the Committee as Communists or members of Communist fronts had been mentioned as having participated in the affairs of the Miami branch of the N.A.A.C.P. As to these fourteen, Gibson was asked to check his lists to ascertain whether they were in fact members. At the same time, he was advised that he was not being asked to turn the lists over to the Committee. Nevertheless he refused to consult the lists and for this refusal was adjudged in contempt.

Florida tried to support the decision of the state courts by pointing out that the Court had upheld the right of congressional and state legislative committees to require testimony and the production of evidence in comparable circumstances. For example, it had upheld the right of congressional committees to investigate Communist

---

Perelman, Wisdom is interested not merely (and not so much) in persuading as in arriving at the truth. For Wisdom, deduction is not the only means of deriving true conclusions, and he uses legal illustrations in order to demonstrate his contention.

[89] 372 U.S. 539 (1963).

infiltration of the universities[90] and of basic Southern industries[91] and had refused an invitation to hold a congressional committee could not investigate alleged Communist infiltration of the press.[92] Finally, in *Uphaus* v. *Wyman*,[93] it had upheld Uphaus' conviction for contempt for refusing to produce lists with the names of all persons who had been guests at a camp maintained in New Hampshire by World Fellowship, Inc. Uphaus was the Executive Director of World Fellowship Inc.; and Wyman, the Attorney General of New Hampshire, had been constituted a one-man legislative investigating committee by a joint resolution of the New Hampshire Legislature. The record developed before Wyman contained testimony that Uphaus had participated in 'Communist front' activities and that nineteen speakers invited to speak at World Fellowship had either been members of the Communist Party or had been affiliated with it or with organisations listed in the United States Attorney General's list of subversive or Communist-controlled organisations.

Against this background, it is difficult to understand how the Court could reverse Gibson's conviction without overruling at least some of the prior cases. And yet this is what the Court did. In an opinion written by Justice Goldberg, it stated that the 'thrust of the demands on the petitioner' was that he disclose whether certain persons were members of the N.A.A.C.P., a 'concededly legitimate and non-subversive organization'.[94] It then held that there was 'no semblance' of a sufficient connection between the N.A.A.C.P. and subversive activities.[95] This lack of connection, the Court declared, distinguished Gibson's case from that of Uphaus.[96] One might point out in rebuttal,

[90] Barenblatt v. United States, 360 U.S. 109 (1959).

[91] Wilkinson v. United States, 365 U.S. 399 (1961); Braden v. United States, 365 U.S. 431 (1961).

[92] Russell v. United States, 369 U.S. 749 (1962).

[93] 360 U.S. 72 (1959).

[94] 372 U.S. 548.

[95] Id. at 550.

[96] Id. In a footnote, id. at 556, n.7, the Court cited Sweezey v. New Hampshire, 354 U.S. 234 (1957), in support of its decision. But *Sweezey* antedated all the cases cited above and was a case in which petitioner had already been asked whether he was a member of the Communist Party and whether he advocated the violent overthrow of the Government and had answered both questions in the negative. The questions he refused to answer concerned his personal beliefs, the contents of a lecture delivered to a humanities course at the University of New Hampshire, and the membership of his wife and others in the Progressive Party of America. The Court held, with two justices

as did Justice Harlan in his dissent,[97] that the Court had upheld a conviction under the membership clause of the Smith Act in which part of the Government's evidence included the Communist Party's desire to win the support of the Negro population of the South for its program of violent revolution.[98] The Court might nevertheless have found a possible distinction between the *Gibson* and *Uphaus* cases if there were some basis for finding that, unlike the N.A.A.C.P., World Fellowship, Inc., was a subversive organisation. But nothing in the record would permit that conclusion: World Fellowship was not even on the discredited United States Attorney General's list. With such evidence, the distinction would be plausible, and the decision reversing Gibson's conviction without overruling *Uphaus* would therefore have been proper. Without such evidence, whatever the 'proper' reach of legislative investigating committees or the 'true' rule of constitutional law, the asserted distinction totally fails and the decision is improper. Indeed, Gibson's conviction should have been easier to support because he was not asked to turn over the lists but only to refresh his recollection by examining them.[99]

The approach towards precedent exhibited by the Court in *Gibson* was repeated in *United States* v. *Brown*,[100] where the Court struck down, as a Bill of Attainder, a statute making it illegal for someone

---

dissenting, that these questions were not pertinent to an investigation of subversion. There was no 'opinion of the Court'. According to Justice Goldberg in *Gibson*, 372 U.S. at 556, n.7, Sweezey's case involved more of a connection with subversive activities than Gibson's, a position which I find difficult to accept.

[97] Id. at 579.80.

[98] Scales v. United States, 367 U.S. 203, 244-57 (1961).

[99] The Florida state courts had already ruled, in a prior proceeding, that petitioner could not be compelled to produce the list, but could only be asked to refresh his memory. 372 U.S. at 540-1. This alone would make somewhat inapposite the reliance by the Court in *Gibson* on the fact that it had said in *Uphaus* that as to the 'lodgers', the operators of the camps were required to maintain a register open to inspection by police officers. 360 U.S. at 80. In *Gibson* Justice Goldberg interpreted the requirement to mean that the 'disputed list was already a matter of public record'. 372 U.S. at 550. The conclusion embodies a factual error as well, for the court in *Uphaus* noted that 'the lists sought were more extensive than those required by the statute', although 'most of the names were recorded pursuant to it'. 360 U.S. at 80, n.7. See also id. at 81; id. at 97, n.7 (dissenting opinion of Justice Brennan). Is it possible, therefore, that Justice Goldberg was suggesting that, if the N.A.A.C.P. were required to maintain a list of members by statute, he would have been governed by *Uphaus*? A large measure of scepticism on this point would appear justified.

[100] 381 U.S. 437 (1965).

who had been a member of the Communist Party within the previous five years to be an officer of a 'labor organisation'. In presenting its case, the Government had proceeded on the basis that, whatever the 'true' definition of a Bill of Attainder, the Brown case was controlled by *Board of Governors of the Federal Reserve System* v. *Agnew*,[101] in which a statute making it illegal for a person engaged in the 'underwriting . . . of securities' to serve as a director of a member bank of the Federal Reserve System was upheld over the challenge that it was a Bill of Attainder. While the two cases could have been distinguished on several other possible grounds,[102] the main apparent basis on which the Court distinguished them was that 'communist' and 'person likely to cause political strikes' *were not* synonymous, whereas 'employee of underwriting house' *was* synonymous with 'person likely unduly to influence the investment policy of a bank'.[103] One would like to have seen some evidence demonstrating that a communist was less likely to cause political strikes than an underwriter unduly to influence the investment policies of banks. Without further empirical evidence, the distinction offends common sense.

United States v. *Philadelphia National Bank*[104] is a final example showing that the significant difference test provides sufficiently objective criteria of the correctness of judicial decisions to permit us to say that the process is, in a meaningful sense, objective. Unlike the previous cases, this case involved economic regulation and raised only a question of statutory construction with no constitutional overtones. The decision turned on the construction of Section 7 of the Clayton Act which, prior to 1950, read as follows:

That no corporation engaged in commerce shall acquire, directly or indirectly, the whole or any part of the stock or other share capital of another corporation engaged also in commerce, where the effect of such acquisition

---

[101] 329 U.S. 441 (1947).

[102] For example, the statute involved in *Brown*, like the historical Bill of Attainder and unlike the statute involved in *Agnew*, was aimed at political conduct. Moreover, under the statute involved in *Agnew*, the Federal Reserve Board could grant individual exemptions, while no such exemption was possible under the statute involved in *Brown*. Although it noted this difference, the Court expressly declined to hold that the possibility of individual exemption made the statute constitutional in one case and unconstitutional in the other. 381 U.S. 437, 454-5 (1965).

[103] Id.

[104] 374 U.S. 321 (1963).

may be to substantially lessen competition between the corporation whose stock is so acquired and the corporation making the acquisition, or to restrain such commerce in any section or community, or tend to create a monopoly of any line of commerce.[105]

An earlier case had construed the section not to cover acquisitions of assets. Then, in *Arrow-Hart & Hegeman Electric Co.* v. *FTC*,[106] a divided Court held that a merger or consolidation of two manufacturing corporations, when followed by the combination of their assets, was also not an acquisition of stock but merely an acquisition of assets and was thus not covered by the Act. The Federal Trade Commission accordingly had no power, after the transfer of the assets, to order the resulting corporation to divest itself of any of the acquired assets.[107]

In 1950, Section 7 of the Clayton Act was amended to read, insofar as pertinent, as follows:

No corporation engaged in commerce shall acquire, directly or indirectly, the whole or any part of the stock or other share capital *and no corporation subject to the jurisdiction of the Federal Trade Commission shall acquire the whole or any part of the assets* of another corporation engaged also in commerce, where *in any line of commerce in any section of the country*, the effect of such acquisition may be substantially to lessen competition, or to tend to create a monopoly. (Emphasis supplied)[108]

The Federal Trade Commission Act expressly provides that banks are not corporations subject to the jurisdiction of the F.T.C.[109] Relying on this provision, the Philadephia National Bank and the Girard Trust Corn Exchange Bank of Philadelphia decided to merge by consolidating assets in a new corporation. The Comptroller of the Currency approved the plan, stating in his annual report to the Congress that, although the scheme would have an unfavourable

---

[105] Act of Oct. 15, 1914, c. 323; 7, 38 Stat. 731-2.

[106] 291 U.S. 587 (1934). See also the three cases decided *sub nom.* FTC v. Western Meat Co., 272 U.S. 554 (1926).

[107] The House Report accompanying the 1950 Clayton Act amendments described *Arrow-Hart* as holding 'that if an acquiring corporation secured title to the physical assets of a corporation whose stock it had acquired before the Federal Trade Commission issues its final order, the Commission lacks power to direct divestiture of the physical assets . . .' *H.R.Rep.No.* 119, 81st Cong., 1st Sess. 5 (1949).

[108] Act of Dec. 29, 1957, ch. 1184, §7, 64 Stat. 1125, *amending* 38 Stat. 731 (1914) (codified at 15 U.S.C. §18 (1964).

[109] 15 U.S.C. §45a(6) (1964).

effect on competition, the consolidated bank would better serve the needs of the community.[110] The United States sued to enjoin the proposed merger, alleging that it violated Section 1 of the Sherman Act and Section 7 of the Clayton Act. The major focus at the trial was on the Sherman Act issue. The district court rendered judgment for the defendants, and the United States appealed. The Supreme Court reversed and held that the proposed merger was unlawful under Section 7 of the Clayton Act.

The Court produced many reasons for its conclusions that the proposed merger was undesirable, but it did not hold that the *Arrow-Hart* Court misinterpreted Section 7. This holding would have been possible, although the relative antiquity of the case and the acquiescence of Congress in it would have made such a course very awkward. Nor did the Court attempt to show that *Arrow-Hart* had been misunderstood by Congress and the bar. Instead, it held that the addition of a clause—

and no corporation subject to the jurisdiction of the Federal Trade Commission shall acquire the whole or any part of the assets [of another corporation]

—which admittedly did not apply to banks changed the meaning of the first clause—

[no] corporation engaged in commerce shall acquire, directly or indirectly, the whole or any part of the stock or other share capital of another corporation,

—which had not been amended at all. Thus it concluded that the *Arrow-Hart* case was no longer applicable. This astounding reasoning must have surprised the Government as much as anyone else because even as late as 1957—seven years after the amendment of the Clayton Act—the Department of Justice concluded that it had no jurisdiction to challenge bank mergers under the Clayton Act.[111] Undoubtedly, it was for this reason that the Government and the defendants in *Philadelphia National Bank* devoted almost all of their argument before the Court to the Sherman Act.[112] In terms of the proposed model, the

---

[110] Cf. *Comp't. of the Currency, 99th Ann. Rep't* 18 (1961),.

[111] The position of the Justice Department is stated in the materials quoted by Justice Harlan in his dissent. 374 U.S. at 377-8.

[112] Only ten out of eighty pages of argument in the Government briefs were devoted to the Clayton Act issue.

Court's disposition of the case amounts to a decision that the amendment of a statute by the addition of a provision expressly not applicable to the parties in the instant case creates a significant difference between the instant case and a prior case. Appreciable research devoted to discovering cases in which a similar technique of statutory interpretation was used has uncovered few even moderately similar instances and none in which the reasoning is so clearly implausible.

(iv) *Additional remarks*

It must be stressed that under the model that we have constructed, a court may not decide any two cases differently unless *it* can demonstrate a plausibly significant difference between the cases. The fact that different results in different cases could have been adequately justified is no answer to a charge that the decision was improper, if the court itself was unable to supply the necessary justification.[113] This is not so much because courts, particularly the Supreme Court, must give guidance to future litigants and to inferior courts, but because our criteria of fairness and objectivity empower a court to decide only these cases whose decision *it* can justify. It is only by vigorously trying to fulfil these criteria that legal reasoning is able to support its claim that it achieves a more rigorous degree of consistency than other forms of informal argumentation.

While the model we have constructed requires a legal system in which past cases are not lightly overruled, the model does not require that a rigid system of stare decisis prevail. Nevertheless, although the model does permit the overruling of past cases—that is, the removal of cases from the body of case law which controls courts unless they can justify new decisions by finding significant differences—it requires that precedents be overruled only in certain ways. It requires that, when the validity of a particular precedent is questioned, the precedent cannot be looked at in a vacuum but must be examined in the context of the entire body of the law. Thus Case *X*, which held that a go-kart is not a motor vehicle for purposes of the road tax, may

---

[113] In 'Racial Discrimination and Judicial Integrity: A reply to Professor Wechsler', 108 *U.Pa.L.Rev.* 1 (1959), Professor Pollak attempts to supply rationales to meet criticism of the school segregation and restrictive covenant cases. Under the model, such commentary cannot add to the objectivity of past decisions.

be considered indirectly overruled by a subsequent decision in Case *Y* that a farm tractor is a motor vehicle for such purposes—i.e., that for purposes of the statute there was no significant difference between a farm tractor and the paradigm case, the family motor car. Such a conclusion can be drawn if, but only if, one is also willing to maintain that there is no significant difference between a go-kart and a farm tractor for purposes of the statute. If there are significant differences, then the decision of Case *Y* is not a sufficient basis for overruling Case *X* or for treating Case *X* as overruled.

Under the model one can also overrule Case *X* directly through the decision of another go-kart case, Case *Z*, but only if one can demonstrate that the significant difference between a go-kart and the family automobile put forth in Case *X* does not in fact obtain. One could do this by pointing to some overlooked legislative history making clear that the distinction is not one that should be recognised or by showing that the factual premises of the distinction are not sound. One might show that the legislature considered and denied an express statutory exemption for go-karts or for analogous vehicles like formula-one racing cars. Alternatively, one might show that the court's assumption in Case *X* that go-karts rarely travel on public highways was factually incorrect. Unless one of these showings can be made, however, Case *X* cannot be overruled and must be taken into account in the decision of future cases. In a like manner a case involving a matter of common law can be overruled if it is no longer significantly different from other cases in which a conflicting result was reached or if its factual assumptions are subsequently proved incorrect.[114]

It should finally be mentioned that, in point of fact, the method of reasoning described in these pages is the predominant method of argument in many areas of the law. Under a rule-oriented method of reasoning, the judicial application of vague notions like 'negligence' and 'recklessness' would often appear completely arbitrary; yet

---

[114] In Escobedo v. Illinois, 378 U.S. 478 (1964), the Court did not attempt the difficult task of distinguishing the facts before it from those in Cicenia v. Lagay, 357 U.S. 504 (1958). The *Escobedo* Court distinguished *Cicenia* on the ground that it was decided in reliance upon Crooker v. California, 357 U.S. 433 (1958), a case in some important respects distinguishable from *Escobedo*. See 378 U.S. at 491-2. Under the model of legal argument that has been presented in these pages, the Court could not properly employ this artifice to avoid the necessity of distinguishing *Cicenia*.

because of the many decided cases involving such concepts, they are sometimes easier to apply than even a seemingly precise statute.[115] Therefore, while the model is in many respects a great departure from the way courts *say* they decide cases, it does not represent so great a departure from the way courts *in fact* decide them.

6. *Conclusion*

The search for objectivity in the law is undoubtedly motivated by the desire to justify the great powers that courts are granted and to explain why the public should have confidence in the courts' proper performance of their function; without such justifications and explanations, the judicial system is merely a vehicle for the application of public power.[116] It is our contention that we have supplied a model of legal argument that permits one to make a limited claim of objectivity for judicial decision-making, a claim that is both meaningful and useful. In deciding new cases in accordance with the model, courts inevitably must and do legislate, but they can do so only in a restricted and stylised manner. In many ways our present legal system approaches this model; if it wishes to lay the strongest claim to objectivity that can be made, it will have to embrace the model completely. Naturally, accepting the model entails recognising that there are certain things that a court cannot do, whether in constitutional law or in the creation of new 'common law'. One cannot choose to be objective and not objective at the same time. To be objective means to accept limitations upon what one can do. To act objectively is not merely to act in a manner whereby one convinces oneself that one has acted objectively, but to operate in a manner that will convince others—particularly unsympathetic others—that one has. It is only by so proceeding that legal reasoning is able to make any claim to consistency. In this regard, legislatures must not make the task of the courts more difficult by saddling them with broad statutes that cover large, important areas of social and economic activity and yet give the courts very little guidance as to their scope and application.

---

[115] Cf. Christie, supra note 80, at 898-910.
[116] See L. Hand, *The Bill of Rights* 73 (1958).

One might object that the courts, particularly the Supreme Court, have a constitutional role to play which requires that they legislate and make policy in addition to deciding legal disputes. This may be so, and yet it is not unreasonable to believe that the Court was given its great constitutional role not in the hope that political decisions could be subsumed under the rubric 'law', nor in the belief that autocratic decision alone could hold the country together in the face of divisive controversy, but in the expectation that the Court *qua* court could bring something to the resolution of difficult issues.[117] Assuming, for the moment, however, that no reconciliation between the Court's legislative and judicial functions can be effected and granting that the Court must perform a basically legislative function, we will be obliged to conclude that there is no objectivity in constitutional adjudication: one can only hope for wisdom, compassion, and common sense. One might nevertheless urge that, in *applying* its constitutional choices as opposed to making them initially, the Court should follow the proposed model of legal argument. Such a course would spare the Court the criticism of those who are unwilling to recognise its dual role. One might further urge that the Court not carry into the arena of nonconstitutional litigation—where it exercises a judicial function—habits and methods developed in dealing with constitutional questions.

---

[117] An attempt to construct a model of constitutional adjudication involving judicial review of legislation that reconciles a relatively broad role for the courts with traditional notions of judicial function is presented in G. Christie, 'A Model of Judicial Review of Legislation', 48 *So. Calif. L. Rev.* 1306 (1975).

Part III

Authority, Legitimacy, and the Law

1. *Introduction*

The concepts of authority and legitimacy approach the question of the 'oughtness' of law—the sense of psychic compulsion that people associate with things legal—from other perspectives. At times, of course, discussions of authority and legitimacy have tried to answer the question of how is the law binding, the question to which the theory of norms is directed. But the basic question to which the notions of authority and legitimacy are directed is that of *why* is law binding; i.e., why ought it to be obeyed. This is a very different question from that of whether or not any law or set of laws is binding or that of how, in point of fact, the sense of psychic compulsion associated with the notion of binding law is generated in human beings.

2. *Legitimacy and the 'logic of the law'*

Writers who have been attracted to the theory of norms have tended to make the question of why a given law or set of laws is 'binding' largely a logical one. A given law or set of laws is valid, and therefore ought to be accepted as binding, because it has been derived from some basic rule or norm—Kelsen calls it the 'grund norm', Hart the 'rule of recognition'—in accordance with the procedures specified by the basic norm and the norms or rules previously generated by it.[1] The basic norm or rule is simply 'accepted'. That is, the legitimacy of the legal order must be accepted as given but the legitimacy of subsidiary norms depends on the logical feature of derivation from

[1] See H. Kelsen, *The Pure Theory of Law* (2d ed. M. Knight transl. 1967) (hereafter *Pure Theory*); *General Theory of Law and State* (A. Wedberg transl. 1945) (hereafter *General Theory*); H. L. A. Hart, *The Concept of Law* (1961) (hereafter *Concept of Law*).

this basic norm or rule. The difficulties with this method of approach are, however, very great. Assuming for the moment that it is in fact possible to specify with any degree of precision what the basic norm of a particular society is, tracing all the asserted rules or norms of that society to that particular basic norm is a very difficult task, indeed. This is one of the major thrusts of Raz's extended criticism of Kelsen's theory.[2] Perhaps a more difficult problem, however, is the logically prior question of in fact determinining, with any degree of precision, what this so-called basic norm is. Hart quite frankly admits that his 'rule of recognition' is open-textured to an extent even greater than is inevitably the case with any so-called rule of law.[3] Hart's rule of recognition is always in a state of becoming. Since the rule of recognition is a statement of what it is people are fundamentally prepared to accept, it is impossible to state the rule with a high degree of assurance even if one were, somewhat arbitrarily, prepared to restrict drastically the number of people whose 'acceptance' counted, say only 'officials' or certain *high* officials. Indeed, Hart takes to task attempts by previous observers to state definitively what the rule of recognition in the United Kingdom is.[4] His point is that one can never be sure, and furthermore that, when a question as to the rightful exercise of fundamental legal power is raised, acceptance often comes after the fact. One justifies a claim to have the right to exercise legal power by acting and securing the acquiescence of others in this exercise of legal power. 'Nothing succeeds like success' or perhaps, to put it more badly, 'success is its own justification'.[5]

This fundamental imprecision undermines the central coherence of Hart's theory. It is a point that Dworkin has stressed. Hart, for example, uses the concept of a rule of recognition to support a great many aspects of his theory of law. He thus contends that the very claim that a given society actually has a legal system requires that at least the officials of that society accept the rule of recognition and the rules generated from it in accordance with the rules of change and of

[2] J. Raz, *The Concept of a Legal System* 95-109 (1970) (hereafter *Concept of a Legal System*).

[3] *Concept of Law* at 144-50. See also id. at 114-20.

[4] Id. at 145-8.

[5] See id. at 149-50. 'Here all that succeeds is success.'

[6] R. Dworkin, 'Social Rules and Legal Theory', 81 *Yale L.J.* 855, 868-74 (1972).

adjudication of that society.[7] But the conceptual framework constructed by Hart for recognising the existence of a legal order breaks down if one can never be sure of what the officials accept. There are, of course, other difficulties. What is it for anyone, including an official, to accept the rules of a system? Hart tells us that one shows his acceptance by acting in the manner in which the rules prescribe and by criticising others who deviate from the conduct prescribed by the rules. But, even if one could agree as to what the precise formulation of the legal rules is, it is doubtful if anyone always obeys what he accepts as the legal rules governing his behaviour or is always prepared to utilise these rules to criticise the deviant behaviour of others; and this is true of officials as well as of private citizens.

One could, of course, make the more guarded claim—which is probably all that Hart is asserting—that the existence of a legal order requires at least that officials *acting in an official capacity* accept the rules of that society. Even this claim, however, is unwarranted. First, for the claim to be worth making, it is important that the officials not only should be clear in their own minds as to what the rules binding them are but they should agree among themselves as to what these rules are. It simply is not true that, at any reasonably concrete degree of specificity, there is any such agreement. Secondly, and more important, even if all that one wants is that each official should behave in accordance with how he conceives the rules prescribe that he should behave—regardless of whether other officials interpret the rules differently—the fact remains that officials, even judges, do sometimes consciously deviate from what they conceive the rules to prescribe. Put in another way, an individual's acceptance of the legitimacy of a particular legal order—for example, he accepts its 'rule of recognition'—does not necessarily mean that he accepts the legitimacy of its validly derived subsidiary norms in the sense that he will necessarily obey them or punish or criticise others for deviating from them. If a correspondence between official behaviour and official beliefs were the *sine qua non* of the existence of a legal order, one would be forced to conclude that there probably never was nor ever will be any such thing as a legal order, let alone a legitimate legal order. Without pursuing the point overly far it is sufficient to conclude that questions as to the existence of a legal order and the

[7] *Concept of Law* at 111-14.

legitimacy of its so-called norms cannot be answered by appeals merely to logic, even to the logic of the law.

AN EXAMINATION OF THE CONCEPTS OF AUTHORITY AND LEGITIMACY

3. *General*

Few questions have been a greater source of difficulty to the philosophers and other scholars who have considered them than those relating to the concept of authority and its relationship to concepts like 'legitimacy'. One frequently recurring feature of the attempt to come to grips with the concept of authority is that the writer, after subjecting the concept to his arsenal of analytical tools, is not altogether satisfied with his conclusions.[8] While a certain amount of diffidence in one's conclusions is an admirable and perhaps even necessary quality in the true scholar, the diffidence seems particularly marked in inquiries into the nature of authority.

4. *The various types of authority*

An examination of the voluminous literature on the nature of authority reveals that statements about authority fall into at least three broad categories. There are, first, statements about what is often called *de jure* authority. The paradigmatic illustration of this kind of authority is that whose basis or justification depends upon legal criteria, but, as used in the literature, the notion of *de jure* authority has a broader reach. It refers to any type of authority whose exercise is dependent upon a set of rules, which includes that arising out of the rules of a game. The authority possessed by a baseball umpire or a basketball referee would be typical examples.

---

[8] See, e.g., Peter Winch's postscript to his excellent paper 'Authority', which originally appeared in 32 *Supp. Vol., Proceedings of the Aristotelian Soc'y* (1958) which is reprinted, together with his postscript in *Political Philosophy* 96, 109-11 (A. Quinton ed. 1967) (hereafter cited as Winch; page references will be to the paper as reprinted in *Political Philosophy*). See also A. Duncan-Jones, 'Authority', 32 *Supp. Vol. Proceedings of the Aristotelian Soc'y* 241, 260 (1958).

Another instance of what might be called *de jure* authority is that which arises from an agency relationship in which one person is authorised to act *for* another. Applying this notion on a larger scale, Hobbes sees the agency relationship as the foundation of the state.[9] *Authorisation* is for him the key concept and the person who is authorised has authority. By focusing on the quasi-juridical act which creates the relationship, the agency notion of authority shares some of the features of the paradigmatic instances of *de jure* authority, such as the authority exercised by the officials of a modern nation-state. On the other hand, although the creation of an agency relationship between Hobbes' sovereign and the citizens of the Commonwealth requires an underlying framework of natural law, the actual exercise of authority by Hobbes' sovereign—the person whose acts are authorised by the citizens—is relatively free from any legal constraint under either natural or positive law. The Hobbesian notion of authority, as based on authorisation to act for another, thus also has some of the features of what is often called *de facto* authority, to the examination of which we shall now turn.

What is often called *de facto* authority is a second general type of authority widely recognised in the literature. Depending upon the point of view of the writer, this term is used to indicate that the authority in question either is not dependent at all upon a structure of rules or that, at first glance, the authority in question does not seem to be dependent upon a structure of rules. The latter move is made by those who, as we shall see, have tried to merge all forms of authority into one analytical framework. A frequently given type of *de facto* authority—indeed one might even say it is the paradigmatic instance of such authority—is what Weber has called 'charismatic authority'.[10] This is the authority exercised by those who, on the basis of their personal qualities, seem to possess the ability to command others. Types of authority which seem to be on the border line between *de facto* and *de jure* authority are the authority based on tradition and the authority based upon the self-interest of those subject to the authority. Some people, of course, might deny that self-interest can ever be the basis of authority. Certainly, someone who obeys another out of fear of a sanction may be acting out of self-interest, but

[9] T. Hobbes, *Leviathan* 87-96 (cc. 17-18) (Everyman ed. 1914).

[10] M. Weber, *Economy and Society* 215-16, 241-5 (G. Roth and C. Witlich ed. 1968) (hereafter *Economy and Society*).

he is usually not considered to be recognising the authority of the commander. He is only recognising the power of the commander. But, as Hume saw, there is no reason why people may not submit to authority not because of any fear of physical sanctions but because they recognise the long-run advantages to them of doing so.[11] And, if they do so, there is no logical reason, as Hume again argues, to invent a social contract, as Hobbes and Locke did for example, to provide a logical or even moral basis for the exercise of this type of authority. That is not to say, of course, that at times it may not be expedient to construct this or other fictions to provide a supposed logical or moral basis for authority.

As to tradition, which unlike self-interest, is generally seen as a sufficient basis of authority,[12] whether it generates a *de jure* or *de facto* type of authority is not a question that can be answered in the abstract. It all depends upon the tradition. Some traditions are very structured and can almost be described in a set of rule-like statements; others cannot. Moreover, even within any single tradition, some features may seem rule-like while other features can be so viewed only with the greatest of difficulties. Almost all authority which is based upon tradition evidences some features that resemble *de jure* authority and some features that resemble *de facto* authority.

A third type of authority statements concerns the notion of 'being *an* authority'. Someone is considered an authority on chess, another on the Italian Renaissance, another on medical matters, etc. The notion of being an authority has some features that resemble both *de jure* and *de facto* authority. For, on the basis of self-interest or of some other reason as well, we often will, in appropriate circumstances, accept the right of those who are authorities in this sense to issue commands or other authoritative pronouncements which are accepted as being rightfully issued and worthy of acceptance. Being an authority can thus be a means of achieving and exercising authority, that is to say, of having authority. But, as we shall see, the notion of being an authority also possesses features which do not readily seem to resemble either of those other types of authority. This later characteristic has been one of the factors that has complicated the attempt to amalgamate all types of authority, and the statements

[11] D. Hume, *A Treatise of Human Nature*, 477-501 (Bk. III, Pt. II, §§1-2) (L. Selby-Bigge ed. 1888) (hereafter *Treatise*).

[12] See, e.g., *Economy and Society* at 215, 226-41.

about authority that they justify, into one overall analytical framework. For, one of the recurrent features of the scholarly discussion about authority has not only been the initial attempt to separate out all the different types of statements in which the term authority appears, but also the attempt to show that all authority statements have some overriding features in common, features which are so important that they permit the reduction of all the separately identified types of authority into one particular type of authority. An examination of these attempts will, of course, be crucial for any study of the concept of authority. Before this can be done, however, it will first be necessary to examine the purposes for which authority is said to exist. Or, to put the matter another way, it is necessary to examine what it is that can be done with authority.

5. *The functions of authority*

Perhaps the most frequent usage of the term authority is that which refers to the ability to gain the voluntary assent of others.[13] As such, authority is frequently contrasted with power, which is the ability to command others regardless of their voluntary consent.[14] Thus, one particular and very important use of the term authority is to refer to the ability to 'get one's proposals accepted by others'.[15] Authority in

[13] See, e.g., B. de Jouvenel, *Sovereignty: An Inquiry into the Political Good* 29-30, 33 (J. Huntington transl. 1957) (hereafter *Sovereignty*).

[14] See, e.g., R. Peters, 'Authority', 32 *Supp. Vol., Proceedings of the Aristotelian Soc'y* 207 (1958) (hereafter *Peters*), reprinted in *Political Philosophy* (A. Quinton ed. 1967), at 83. Where this work is cited, page references will be to *Political Philosophy*. In the instant case the reference is to pp. 92-4.

[15] See, e.g., *Sovereignty* at 31. 'What I mean by "authority" is the ability of a man to get his own proposals accepted.' For de Jouvenel the core notion of the concept of authority is contained in its Latin roots, 'auctor', the creator of a work, founder of a family or a city, etc. Id. at 30. Building upon J. Lucas, *The Principle of Politics* (1966), Joseph Raz, in a recent work which appeared after I had written this book, describes authority as 'normative power', that is the ability not only to give a person a *reason* to do an act but also a *reason* to *exclude* consideration of some other reasons for not doing the act. See J. Raz, *The Authority of Law* 3-27 (1979). Law therefore can be an instance of the effective exercise of authority. This is an interesting description of how authority operates, but it does not address itself to the questions with which I am concerned. Moreover, for reasons that will appear I do not think that Raz is correct in maintaining that it is meaningful to distinguish between legitimate authority—Raz maintains that 'it is an essential feature of law that it claims legitimate authority'

this sense can, of course, be a source of power. Depending upon whether one focuses upon the rightfulness of an exercise of authority or upon the end results of such an exercise of authority, one will be inclined, using the classification described in the preceding section, to characterise the authority in question as either *de jure* or *de facto*. But one will also often use the term authority to describe not only situations in which one person attempts to organise others to achieve some concrete goal but also situations where one person is looked to by others to resolve disputes between people involved in some kind of joint enterprise. The joint enterprise can be some kind of more or less specific activity directed to some concrete goal or it may only be a condition of mutual coexistence between relatively independent persons whose activities to some degree inevitably interact with each other. The sense of authority that corresponds with the concepts of an arbiter or reconciler is what de Jouvenel describes as the authority of a *rex*, or rectifier, which he contrasts with the authority of a *dux*, a leader or organiser of human activity.[16]

The kind of authority exercised by an arbiter bears a relationship not only with *de jure* and *de facto* authority, particularly *de jure* authority, but also with the notion of being an authority. People may turn to a particular person as an arbiter because he is legally designated as one or because he possesses personality traits which lead others to seek and to trust his judgment or because he possesses some special knowledge which it is felt will resolve the dispute. The use of the term authority to refer to some of the situations where one person is looked to by others to arbitrate their disputes and to regulate their conflicting activities does not, however, exhaust the range of situations in which people commonly use the notion of being an authority. That notion is also used to describe situations in which a person possesses, or is perhaps thought to possess, a special kind of knowledge regardless of whether other people actually turn to him for guidance. We shall further explore the different uses of the notion of authority during the course of the discussion in the next few sections. For the present, it is sufficient to conclude that the use of the term authority to refer to activities related to such important but

---

(p. 30)—and so-called other authority (whether called *de facto* or what have you). By 'legitimate authority' Raz means *de jure* authority (p. 18), and, for Raz, 'the notion of legitimate authority is the primary one'. (p. 8).

[16] *Sovereignty* at 33-4.

nevertheless somewhat different aspects of human existence profoundly complicates the attempt to subsume all uses of the term authority under one analytical framework. It is time now that we should turn to an examination of this enterprise.

6. *The attempt to include the various uses of the term authority within a common analytical framework*

The most frequently taken approach is to attempt to subsume *de facto* authority under *de jure* authority. Thus, R. S. Peters states:

> In so far as the *de facto* sense implies that, in an indeterminate and embryonic sense, the person who exercises authority is regarded as 'having a right' to be obeyed, and so on, the *de facto* sense is parasitic on the *de jure* sense.[17]

Peters seems to assume that when a person is regarded as 'having a right to be obeyed' the term 'right' refers to a structure of so-called rules and norms that is similar to that which we find in the legal sphere. I am not at all sure that this assumption is warranted. The acceptance of a person's right to command and of his right to be obeyed does not necessarily seem to imply the existence of any such rule-like superstructure. Peters, however, does not subsume all *de facto* authority under *de jure* authority because he apparently assumes that some exercises of *de facto* authority, though not mere exercises of power, are nevertheless not accompanied by any mutually accepted claims of a right to command and to be obeyed. It is on this point that he is attacked by Peter Winch who asserts that all exercises of what are commonly called *de facto* and *de jure* authority are accompanied not only by claims of a right to be obeyed but are actually obeyed because it is further assumed that what is commanded is the right thing to do under the circumstances. To quote Winch's own words:

> . . . [T]o submit to authority (as opposed to being subject to power) is not to be subject to an alien will. What one does is directed rather by the idea of the right way of doing things in connection with the activity one is performing . . .[18]

In the paradigm cases, when the exercise of authority is said to be *de jure*, the action commanded is the right thing to do, in the circum-

[17] Peters at 92.

[18] Winch at 100.

stances in which the individual finds himself, because it is legally
prescribed. When the exercise of authority is not so easily made to
follow for some pre-existing legal prescriptions, such as when we are
concerned with basic policy choices made by political leaders, the
exercise of authority is accepted as rightful by those subject to it
because they assume that it aims at the right sorts of goals for that
particular society.[19] Authority exercised outside of a political context
is also accepted because of a similar belief about the appropriateness
of the actions commanded for the particular group of individuals
involved, however small or *ad hoc* that group might be. The
assumption is that all human activity is goal-oriented and that therefore all authority, whether initially classed as *de facto* or *de jure*, is
accepted because it is presumed to be an appropriate means to the
goals sought by the individuals involved. In short, an exercise of
authority is accepted as right because it is assumed that it aims at the
right. For Winch, the fundamental point is that human activity is in
some sense rule-governed—that is why man is considered a rational
animal—and therefore all exercises of authority ultimately refer to a
structure of rules,[20] although in some instances, namely those
commonly referred to as instances of *de facto* authority, the structure
of rules may be very broad and uncertain indeed. Thus, for Winch,
all *de facto* authority becomes a species of *de jure* authority, if by the
term *de jure* authority one means an authority ultimately dependent
upon a structure of rules.[21]

It is evident that it does not require too many steps to extend this
analysis to cover the notion of being an authority not only when this
term is used to refer to an expert on games, such as chess, who may

---

[19] ' . . . [W]e have to deal with genuine authority, as opposed to bare power or ability
to influence, only where he who decides does so under the idea of what he conceives to
be the *right* decision. This fundamental fact is not altered by the controversial
character of the distinction between right and wrong here.

'Again, certainly not everyone would agree that the Labour Government acted rightly
in nationalizing the steel industry. Nevertheless, part of the act's authoritative
character derived from the fact that it was *claimed* to be the *right* thing to do in the
circumstances . . .' Id. at 105-6 (emphasis in the original).

[20] For Winch, furthermore, 'to participate in rule governed activities *is*, in a certain
way, to accept authority'. Id. at 99 (emphasis in original).

[21] This point comes out clearly in the concluding pages of Winch's paper. See id. at
106-9.

be viewed somewhat like an arbiter or even a judge to whom difficult
questions of interpretation may be referred, but also when the term
'an authority' is used to describe any so-called expert, such as an
authority on nuclear physics or molecular biology. The pronouncements of this authority are accepted as true because it is assumed that
they are correct. Something like this move is made by Carl Friedrich
who asserts that when a person is considered to possess authority it is
because his commands are deemed 'worthy of acceptance'.[22] For
Friedrich, the worthiness of a command for acceptance depends upon
its susceptibility to 'reasoned elaboration'. Authority, for him, is a
quality of communication, rather than of persons. When one speaks
of the authority of a person one is really using a shorthand expression
to indicate that he possesses the capacity to issue authoritative
communications. In Friedrich's scheme of analysis there is, thus,
little place for what Weber calls charismatic authority. Presumably,
insofar as something resembling the exercise of charismatic authority
is seen to exist, it must be considered a form of psychological power of
one person over another.[23] Winch, on the other hand, specifically
does consider charismatic authority. He is, however, able to subsume
it under his general analytical framework because, although he
accepts Weber's contention that charismatic authority is divorced
from any specific tradition, nevertheless it is exercised in the context
of some particular social condition and, to Winch, this necessarily
implies the existence of some broad rule-like structure.[24] Possibly this
is all that Friedrich is saying, in which case he could perhaps
accommodate the exercise of charismatic authority into his analytical
framework as well.[25] But it seems to me that to do so would be to
water down, almost to the point of meaninglessness, his insistence
that the exercise of authority depends upon the potential amenability

[22] C. J. Friedrich, 'Authority, Reason, and Discretion', *Authority and Social Work:
Concept and Use* (S. Yelaja ed. 1971) at 17-34 (hereafter Friedrich) (reprinted from
Nomos III, Authority 28-48 (1958)). On the points discussed in the text see id. at 23-5.
[23] Id. at 31-2, 33-4.
[24] See Winch at 107-8.
[25] See Friedrich at 27 where rather than referring to these cases as instances of
'psychological power', he states that: ' . . . The opinions and commands of a Stalin or
a Hitler, oriented to the regime's ideology . . . could as a rule be elaborated by
extensive reasoning. It is important to bear in mind that such reasoning may well
appear wholly "irrational" to any outside the particular belief and value system.'

of the commands issued to reasoned elaboration.[26] Indeed, in order to extend his analysis to cover charismatic authority, Winch is forced to water down the notion of rule-governed activities almost to the point of unrecognisability.

A somewhat similar result is reached by David Bell, who approaches the subject from a different prospective from most other writers. For him, the core situation is that of being an authority. 'To designate someone as an authority is necessarily to raise a question as to what they are an authority on, over what range of matters their view is taken.'[27] Furthermore, according to Bell, 'we tend to speak of human sources of knowledge as authorities only where the knowledge rises above the level of accidental acquaintance with some particular circumstance'.[28] In short, he characterises 'the notion of authority by the concepts of knowledge, belief, and trust rather than through the concepts others have thought central here, namely those of power, imperative control, order and command'.[29] Thus, when we say that authority implies a belief as to right—a situation where others have focused on a right to command and a right to be obeyed— Bell asserts that this belief as to right concerns 'the correctness of someone's view on a matter of fact or theory . . .' By extension, in practical affairs, the belief as to right associated with the notion of authority concerns 'the correctness of someone's practical judgment or advice'.[30] Thus to state that someone exercises authority is not merely to say that he has authority in the *de facto* sense, nor does such a statement necessarily imply, as Winch claims, that the authority in question is *de jure* because it is dependent on a notion of rule-governed activities. Rather, to state that someone exercises authority is to assert that the person in question *is* an authority. He is what might be called an

[26] In elaborating on the Hitler illustration quoted in the previous note, Friedrich adds, id. at 27, n. 18; 'This insistence is particularly worthy of attention because Hitler's position appears to any outsider to have been utter madness. His conduct was not only irrational, but contrary to all common sense and reason. But reason in the general sense and "reasoning" in the sense here suggested, namely related to values, opinions, and briefs [beliefs], are not the same thing.'

[27] D. Bell, 'Authority', *Royal Institute of Philosophy Lectures, 1969-70*, 190, 195 (1971) (hereafter *Bell*).

[28] Ibid.

[29] Id. at 195-96.

[30] Id. at 197, for the quotations in this and the preceding sentence. Cf. G. Young, 'Authority', *Can. J. Phil.* 563, 582 (1973).

expert because he possesses some special kind of knowledge. The belief, held by some people, that social problems, including even those concerning ultimate social values, could be solved if only we would turn them over to experts would seem to be a logical extension of this view.

7. *An irreducible difference between the notion of being an authority and those of* de jure *and* de facto *authority*

Is it possible for people who accept someone as an authority to be mistaken about his possession of authority? In other words, is it meaningful to say of a person, 'he was accepted by people as an authority but he really was not one'? Conversely, is it meaningful to say, as one might have of Cassandra and Laocoon, 'he was not accepted as an authority as to what would happen in the future but he really was one'? Insofar as a purported authority is someone who functions as an arbiter or judge to whom people take their problems for resolution, the answer seems to be that as long as people accept his answers as authoritative that person is an authority. The fact that his advice may be wrong or even downright ridiculous does not alter the situation. It is the acceptance of his responses, by those who have sought his opinions, as authoritatively resolving their problems that is crucial. But, if a person is considered an authority because of his special knowledge alone and not because people may have turned to him to resolve their dilemmas, the situation alters. In this case it does seem possible to say 'he was considered an authority on the composition of the atmosphere, but now, after the isolation of oxygen, we see that he really was not an authority on those questions'. Certainly, it would seem that we are making this kind of statement when we say that some successful medical practitioner is really a 'quack'. Conversely, it does seem to make sense to say 'X really is (or was) an expert authority but, unfortunately, no one recognised him as such'. For example, the work of Mendel was for a long time unappreciated by others working on problems of genetics. Yet, it does not seem strange to assert that Mendel really was an authority on that subject, despite the fact that almost no one recognised him as such.

The question is then, 'Is it possible to apply the same type of analysis to statements about *de facto* and *de jure* authority?' This is . where the notion of legitimacy enters the picture. For, another way of asking the question of whether someone who exercises authority can nevertheless be said not really to possess authority is to ask, 'Is it possible for authority to be illegitimate?' It is my contention that it is not very useful to ascribe the notions 'legitimate' or 'illegitimate' to the concept of authority. Failure to recognise this feature is a major source of confusion for political philosophers. If one nevertheless insists on seeking some relationship between the concept of legitimacy and that of authority one must ultimately recognise that, in a sense, all effective authority is legitimate, at least from the point of view of those exercising the authority in question and those subject to it. Unlike the case of being an authority where, in some circumstances, it does seem possible for someone to act like an authority but not be one or for someone actually to be an authority but not to be recognised as such, it is not particularly meaningful to ask of someone who exercises what is usually called *de facto* or *de jure* authority whether he really has authority, nor to ask, alternatively, whether his authority is legitimate. In the discussion that follows I shall try to support these assertions.

8. *Is there any relationship between the concept of legitimacy and the concept of authority?*

Legitimacy is a term of many shades of meaning. It can, of course, be used as a legal term of art whereby it refers to one of the bases of authority without implying anything as to whether all authority is necessarily either legitimate or illegitimate. For example, in this restricted context, authority may be said to be legitimate because it was created in ways specified by some existing legal system. When Hume speaks of the authority of governments based upon 'long possession' or upon 'positive law' he seems to be referring to situations where more modern writers would term the authority 'legitimate' in this narrow sense.[31] Authority so based is contrasted by

---

[31] *Treatise* at Bk. III, Pt. II, §10. By authority based upon 'long possession' Hume means authority based on long-established custom which we might also describe as 'fundamental law'. Hume claims this is the firmest basis upon which authority can rest. If, to use the United Kingdom as an example, a sovereign based upon long-established custom such as the Crown in Parliament were to transfer the sovereignty of the United Kingdom to some new sovereign, such as a European Federation, then the authority of this latter would rest merely upon positive law, a much weaker basis. The

Hume with authority premised upon some other basis such as self-interest and even conquest.[32] In much of the philosophical literature, however, the term legitimacy is used in a more extended sense in which it pre-empts the field. It refers to a quality of authority and not to one of its possible bases. In this usage, authority is either legitimate or illegitimate, there is no third possibility. It is the relationship of the notion of legitimacy in this extended sense to the concept of authority that we shall now be considering.

At the outset we might note that, insofar as one is considering what is normally called *de facto* authority, it does indeed seem at first glance that there is no sense in asking whether the authority in question is legitimate. Either a person has *de facto* authority or he does not, and that seems to be the end of the matter. It is precisely in order to change the nature of the discussion so as possibly to make talk of legitimacy and illegitimacy meaningful that political philosophers have tried to amalgamate *de facto* authority with *de jure* authority. A similar motive lies behind the attempt to subsume both *de facto* and *de jure* authority under the notion of being an authority. This latter concept does seem to relate to knowledge and belief; and it certainly is possible to characterise knowledge and belief as either correct or incorrect. It therefore is not surprising that under some circumstances, as we have seen in the proceeding section, it does seem to make sense to deny that someone is an authority even if he seems quite effectively to function as an authority. If the exercise of all authority ultimately depends on actually being an authority, then it would seem that we could also quite properly sometimes deny that someone who successfully exercises authority really is an authority. Surely, however, enough fools and madmen have quite effectively exercised authority over such very long periods of time as to make it seem a very perverse use of language to claim that authority based on ignorance is not, in point of fact, authority.

The problem is, of course, somewhat more complicated when the question concerns ultimate choices of social value and the ignorance relates, not to the material world, but to issues of morality. Does even asking the question of correctness of knowledge in this circumstance,

---

fact that in 1975 the Labour Government felt that it was necessary to hold a plebiscite upon the United Kingdom's accession to the European Economic Community, which had already been ratified by Parliament, shows that Hume probably had a point.
[32] Ibid.

which, of course, is what one does when one asserts that there are authorities on these subjects, imply the belief in the existence of a universal natural law? If so, whether the question can even be asked will depend on the proof of the existence of this natural law and, even more, upon the accurate derivation of its content. The insurmountable difficulties that have been encountered in trying to perform this task justify the conclusion that it does not appear to be very useful to try to subsume all instances of the successful exercise of *de facto* and *de jure* authority under the notion of being an authority.

As a postscript one might add that, even if Bell were correct that the notion of being an authority is at the core of our concept of authority, it clearly would not be true that one must actually be an authority in order to possess either *de jure* or *de facto* authority. Rather all that would be required is that people must believe that those exercising *de facto* or *de jure* authority over them are authorities, even if in fact they are not. If, however, the nexus that connects all the different types of authority is the '*belief* that someone is an authority' then the discussion has been shifted away from the notion of authority and has become instead a discussion of the related but different question, why are people prepared to accept the authoritative pronouncements directed to them by others? This latter is, of course, a question concerning the psychological make up of human beings.

Despite the fact that it does not seem possible to reduce the notion of exercising *de jure* or *de facto* authority to that of being an authority, one might nevertheless persist in claiming that it does make sense to talk about its 'being right' for someone to exercise *de facto* or *de jure authority*. Furthermore, one can also speak of particular exercises of such authority, as 'being right'. After all, 'being right' not only can refer to the correctness of the knowledge or belief of an authority and of the authority which he might be said to exercise on that basis; it can also refer to being right *simpliciter*. But, if the term right, in this context, is divorced from knowledge and its related concepts, then the possibility of any necessary connection between the exercise of *de jure* or *de facto* authority and 'being an authority' totally disappears. We are left rather with something that looks like *de jure* authority. Indeed, we are left with our original question, 'Is it possible to say of an exercise of purported *de jure* authority that it was not really an exercise of authority?' Or, put another way, is it possible to say that *de jure* authority may be illegitimate? If it is not possible to make such statements then, whether or not what is called *de facto* authority is really only a species of *de jure* authority will not matter. In neither case will it make sense to speak in terms of legitimate or illegitimate authority.

Suppose, on the other hand, we find out that it is possible and meaningful to apply the notions of legitimacy and illegitimacy to the concept of *de jure* authority. What is the significance of that finding? Have we now shown that authority can indeed be illegitimate or have we shown something very different? In order to find out, it is time to examine the relationship between the concept of legitimacy and that of *de jure* authority. This is the subject to which we shall turn in the next section. We shall then return to the relationship between *de facto* and *de jure* authority. Contrary to what Winch asserts, we shall see that, rather than *de facto* authority being reducible to *de jure* authority, in point of fact all *de jure* authority ultimately depends upon *de facto* authority.

9.   *The relationship between legitimacy and* de jure *authority*

At the outset of this critical part of the discussion, it would seem prudent to set out clearly what we mean by authority. A definition, that seems to capture the core of what many different writers on the subject have assumed is the essence of what it is to have and to exercise authority, is: the ability of a person to command under a claim of right that is accepted as such by those over whom the person commanding is said to have authority. Since, however, those who have and exercise authority do more than issue commands, it is necessary to expand this definition to encompass all those situations where one person issues pronouncements that are accepted as authoritative by those to whom they are addressed. The person issuing these pronouncements must do so under a claim of right that is accepted as such by those to whom the pronouncements are addressed. These pronouncements may consist of commands but they may also include statements resolving disputes or interpreting previous utterances, as well as other types of statements which do not necessarily imply any commands. When we say that the pronouncements of the person possessing authority are accepted as authoritative by those to whom they are addressed, we mean that these latter people accept the statements as dispositive of the matter under consideration. In the case of pronouncements which are commands, they are dispositive of what these people ought to do. In the case of pronouncements that are not commands, they are dispositive of what it is those to whom they are addressed should accept or what it is they should believe. It is this core concept of authority, which seems to be accepted by writers with as diverse viewpoints as de Jouvenel and Winch, that will be utilised in the subsequent discussion.

Before proceeding further, however, I might note that there is a tendency towards equivocation in the usage of the term authority that I hope to avoid. When writers, such as those that have been mentioned, give their undivided attention to the concept of authority they treat it as something that some people *have*—the ability to issue authoritative pronouncements under a claim of right that is accepted, etc. In this full-blown treatment the notion of acceptance is included in the notion of authority. It is only this move that makes it possible to distinguish authority from power. Sometimes, however, writers use the term authority to include only either the effective issuance of commands (or other pronouncements) or the mere attempt to issue such commands or pronouncements. When either of these moves is made, it does become possible to speak of authority that is either accepted as rightfully exercised or is not accepted as such. But, under this usage, authority becomes synonymous with power or the attempt to exercise power, despite the fact that almost all writers seek to contrast authority with mere power. In the discussion that follows I shall endeavour to be consistent in treating authority as authority and in not confusing it with power or the ability to dominate or coerce others.

(i) *Some logical considerations*

When a person denies that someone who seems ostensibly to exercise authority actually has authority what is it that he is saying? He may, of course, be using a statement of this sort to deny that the person in question actually is exercising authority: i.e., to deny that the person in question is issuing authoritative pronouncements under a claim of right that is accepted by those to whom his pronouncements are addressed. Our speaker might be claiming, for example, that the person in question is getting people to do what he wants because they fear him. If our speaker is misusing the term 'authority' as a synonym for the term 'power' he might be stating this claim in the form 'X's authority is not accepted'. But what if this is not the case, that is to say, what if, as a matter of fact, it is incontrovertible that the person whose authority is denied actually does issue authoritative pronouncements under a claim of right that is accepted by those to whom the pronouncements are addressed? Under these circumstances, a speaker who still denies that someone actually has authority may simply be stating that he does not like the fact that the person about whom he is speaking possesses authority. From the point of view of the present discussion, however, this is not a particularly interesting type of statement.

Another possible, and not too dissimilar usage, of statements denying that someone who in point of fact exercises authority actually does have authority is in order to assert that the person whose authority is in question ought not to be able to exercise authority. Under this usage, one possible meaning of such statements is that the speaker is asserting that, were the pronouncements issued to him, he would not accept them as rightfully issued and that the people to whom in point of fact they are issued ought not to accept them either. In making such a statement, the speaker could be further asserting that the person who is exercising authority does not have the *right* to exercise that authority. Since, however, to issue authoritative pronouncements under a claim of right that is accepted by those to whom the pronouncements are addressed is to possess authority, to deny that someone has such a right, despite the fact that he successfully asserts that he does have such a right, is tantamount to claiming that he has no authority to have authority. Given the possibilities of infinite redress—no right to have a right to have authority—one may wonder whether such statements are particularly useful. Certainly, outside of the situation, which will be discussed in due course, where there is clearly defined hierarchical structure of authority that is generally recognised by all those involved in the discussion, including the person exercising authority and those accepting it, such statements do not seem to have much descriptive content. It is perhaps in order to disguise this problem that those who wish to deny that someone really has authority, despite his successful exercise of authority, are inclined to express their view in terms of legitimacy. It may seem odd to say that someone does not have authority as illegitimate? Obviously such a challenge does not deny particular instance of the successful exercise of authority is not a case of legitimate authority. A claim of this sort is made by Winch who argues that true authority requires that there be some aura of rightfulness about it in something like an objective sense.[33]

What then is it to challenge a particular successful exercise of authority as illegitimate? Obviously such a challenge does not deny that a particular person is issuing pronouncements—this is an objective fact and, in the case under consideration, is a given. The challenge then must be to the propounding and acceptance of these pronouncements as authoritative. That is, the challenge must be to the propounder's claim of right to issue these pronouncements and/or to the recipient's acceptance of these pronouncements as having been rightfully issued. But, the acceptance by the recipients of the pronouncements that the pronouncements were rightfully issued is again an objective fact. Whether one likes it or not it, too, is a given. Accordingly, unless there is some higher authority accepted by the recipients of these purportedly authoritative pronouncements to whom one can appeal, from a descriptive point of view all that one can be saying is that he does not like the fact that a particular person, X, exercises authority and that, if he were one of those to whom these authoritative pronouncements were addressed he would not accept them. One might even be contending that the recipients of authoritative pronouncements are wrong to accept them. But, as far as the intentional act of the recipients in accepting X's claim of right to issue authoritive pronouncement is concerned, statements challenging it as illegitimate on this basis are devoid of descriptive content.

The only other possible descriptive meaning of a challenge to authority on grounds of legitimacy is, then, a challenge to X's claim of right to issue authoritative pronouncements, regardless of the fact that they are accepted by the recipients. But this amounts to the

---

[33] Winch, it should be recalled, does not condition the *having* of authority upon *being* an authority. Bell, however, contended that, given the tenor of Winch's argument, this move must have been an implicit part of Winch's thesis. Bell at 196. Winch's subsequent retreat from some of his original positions indicates that he was not making this move. See the discussion at pp. 110-12, *infra*.

assertion that X does not in fact have authority. Accordingly, to say that X's authority is illegitimate is to say that X in fact has authority—after all it is a given that he issues authoritative pronouncements under a claim of right that other people accept—but in fact he does not have authority. This interpretation leads to absurdity. Alternatively, we can interpret statements to the effect that X's authority is illegitimate as statements asserting that X has no authority to have authority. Since, as we have already seen, this second order authority can also be challenged as illegitimate, we are in danger of embarking on the treadmill of infinite redress, unless we are confronted with an accepted finite hierarchy of authorities about which, as we have already noted, more will be said later. And yet, with one possible exception that we shall discuss at the end of this subsection, these seem to exhaust the possible descriptive means of ascribing the concept of legitimacy (or illegitimacy) to that of authority.

The concept of legitimacy, of course, can and usually does have a primarily evaluative sense as well, typically relating to whether the speaker believes it is good or bad for X to have the authority that he in point of fact possesses. But, if all that is intended by the use of the terms legitimate and illegitimate is this predominantly evaluative type of statement, it is better to replace them by terms such as good or bad, desirable or undesirable, useful or not useful. To continue to use the terms legitimate and illegitimate under these circumstances is to imply that the statements being made have a descriptive content which, in point of fact, is non-existent. This can be misleading and even dangerous.

People often intuitively sense this limited descriptive content of the terms legitimacy and illegitimacy. For example, while people do assert that someone's having authority in the past was good or bad—say the authority of the Roman consuls—people rarely say that such authority, when the claim of right underlying it was in fact accepted, was illegitimate. The case of the Roman consuls is again illustrative. It is only in more emotionally charged current circumstances that people are tempted to make statements of this kind. It makes political arguments seem more objective than they really are. But, as we have seen, with one possible exception which will soon be discussed, statements about legitimacy have only two kinds of descriptive uses, one internal and the other external, that make sense.

From an internal point of view they tell us something about the state of mind of the speaker. They tell us, for example, that the speaker does not accept the claim of right of those trying to exercise authority over him or that, if the speaker were himself subjected to such claims of right, he would not accept them or, finally, that he does not think that those who do accept such claims are well advised to accept them. From an external point of view, on the other hand, statements about legitimacy can only refer to the question of whether or not people subjected to such claims of right actually do in fact accept them. They have no other meaning. If the members of the political orders known as Israel or Soviet Russia accept the claim of right to issue authoritative pronouncements put forth by those who in fact issue such pronouncements to them, that is the end of the matter. From a descriptive point of view, those political orders are legitimate. To attempt to assert the contrary is to attempt to elevate epithet into the status of reasoned argument with the potential for disastrous consequences for mankind by making power struggles into crusades.[34]

One must not be misled by the distinction made in international law, and in the law of most nation-states, between the recognition of a government (or occasionally even a state) as either *de jure* or *de facto*. This distinction has to do with the extraterritorial effects of actions taken by the government described as being either *de jure* or *de facto*. To recognise a government as *de jure* means that one commits oneself, at the very least, to according the actions of that government the extraterritorial effect to which those actions are entitled under international law. To refuse to recognise a government as *de jure*, is among other things, to attempt to justify the refusal to accord the acts of that government any extraterritorial effect. But the refusal to recognise a *de facto* government as being *de jure* has no effect whatsoever on its otherwise effective exercise of authority within its own territorial confines. The law of the United States, for example, recognises that even *de facto* governments can effectively transfer legal title to

---

[34] It must be kept in mind, as stated at the outset of this portion of our discussion, that we are speaking about 'legitimacy' in its more extensive sense in that all authority and any particular exercise of it is conceived to be either legitimate or illegitimate. There is, of course, a narrower sense of legitimacy, adverted to at the beginning of section 8, supra, in which legitimacy, i.e., derivation from custom or positive law, is just one basis of authority and in which authority founded upon some other basis can nevertheless be legitimate in the more extensive sense of legitimate that is now under consideration.

property located within the territorial confines ruled by those governments.[35] Admitttedly, the United States, after over thirty-five years, still engages in the charade that a small group of people in Washington represent the 'lawful' and 'legitimate' governments of Latvia, Lithuania, and Estonia. Nevertheless the United States hardly denies that the Soviet Union is, in fact, the entity that exercises authority in those areas. Indeed, this example illustrates the ludicrousness of insisting on using emotionally charged terms like *de jure* and legitimacy in an effort to avoid facing up to facts that are regarded as unpleasant. Before Mr Nixon's trip to Peking a similar ostrich-like approach was taken with regard to China.

One recognises, however, that someone could claim that there are no such things as national states. There is only one international political order of which we are all members.[36] In this event, if most people in the world claimed that the authority exercised by Israeli or Soviet or even United States officials was illegitimate we would perhaps be able to say that most people do not accept the claims of right of those so-called officials, who are not officials at all because they are not designated by valid political orders. But, if Israel and the U.S.S.R. are not political orders, they certainly are social orders, just as the family is a social order, and with regard to all of these social orders all the old problems relating to statements about legitimacy would reappear. Besides, most people do accept that there are such things as nation states.

It is time now to return to an issue that has already been noted several times but not yet discussed. We have examined two general types of descriptive meanings that statements about legitimacy and authority can have. The first related to the internal attitude of the speaker; the second related to the external question of fact of whether the people to whom authoritative pronouncements are addressed

---

[35] See Banco Nacional de Cuba v. Sabbatino, 376 U.S. 398 (1964); Salimoff & Co. v. Standard Oil Co. of N.Y., 262 N.Y. 220, N.E. 679 (1933). Whether or not a foreign court will attempt to enforce the presumed obligation of a state under international law to compensate foreigners for property it has taken or to grant extraterritorial recognition to any such transfer of title to property is, of course, another matter. On this last question, moreover, the courts of a foreign nation may be prepared to intervene regardless of whether their governments recognise the government or state, whose acts are in question, as either *de jure* or *de facto*. See the so-called Hickenlooper Amendment, 22 U.S.C. §2370 (a) (2).

[36] Cf. Kelsen's *General Theory* at 363-76.

accept both those pronouncements and the claim of right under which they are issued. There is perhaps another type of descriptive meaning which assertions that some authority is illegitimate may convey, despite the fact that this authority may be accepted by those subject to it. What I am referring to are statements intended to assert that no authority can be legitimate because, for example, the acceptance of such authority contravenes the principle of human moral autonomy. The usual method of establishing this position is to try to demonstrate that the state is illegitimate and, if this can be shown, it then supposedly follows that authority itself is illegitimate. I shall discuss this contention in section 10, below. First, however, I wish to turn again, with the discussion of this present subsection about the 'logic' of the term authority in mind, to the notion of *de jure* authority as it appears in the philosophical literature. Specifically, I wish to examine in some detail what it is to deny that a particular authority is, in point of fact, *de jure* authority.

(ii) *Denying the existence of* de jure *authority*

As we have seen it is customary to distinguish between *de jure* and *de facto* authority. At the same time, an attempt is also frequently made to establish some kind of relationship between the two. Thus, as we have already noted, R. S. Peters finds that *de facto* authority is parasitic on *de jure* authority. We saw that Peter Winch goes even further and asserts that all authority, including *de facto* authority, must ultimately be reducible to a form of *de jure* authority.[37] It thus becomes crucial to know what it is we are doing when we deny the existence of some purported *de jure* authority, a denial that can also be expressed in the terminology of legitimacy or of some other similar notion. In the case under consideration we are assuming that we have an actual instance of someone issuing authoritative pronouncements under a claim of right that is accepted by those to whom the pronouncements are addressed. What are we saying, then, when we deny the *de jure* authority of such a person?

We may be saying that X, the person exercising the authority in question, does not have the authority to exercise the authority which in fact he has exercised. By this we might mean that there are legal provisions, which are accepted by X, which deny him the authority to

---

[37] See §6, supra for the prior discussion of the theses of Peters and Winch.

act as he has done. An alternative way of saying substantially the same thing would be to say that there are legal provisions, which are accepted by X, which so limit his authority as to prohibit him from doing what he has done. Regardless of which way we make our objection to what X has done, we are implying that, were the appropriate legal provisions brought to X's attention, he would not have done what he did or, if these provisions are only brought to his attention after he has acted, he will attempt to undo what he has done. But what if he does not take any such steps after his 'error' is pointed out to him? What then?

Of course, in appealing to legal provisions that constrain someone's apparent exercise of authority, we may also be implying that there is some higher authority recognised by X to whom appeal may be made and who will countermand X's wrongfully issued purported authoritative pronouncement. When such a hierarchy of authorities exists, as in any modern complex legal order, it does indeed make sense, as we have already noted, to speak of someone having or not having authority to have authority. Unfortunately, as a practical matter, even when it is clearly shown that a person, X, does not have authority to have authority, it does not necessarily follow, even as a matter of law, that he did not in point of fact have legal authority. For example, in the United States, the Supreme Court has permitted the actions of improperly apportioned state legislatures to stand.[38] Indeed not only has the validity of the past actions of these legislatures not been denied but even the future acts of such legislatures—those actions taken after the Court's decision but before a properly apportioned legislature has been elected—have been accorded validity.[39] All this has been done despite the fact that the legislatures were apportioned and elected in violation of the Constitution. Similarly, congressmen elected as a result of a constitutionally defective system of drawing congressional districts have not ceased to be congressmen capable of exercising the legal authority of congressmen.[40] In a similar vein, although the Constitution provides

---

[38] See Connor v. Williams, 404 U.S. 549, 550-1 (1972).

[39] Georgia v. United States, 411 U.S. 526, 541 (1973); Fortson v. Morris, 385 U.S. 231, 235 (1965) (election by mal-apportioned legislature of governor when none of candidates in general election had secured a majority).

[40] Cf. Kirkpatrick v. Preisler, 394 U.S. 526 (1969). In this case the lower court (the U.S. District Court) had, in 1967, ruled that the redistricting of congressional seats by

what shall constitute a quorum of both houses of Congress, if the journals of both houses indicate that a quorum was present in their respective houses, the courts will not look beyond these journals to ascertain whether in point of fact a quorum was present.[41] Similarly, the courts will not look behind the enrolled bill as certified by the Speaker of the House and the President of the Senate, to determine whether the enrolled bill is the bill actually passed by the Congress.[42] The practice in Great Britain is similar.[43]

Nor are the instances where an exercise of authority is upheld as *de jure*, despite the fact that it turns out that there really was no *de jure* authority, confined to the legislative level. The Supreme Court declared unconstitutional not only portions of the initial legislation establishing the Federal Election Commission but also declared that the Commissioners themselves were appointed in a manner that contravened the Constitution.[44] Nevertheless the Supreme Court not only validated the past actions of the Commission but twice allowed this unconstitutionally established Commission to continue to function for two brief additional periods totalling fifty days altogether.[45]

---

the Missouri state legislature was unconstitutional. In 1968 the Supreme Court stayed the district court's judgement pending appeal and authorised the state to conduct the 1968 congressional elections under the redistricting plan struck down by the district court. In April, 1969, the Supreme Court affirmed the district court's invalidation of the Missouri congressional redistricting plan but did nothing to question the authority of the members elected in the fall of 1968 under the plan held unconstitutional.

[41] See United States v. Ballin, 144 U.S. 1 (1892).

[42] See Field v. Clark, 143 U.S. 649 (1892).

[43] It was established at an early date that, for public acts, the bill enrolled by the Clerk of Parliament and delivered to the Chancery (the whole process being referred to as 'enrolment') was the 'original record'. As such, the only issue is whether this record exists and on that issue the record itself is the only admissible evidence. 'Private Acts' were filed only with the Clerk of Parliament, but they too were 'original records'. See J. Sutherland, *Statutes and Statutory Construction* 48-50 (2d ed. J. Lewis, 1904), which also contains references to the early cases. There have been some changes in the actual record keeping procedures used since 1850, but the Parliament roll is still the final resort. See 32 *Halsbury's Statutes of England* 361 (3d ed. 1971).

[44] Buckley v. Valeo, 424 U.S. 1 (1976).

[45] Id. at 142-3 (30 days); Buckley v. Valeo 424 U.S. 936 (1976) (20 days). The Court's purpose was to allow the Commission to perform its functions while Congress and the President resolved their differences as to how the Commission should be established. The differences were not resolved quickly enough, however; the Court's decision came into full effect and the Commission ceased to function. It was subsequently recreated after the President and the Congress resolved their differences. Pub. L. 94-283, May 11, 1976. The current provision is contained in 2 U.S.C. §437c.

In a similar vein, courts in the United States have come increasingly to reject nineteenth-century dogma to the contrary and to hold that officials acting under legislation subsequently declared unconstitutional are immune from any civil or criminal liability for any actions they may have taken under the legislation in question.[46] Even when there is no legislation to appeal to, officials who are found to have acted under a good-faith belief that their actions are constitutional have been held by the federal courts to be immune from liability under the Civil Rights Acts, even if it turns out that they have acted unconstitutionally.[47] Indeed, it has long been the law that a citizen normally has no right to disobey a judicial order, however unconstitutional it may be. The citizen's only recourse is to seek to have the order vacated; until it is vacated, he has no choice but to obey it.[48] As can be seen, therefore, even when there is a recognised hierarchy of authorities to whom an appeal can be made, the mere fact that an official was not entitled to have *de jure* authority does not necessarily mean that he was unable to exercise both *de facto* and *de jure* authority. These examples seem to show that philosophers are too quick in taking the case of *de jure* authority as the core situation upon which all other forms of authority are parasitic or dependent. Often, in the law, it turns out that the successful exercise of *de facto* authority, even by subsidiary organs of state, takes precedence over *de jure* authority.

The situation is even more complicated where there is no higher authority to which appeal can be made, either because there is no recognised hierarchy of authority or because one has reached the end of a hierarchical chain. What is it to contend, under these circumstances, that someone who successfully exercises authority does not have *de jure* authority? Is it to do anything more than to say that one

---

[46] See Bricker v. Sims, 195 Tenn, 361, 259 S.W.2d 661 (1953); cf. Idaho Code §6-611 (1979). See also Chicot County Drainage District v. Baxter State Bank, 308 U.S. 371 (1940). (Parties bound by judicial determination in which they were participants, even though act of Congress under which court operated subsequently declared unconstitutional by Supreme Court in another case.) For the earlier view, see Norton v. Shelby County, 118 U.S. 425, 442 (1885) (dictum) (case involved validity of county bonds); Sumner v. Beeler, 50 Ind. 341 (1875).

[47] See Wood v. Strickland, 420 U.S. 308 (1975); Scheuer v. Rhodes, 416 U.S. 232 (1974).

[48] See United States v. United Mine Workers, 330 U.S. 258 (1947) (order of a federal court); Walker v. City of Birmingham, 388 U.S. 307 (1967) (order of state court). In

does not like the fact that some person, X, has authority? One might contend that he is doing more than this, provided there is some body of law or similar rule-like structure to which one can appeal to justify one's claim that X does not have *de jure* authority. Certainly, if, after this appeal to the so-called rules, X desists from his attempts to exercise such authority or if, after this appeal, the people to whom X's authoritative pronouncements are addressed no longer accept his right to issue such pronouncements, to deny that X has *de jure* authority is to succeed in destroying X's authority. But what if neither X nor those who accept his authoritative pronouncements and his claim of right to issue these pronouncements alter their behaviour. Will not X now still have authority?

Winch, it will be recalled, maintains that all authority is ultimately *de jure* because authority relates to purposive human activity and all such activity is ultimately rule-governed. At its most basic it is presumably governed by the rules of morality. Winch initially argued that 'the fact that one is a human social being, engaged in rule-governed activities and on that ground able to deliberate and to choose, is in itself sufficient to commit one to the acceptance of *legitimate political* authority'.[49] Winch has now come to abandon this view because he now accepts that social life would not be impossible without the authority of the state and because 'the authority of the state, where it exists,[50] is *sui generis* and somehow imposed from without on other social institutions'. He, nevertheless, does not seem to have abandoned his notion that all authority is ultimately *de jure* in nature because he continues:

[T]hough the state faces other social institutions as something like an external force with its own, in a way independent, sources of authority, still this force and this authority are what they are by virtue of the fact that there exists a *concept* of the state in the society within which they are exercised—a concept which enters into what subjects will or will not submit to from the state. This concept is not itself *imposed* by the state; it manifests itself in the spontaneous

---

both cases, the most that the Court was prepared to concede was that there might possibly be some cases where the judicial order was so 'frivolous' or so 'transparently invalid' that the normal doctrine would not be operative.

[49] Winch at 105. In this quotation the emphasis has been supplied. When Winch retracted this view (see note 50, infra) he himself supplied the emphasis.

[50] Id. at 110.

life of the society even though its existence makes possible the imposition of certain things in a way which would not otherwise be possible.[51]

Indeed, in reiterating his contention that all authority is ultimately *de jure*, Winch has also now more fully spelled out what he means by *de jure*. It seems that, unless there is some recognised hierarchy of authority to whom an appeal can be made or unless there are some clearly agreed upon legal or law-like provisions that are accepted as governing the exercise of authority, what is meant by the assertion that all authority is ultimately *de jure* is that all authority is ultimately based upon consent. But, this tells us nothing that we did not already know. The most widely accepted common element of the various definitions of authority, the one even used by Winch, is the ability to issue commands (or other authoritative pronouncements) under a claim of right that is accepted by those to whom these commands (or pronouncements) are addressed. To say, therefore, that authority depends on consent is merely to say that having authority depends upon having authority, since the concept of authority already has the notion of consent built into it. It is only, as we have already seen, when one has unconsciously shifted the meaning of the term authority to refer instead to power or to the attempt to exercise power, that it makes sense to talk about authority that is accepted or not accepted.

Winch, furthermore, seems to be asserting that, since men are rational animals engaged in purposive activity, men's consent—men's acceptance of the authoritative pronouncements of others as rightfully issued—is somehow rule-governed.[52] Leaving aside that it is not altogether clear that all human activity is purposive, Winch's reduction of the term *de jure* authority certainly seems to swallow up the distinction between *de jure* authority and *de facto* authority. It also swallows up the distinction that many people, including Winch, wish to make between legitimate and illegitimate authority. If one pursues Winch's argument to its ultimate conclusion one would be forced to conclude that all authority is by definition legitimate. While I stated at the outset that it was not particulary helpful to describe authority as either legitimate or illegitimate, it seems to me that Winch's whole approach is wrong even if its implications, were they fully developed, would force him to reach the

[51] Id. at 110-11.
[52] Cf. pp. 11-12, supra.

same conclusion I have. At any rate, however, whatever the implications of his theory, Winch does believe that the distinction between legitimate and illegitimate political authority is a meaningful one, although he has not shown us why.

I have approached the problem from another point of view. I have asserted that all authority is ultimately *de facto*. I have shown that when there is a recognised hierarchy of authorities to whom an appeal can be made it is sometimes useful to distinguish between *de jure* authority and *de facto* authority and that, if the authority in question is found not to be *de jure*, the practical effects of that authority will usually be undone. I have shown, however, that this is not always the case, that sometimes even within an ongoing hierarchically organised legal order the *de facto* exercise of unlawful authority makes that authority *de jure*. The remaining point to be made is that this is even more true when there is no such hierarchy of authority or when one has reached the end of a hierarchical chain and there is no higher authority to appeal to. Kelsen clearly recognised that this was true and H. L. A. Hart was certainly prepared to concede that there was some warrant for the conclusion.[53] We will have occasion to return to this issue later when the time comes to draw our ultimate conclusions. For the present, I merely wish to submit that I have shown that the validity of my conclusions about the relationship between *de jure* and *de facto* authority is not at all affected by whether the activity in question—the one in which authority is exercised—is rule-governed in any meaningful sense of that term. *Contra* Winch, I wish to assert that it is indeed pointless to use the terms 'legitimate' or 'illegitimate' to *describe* authority, not because the exercise of all authority is conditioned upon the existence of rules, but rather because the existence of authority is more basic even than the existence |of rules Whether or not authority exists is, in the last analysis, a purely factual question and not a question of logical derivation.

The justification of all these assertions will require an examination of the relationship between law and authority. I shall undertake this examination shortly. First, however, I wish to turn to one other unfinished matter, namely the question of the relationship of the legitimacy of the state to the legitimacy of authority. Several questions present themselves. First, if the state is shown to be

---

[53] *General Theory* at 110-19, *Pure Theory* at 193-205; *Concept of Law* at 149-50.

illegitimate does this show that all authority, at least that exercised over adults in command of their mental faculties, is illegitimate? Some, of course, have so maintained. Secondly, even if one is not prepared to go so far as to deny the legitimacy of all authority, if one has nevertheless shown that the state in general (or some particular state) is illegitimate, does it follow that the authority it successfully exercises is likewise illegitimate? Winch's use of the term 'legitimate political authority' suggests that it does. It is to these questions that I shall now turn.

10. *The relationship between the legitimacy of government and the legitimacy of authority*

Perhaps as a result of the discontent produced by the Vietnam war or perhaps as a by-product of the increasing affluence in what is popularly known as the 'Western World' or perhaps as a combination of these and other causes, there has been an increasing tendency to question the moral legitimacy of the state and other institutions that exercise political authority. Two of the best known critiques of the concept of the state are those of Robert Paul Wolff and Robert Nozick. Although they arrive at somewhat different conclusions, both Wolff and Nozick start out from the position that the principle of human moral autonomy is the most fundamental postulate of morality and that, if the existence of the state cannot be harmonised with that principle, then the state is illegitimate. In the discussion that follows we shall examine their arguments. We shall be particularly concerned with what, if any, consequences their conclusions about the legitimacy of the state may have on the appropriateness of regarding authority as either legitimate or illegitimate.

Wolff starts out with certain assumptions about the importance of human moral autonomy that make it difficult, for anyone who might accept these assumptions, to quarrel with his conclusion that the state is illegitimate and that the moral man must opt for anarchy as the only possible form of social organisation that is morally justifiable. Given his assumptions, his argument is in a very real sense superfluous. Wolff postulates that the most important thing that a person can do with his time and energy is to make his own personal decisions whenever he is confronted with the possibility of choice in the conduct of his practical affairs.[54] He recognises that one may be justified in entrusting the power to make decisions in matters involving his physical health to so-called experts, like physicians, but not in other practical matters, and particularly not in those matters which fall into the realm of political affairs.[55] Admittedly, we usually lack the knowledge necessary to make rational decisions in matters concerning our health and it would be terribly time-consuming to try to acquire this knowledge as occasions arise which require it. But we often lack sufficient knowledge to make other practical decisions as well. Nevertheless, according to Wolff, we are not morally justified, in these other types of situations, in delegating our decision-making power to others, however much more knowledge and experience these others might have. This is not to say that, in exercising our power to make our own decisions, we should ignore the need for group action; we might very well go along with decisions which we regard as less than optimal in order to make group action possible. Nevertheless, each time we are confronted with the possibility of moral choice we must reserve the ultimate choice for ourselves and gather the necessary information to permit us to exercise that choice ourselves. Blanket approvals in advance of what others may decide are, from a moral point of view, never justified. To grant such blanket approval to the decisions of others represents moral cowardice or sheer laziness on our part. The only possible kind of state that can make a claim to moral legitimacy is what Wolff calls 'unanimous direct democracy'.[56] This is a state in which every person votes on every issue and decisions can only be reached under a rule of unanimity. Because the individual is only bound by decisions he has already accepted, unanimous direct democracy is, for Wolff, a 'genuine solution to the problem of autonomy and authority'.[57] Curiously, perhaps, Wolff believes that in the area of economic relations some intermediate position is available between total abdication of human autonomy and the reservation of decision-making authority on all specific questions of choice. Thus Wolff asserts that 'a community may agree unanimously on some principles

[54] R. P. Wolff, *In Defense of Anarchism* 12-18 (1970) (hereafter *Anarchism*).
[55] Id. at 15.
[56] Id. at 22-7.
[57] Id. at 27.

of compulsory arbitration by which economic conflicts may be settled'.[57a] An individual who has participated in this process 'will have a moral obligation to obey the commands of the mediation board or arbitration council, *whatever it decides*, because the principles which guide it issue from his own will. Thus the board will have authority over him (i.e., a right to be obeyed) while he retains his moral autonomy'.[57b] Wolff does not however seem to accept that such prior agreement to be bound by the application of principles of conflict resolution are applicable in the area of political decision-making. Were he to do so, unanimous direct democracy would then not be the only possible legitimate state. Any number of possible types of state could have the potential of legitimacy, including a state established upon John Rawls' principles of justice.

As we have already noted, at the level of its most basic postulates, it is hard to criticise Wolff's argument. Perhaps the most effective criticism that can be made is that made by Lisa Perkins.[58] She points out that the moral choices, which Wolff wishes to reserve for each adult individual, can only be made in a climate which presupposes the existence of the state. Only when a political order that effectively exercises authority actually exists, will we have the opportunity to try to make rational moral choices. Therefore, Perkins persuasively argues, only by recognising the legitimacy of the state can we have the opportunity to function as morally sensitive individuals, the goal which Wolff so ardently desires. In constructing this argument Perkins points out that Wolff himself seems implicitly to recognise the force of her argument.[59] For example, and the point is an important one, Wolff is not claiming that the principle of human moral autonomy requires that an individual must be free to do whatever he might wish to do at any given moment of time. Wolff recognises that an individual can morally bind himself by his prior commitments on specific issues. This is why he recognises unanimous direct democracy as a 'genuine solution to the problem of autonomy and authority'. Indeed, as we have seen, in the area of economic

---

[57a] Id. at 24.

[57b] Id. at 25 (emphasis in original).

[58] L. H. Perkins, 'On Reconciling Autonomy and Authority', 82 *Ethics* 114 (1972) (hereafter *Perkins*).

[59] Id. at 118-22.

interaction, one can even agree in advance to arbitrate economic conflicts so long as it is possible to agree in advance upon the principles to be applied in the resolution of those conflicts. What the individual may not do in the area of political decision-making, however, is give blanket prior commitments which are morally binding upon him. But, it seems fairly clear that there will be time lags, even in a unanimous direct democracy, between decisions and their execution. Inevitably, Perkins contends, there will be instances in which conditions change or, even if they do not, there will be instances in which we succeed in obtaining greater knowledge than we had at the time of the decision. I might add that, even where there is no change of conditions and we have obtained no greater amount of information, we may, on further reflection, conclude that we were just plain mistaken.

If we are prepared fully to accept Wolff's presuppositions about the overriding importance of individual human autonomy, why should we eschew any moral right to question or oppose the execution of prior specific political decisions? And yet Wolff believes that, in unanimous direct democracy we can, with no moral impropriety, give up our moral right to do so. Perkins believes Wolff is driven to this position because Wolff implicitly recognises that an individual can only effectively exercise this human autonomy in the context of the state—presumably some kind of just state. This is the germ of truth in the old saw that freedom is only possible under law. At any rate by recognising the 'legitimacy' of unanimous direct democracy Wolff concedes that individuals can bind themselves in advance to doing what they might come to consider to be morally objectionable. How much commitment to how many prior decisions is, of course, another matter, but it all becomes a question of degree; there are no *a priori* answers. And, if the essence of being a human being is exercising moral choice, then a fairly complex state is necessary to give the individual the leisure to devote himself to moral issues rather than having to spend all his time and energy in the struggle for physical survival. To meet these objections, of course, Wolff might be prepared to reject the legitimacy even of unanimous direct democracy. As to the fact that, in a state of anarchy, the individual has less time to make moral choices and probably fewer moral choices to make, Wolff might answer that it is better for a person to be morally free in all of the few moral choices he has an opportunity to make than to expand his field of moral choice by accepting some restrictions on his freedom. At this level, Wolff's argument, for what it is worth, is unassailable. Either one accepts it or one rejects it.

For those who are unwilling to make the extreme choices Wolff may be prepared to make, another objection to Wolff's thesis that comes to mind is why is it so wrong for individuals to wish to engage in large scale group efforts, efforts which require the effective exercise of authority if they are to succeed? Is it wrong for us to wish to put a man on the Moon or on Mars? Is it wrong to wish to eradicate hunger? Is it wrong for us to wish to spend most of our time producing music or other works of art rather than continually engaging in moral deliberations? Wolff presumably thinks it is, for he would leave us no time for these activities. Whatever energies man can spare from the struggle for sheer physical survival he must devote to moral deliberation. I am not suggesting that people should do what they believe to be morally wrong just because someone else has told them to do so. As we shall see in section 11, below, our acceptance of the claim of right of others to issue authoritative pronouncements to us does not entail this result. But why is it wrong, when we are unable readily to discern the morally correct thing to do, to trust in the judgment of others?

Assuming, however, that Wolff is correct, that the state is not a morally legitimate social order, what follows from this conclusion? In particular, what effect does it have on the concept of authority? At the outset of his study, *In Defense of Anarchism*, Wolff clearly shows that he appreciates that the question of the legitimacy of the state is a different one from that of the legitimacy of authority. To ask whether there is such a thing as authority, however one may characterise it (*de facto, de jure*, legitimate, etc.), is to ask a factual question. It depends solely upon what people believe. Thus, Wolff explicitly states:

What can be inferred from the existence of *de facto* states is that men *believe* in the existence of legitimate authority, for of course a *de facto* state is simply a state whose subjects believe it to be legitimate (i.e., really to have the authority which it claims for itself). They may be wrong. Indeed, *all* beliefs in authority may be wrong—there may not be a single state in the history of mankind which has now or ever has had a right to be obeyed. It might even be impossible for such a state to exist; that is the question we must try to settle. But so long as men believe in the authority of states, we can conclude that they possess the concept of *de jure* authority.[60]

[60] *Anarchism* at 10-11 (emphasis in original).

In the middle portion of his study Wolff proceeds to show that the state cannot be justified, and that therefore the state is not legitimate. Given his assumptions, his conclusion is hardly surprising. What is surprising is that in a brief conclusion he states that what he has shown is that men must 'embrace the doctrine of anarchism and categorically deny *any* claim to legitimate authority by one man over another.'[61] One must abandon the search for 'legitimate collective authority'.[62] A few pages later he states pejoratively that. '[t]hrough the exercise of *de facto* legitimate authority, states achieve what Max Weber calls the imperative coordination of masses of men and women'.[63] I find this all very confusing. By his own admission it may be helpful to consider whether the state is legitimate, that is, to consider whether people should accept authority, but, as Wolff himself recognised at the beginning of his work, if people accept authority then authority exists. In the less abbreviated terminology. I have used, if people accept someone's claim of right to issue authoritative pronouncements to them, then there is authority. One may regret this fact but there it is. After making this concession, which as we have seen is unavoidable, to start talking about '*de facto* legitimate authority' is at best to degenerate into ephithet and at worst to lapse into incoherence. I could not begin to attempt to analyse what that complex term means. The attempt at analysis is not greatly helped by Wolff's assertions that there can be 'no *de jure* state', in contexts in which he presumably means to imply that there can be no '*de jure* legitimate authority', whatever that means other than that Wolff thinks political authority is not morally justifiable. This characterisation does not affect the fact that authority can be seen to exist and that some people believe it is useful to describe some forms of authority as *de jure* because they are premised upon some rule-like structure like law. In short, Wolff's work on the legitimacy of the state has told us nothing about authority, other than that, if we agree with Wolff's conclusion about the illegitimacy of the state, we should not ourselves so act as to permit anyone to exercise authority over us and we should decry and morally condemn other people permitting the establishment of authority over themselves. If this is what Wolff

---

[61] Id. at 72 (emphasis in original).

[62] Ibid.

[63] Id. at 78.

means by his pejorative use of the term '*de facto* legitimate authority' and his suggestion that there can be no *de jure* legitimate authority, then so be it. If enough people accept Wolff's contentions then we may indeed come to witness what is so often decried as the 'erosion' or 'twilight' of authority,[64] although at the present time these fears seem premature, to say the least. Of course, if we reject Wolff's thesis, either because we accept Lisa Perkins' point or because we disagree with Wolff that man is most a man when he becomes so obsessed with making moral choices that he has no time to play or behave whimsically or to engage in joint endeavours whose consequences he can never fully appreciate, then even these modest conclusions do not follow.

Nozick's thesis, as expressed in his recent work *Anarchy, the State, and Utopia*, is more complex and in some ways less sweeping than Wolff's. It is, however, for these and other reasons more difficult to deal with. Like Wolff, he lays major stress on the principle of human moral autonomy. No one, except in certain cases of self-defence, is justified in infringing the rights of another individual without that person's consent. According to Nozick, a rational man would only voluntarily sacrifice his moral autonomy in order to preserve himself and his entitlements from the aggression of others. Thus, a minimal state, which adequately performs these functions, can be morally justified, that is to say, such a state can be legitimate. Nozick shows that, as a logical matter, such a state could arise without anyone consciously desiring to create a state through the device of each individual contracting with private protection societies. In the course of time one of these societies will become dominant in any particular geographic locality and, in order for the individual to achieve the highest degree of protection obtainable, there will be a natural tendency for people to contract with the dominant protective association rather than with one of the less comprehensive associations. The problem of a few hold-outs will, of course, be a likely possibility. The incorporation of these people into the sphere of the dominant protective association to complete the birth of the minimal state is not justified by Nozick by any 'free-rider' theory. Rather, he argues the risk to others presented by a few lone people who insist on enforcing the requirements of justice as they would exist

---

[64] See R. Nisbet, *Twilight of Authority* (1975); cf. de Jouvenel's *Sovereignty* at 33.

in a state of nature in a society where most people belong to a protective association with elaborate and impartial machinery of justice justifies prohibiting these outsiders from taking justice into their own hands. But the right to enforce the requirements of justice in a state of nature is something to which that individual is entitled. It cannot be taken away from someone without paying him compensation. This Nozick is prepared to do, and the minimal state arises because part of the form in which compensation is provided is the furnishing of minimal protective services to the few hold-outs. These latter thus become part of the 'night watchman' state in which one entity, the dominant protective agency now transformed into the minimal state, has a monopoly of the use or authorisation of force by one citizen against another and in which all citizens are accorded some measure of protection by this entity. That the minimal state could possibly, as a practical matter, thus arise indirectly as a result, so to speak, of an invisible hand is a decidedly plus factor for Nozick. Indeed it is one of the major reasons why Nozick concludes that the minimal state can be legitimate.[65]

Among the most effective portions of Nozick's study are his trenchant criticisms of Rawls' *A Theory of Justice* which makes the dominant purpose of the state the ensuring of justice in distribution rather than, as in the case of Nozick's minimal state, the offering of protection to the individual of both his person and entitlements. Rawls, it will be recalled, asserts that inequality in the distribution of social goods can only be justified if the inequality leads to making the position of the least advantaged group in society better off than it would otherwise be. Rawls postulates that one social good, liberty, is more important and, partly for this reason, different from other social goods. Thus the liberty of some can only be restricted if the resulting social arrangements '(a) . . . strengthen the total system of liberty shared by all, and (b) a less than equal liberty [is] . . . acceptable to those citizens with the lesser liberty.'[66] In no event may liberty be traded off for some other types of social goods. To emphasise this

---

[65] This paragraph has summarised the argument of Part I, *The State* (pp. 3-146), of R. Nozick, *Anarchy, the State and Utopia* (1974) (hereafter Nozick). The period between the disappearance of competitive protective association and the incorporation of the hold-outs Nozick describes as the period of the 'ultra-minimal' state.

[66] J. Rawls, *A Theory of Justice* 250 (1971) (hereafter *Theory of Justice*). See also id. at 243-51.

difference he calls liberty a 'basic right' and not merely a social good such as are the vast panoply of ordinary legal rights. Furthermore, even with regard to the other (and lesser social goods) which are subject to the operation of Rawls' difference principle, one such good, freedom of opportunity, can only be restricted to enhance the opportunities of those with lesser opportunities.[67] Rawls justifies his conclusions in two ways. First, he contends that they coincide with what, on reflection, we could consider as most in accord with our intuitive notions of justice.[68] Secondly, as a logical matter, social arrangements embodying his principles could arise from what we would regard as a fair procedure.[69] We come to see what might be the fair procedure and what might be its outcome by asking ourselves the following question: What would happen if individuals, living in a state of nature and ignorant of both their intellectual gifts and of the social position and material possessions they might possess within the social order, met together to decide, on the basis of unanimity, what should be the basic principles upon which they will establish the state. Prudential considerations—the desire to protect themselves against the possibility that they may turn out to be among society's least

---

[67] *Theory of Justice* at 298-303. For other social goods subject to the difference principle, it is the position of the least favoured that is crucial.

[68] That is, Rawls is claiming that his principles of justice would be found to be in accord with our moral sensibilities in, what Rawls calls, the state of 'reflective equilibrium'. This latter condition, as applied to our concept of justice, is one which we have arrived at after a disinterested reflection upon all of the possible principles of justice that occur to us. See *Theory of Justice* at 20-1, 48-53, 120; cf. id. at 432.

[69] Rawls distinguishes between perfect procedural justice and imperfect procedural justices: '[P]ure procedural justice obtains when there is no independent criterion for the right result: instead there is a correct or fair procedure such that the outcome is likewise correct or fair, whatever it is, provided that the procedure has been properly followed.' *Theory of Justice* at 86. In the real world imperfect procedural justice is the most that can be hoped for and the results of following such a procedure will not always be correct (or fair or just), in whatever sense is under consideration. The purpose of the restrictions imposed on the 'original condition', to be described shortly in the text, is to approximate a framework of pure procedural justice. Once a 'just' state has been established in accordance with Rawls' principles of justice, the actual operation of that state will approximate that of an imperfect system of procedural justice (Rawls sometimes calls it a system of 'quasi-pure procedural justice'), which will on the whole, but not always, lead to just legislation, etc. This is why Rawls recognises the validity of conscientious objection even in a 'nearly just' state. See id. at 83-90, 197-201, 356-91.

advantaged people—would lead them to adopt Rawls principles.[70]

I for one have always been surprised that some arrangement should be considered just *because* it arose from prudential considerations[71] That what, in point of fact, we do consider just should coincide with out perceived self-interest under some given set of circumstances—such as Rawls' original position—does not, of course, surprise me. Hume long ago pointed out why this is likely to be the case.[72] Rawls further argues, however, that his principles accord with our own disinterested and considered intuitive notions of justice. Nozick, on the other hand, makes a strong argument that Rawls' arrangements do not even accord with our intuitive notions of justice.[73] There are many important social goods, he persuasively argues that almost all people, even after considerable reflection, agree are part of the entitlements of those who possess these goods. There is no generally perceived sense of justice that requires those who are fortunate enough to possess these social goods to share them with the least advantaged. Indeed, most people would be aghast at any effort to enforce such a presumed requirement of justice and would, indeed, find any such effort to be the epitome of injustice. This is certainly a major contribution to the debate generated by Rawls' work and a welcome antidote to some of the uncritical acceptance Rawls' conclusions have received.

Where Nozick's argument gives me trouble is in its assertion that nothing more than the minimal state can be legitimate; that to accept

[70] See *Theory of Justice* at 136-61, where Rawls discusses the 'veil of ignorance' and the 'reasons leading to the two principles of Justice'.

[71] Nozick argues rather persuasively that it is not even clear that the adoption of the principles of justice is in fact the rational thing for men to do in Rawls' artificial 'original condition'. See Nozick at 189-97.

[72] *Treatise* at 484-549.

[73] Nozick at 213.31. Why, Nozick asks, is a man not entitled to the fruits of his natural talents and abilities and, even more, of his superior character which may permit him more fully to utilise his natural talents and abilities. Moreover, if Rawls is not prepared to take into account people's individual entitlements, why cannot the difference principle be used to justify taking one of a person's corneas to help someone less advantaged (or, I would add, one of a person's kidneys to help someone experiencing total kidney failure). Id. at 206-7. Nozick also is distressed because despite Rawls' talk of 'liberty'—which in his usage refers only to very basic liberties like those of conscience and speech and equality before the law—the citizens of Rawls' society do not have the liberty, through voluntary transactions, of disturbing the end state distributions arrived at by the difference principles. For this reason Nozick considers such distributions, *contra* Rawls, to be highly unstable. See id. at 153-74.

any further authority, or to use the terminology that I have been using through this book, to permit anyone to have any greater authority over one, is not morally justifiable. Indeed, it seems to me that Nozick's own argument, if all its implications are examined, militates against the validity of his conclusion. In the first place it is all very well to talk about people participating in the minimal state in order to protect themselves against aggression directed towards their persons or their entitlements. The important practical question is what, in point of fact, are people entitled to? According to Nozick, what one is entitled to are things that one has acquired under the principle of justice in acquisition or under the principle of justice in transfer.[74] Amplifiying Locke's thoughts on the subject of the acquisition of property in a state of nature, Nozick asserts that the principle of justice in acquisition requires, as a condition of anyone being able to acquire 'a permanent bequeathable property right in a previously unowned thing', that such a person's acquisition of 'the thing' will not result in worsening the position of others no longer at liberty to use 'the thing'.[75] When such an appropriation will result in a worsening of the position of others, the item cannot be appropriated unless those whose position is worsened are paid compensation. In the extreme case, things which are absolutely essential to the life of others cannot be the object of the exclusive domination of one person.[76] In its turn, the principle of justice in transfer specifies that one can acquire things that are already the property of others only by voluntary exchange or by gift.

Now, if one lives in a social condition where people own all sorts of things that they did not acquire in accordance with the two principles of justice that Nozick has enunciated, what should be done? According to Nozick, a third principle of justice comes into play, the principle of justice in rectification. How this principle would operate in practice, particularly if the injustice has persisted over many generations, Nozick never makes clear. It certainly does not seem

---

[74] Nozick at 150-82.

[75] Nozick at 178.

[76] The case is persuasively made that what is essential for life from a physical point of view, as well as from a social point of view, is relative and that, even accepting Nozick's notion of property, a case can be made for providing basic subsistence and even, perhaps, other basic goods to the needy. See T. Grey, 'Property and Need: The Welfare State and Theories of Distributive Justice', 28 *Stan. L. Rev.* 877, 888-97 (1976).

implausible to conclude that one will need much more than the aims and machinery of the minimal state to accomplish this rectification. Indeed, Nozick himself admits as much when he asserts '[a]lthough to introduce socialism as the punishment for our sins would be to go too far, past injustices might be so great as to make necessary in the short run a more extensive state in order to rectify them'.[77] Unless, however, the rectificatory state is to become in large part a coercive order—compare the dictatorship of the proletariat—it will need to possess a great deal more authority, in order to achieve its rectificatory goals, than is required by the minimal state whose purpose is merely to provide its citizens mutual protection against aggression. The conclusion, then, seems inescapable: One can be morally justified in accepting the legitimacy of something more than the minimal state. In short, one can be morally justified in permitting others to possess authority over one that is greater than that which they would possess in the minimal state.

Even if the principle of justice in rectification does not come into play—let us assume there is no injustice to redress—there is a second difficulty with Nozick's limitation of the amount of personal moral autonomy one may be morally justified in surrendering to make the minimal state work. For the minimal state to function, indeed for a protective association to exist, there is a need for an enforcement staff. Now, while this enforcement staff can be recruited by contract, the members of that staff are contracting for more than protection against aggression in return for which they surrender certain of their rights to act on their own initiative in repelling aggression. The members of the enforcement staff quite obviously must assume the obligations of quasi-military discipline. They may do this because the pay is good, because they like the kind of life involved, or because they wish to serve their fellow-men. Nozick believes that men, as morally autonomous agents, are free, in the absence of coercion, to do what they wish, provided they do not infringe the rights of others. Indeed, it is central to Nozick's thesis that no legitimate state more extensive than the minimal state can arise without the consent of all the people subject to its dominion. He considers it unlikely to arise because there would always be some hold-outs and it would be unjust

---

[77] Nozick at 231. See also id. at 152.3.

to force them to join. The whole key is voluntary choice because the ability to make such choices is the essential ingredient of moral autonomy, of being a man. Men are thus free to contract themselves into slavery.[78] Presumably, therefore, the members of the enforcement staff, who must assume some obligations which many would consider similar to those which slaves labour under, are, accordingly, free to submit to the increased obligations which are required for the organisation of an efficient enforcement staff.

But, while people are free to assume these obligations, are they morally justified in doing so? Nozick lays stress on the fact that the enforcement staff is 'hired', but the fact that they receive payment for enlisting surely does not answer the question of whether they are justified in entering into any such arrangements. It may be instructive then to turn to the last portion of Nozick's book in which he discusses the concept of utopia.[79] He criticises previous attempts to state in great detail what a utopian society would look like. People are diverse and their desires disparate and we would not want the facts to be otherwise. Rather, therefore, than trying to describe an actual utopian state, Nozick believes it is more fruitful to construct a framework of utopias. This is a somewhat complicated concept but its essential feature is that it permits individuals to join any associations they wish in search of their individual utopias. Once they have joined an association they lose their right to opt out of any particular arrangement in force in that society.[80] Nozick is prepared to recognise this restriction of individual freedom because he envisages such utopian societies as existing within the overall framework of the 'minimal state'. He suggests that, unlike the larger community that composes the minimal state, these particular utopian communities—which Nozick calls 'face-to-face' communities[81]—may prohibit their members from opting out of particular community arrangements. But, and this is crucial to Nozick's thesis, while individuals cannot opt out of particular arrangements prevailing in

---

[78] Nozick at 331. But cf. id. at 283, where he allows for the possibility that, in a morally jusitifed minimal state, the protective association, which is in effect the executive arm of the minimal state, might choose *not* to enforce such contracts.

[79] Nozick at 297-334.

[80] Nozick at 320-3.

[81] Nozick at 322-3.

a sub-community that they have joined in search of utopia, the utopian framework requires that each individual must always have the right to leave any particular community he may have joined in search of utopia and to seek his utopia in some other community. [82] This is a right so crucial that it is to be enforced by the minimal state.

The implications of this discussion are clear. Rational and moral individuals would not wish to belong to a community from which they would be forbidden to leave whenever they chose to do so. Indeed, the utopian framework is not only protected and preserved by the minimal state; it is the minimal state.[83] The purpose of Nozick's discussion of utopia becomes clear. It is not simply an occasion for him to engage in interesting philosophical speculation; it also represents his argument that there is an alternative route to the minimal state. The minimal state is thus not merely the only morally justifiable state but it is now also seen as the most desirable state for other reasons as well, because it is the best vehicle for permitting each individual to seek his own utopia. Yet, for the minimal state to be possible, there must exist a sub-group of individuals—the enforcement staff who themselves constitute a social order—who are prepared to live in a social environment in which a much more extensive authority exists and has the right to structure their lives for them. The members of such a staff must be bound to execute orders which they disagree with and even find offensive. In addition, an effective enforcement staff clearly must be constrained by minimum terms of enlistment. They must, consequently, give up the aspiration of participating in what Nozick calls the utopian framework. Their sights must be set lower than the quest for utopia and the inalienable freedom of choice that this quest requires. Thus, while they are free to join the enforcement staff or not, their very act in doing so shows

---

[82] Nozick at 316. 329-31. See also id. at 309-12. Nozick has set the stage for this conclusion by first considering what an individual might be prepared to accept as an ideal model of utopia. He suggests that this ideal model would be a stable association—a world, if you will—of human beings which is of such a nature that none of its members can imagine an alternative world they would rather live in and which they believe would continue to exist even if all of its rational members had the same right of imagining other utopian worlds and then emigrating to such new worlds. Nozick at 296-306.

[83] Nozick at 333-4.

them to be lacking in certain very desirable human qualities, namely rationality and a developed moral sense, including a sense of their own moral autonomy. Accordingly, while the only legitimate state is, for Nozick, the minimal state, its very existence requires the existence of a sub-state which is much more than minimal and which requires for its very existence that some people renounce the full range of moral aspiration. The problem is even more complicated if not enough people volunteer to join the enforcement staff and resort must be made to some sort of compulsory service. Presumably, if this is done, the very legitimacy of the minimal state will be threatened if not undermined.

In sum, Nozick rejects anarchy but the only state whose moral legitimacy he is expressly prepared to accept is his so-called minimal state. It is fairly certain that he would accept the legitimacy of Wolff's unanimous direct democracy, but Nozick makes it clear that such universal consent could never be secured in the real world. Indeed, Nozick's derivation of the minimal state is designed to get around the problem that universal consent is impossible and that the legitimacy of the state must be ensured in some other way. Whether Wolff would recognise the legitimacy of Nozick's minimal state is an interesting question. It has been suggested that Nozick has shown that, if Wolff's unanimous direct democracy is legitimate, because its manner of derivation does not offend the principle of human moral autonomy, then an anarchist like Wolff should accept the legitimacy of Nozick's minimal state because its derivation likewise does not offend the principle of the primacy of human moral autonomy.[84] As we have already noted, of course, Wolff might respond by rejecting the legitimacy even of a unanimous direct democracy. At any rate the final point that should be made in connection with Nozick's theory is similar to one that was made with regard to Wolff's. Why is man most a moral agent when all he wants to do is be left alone and to have absolute freedom of choice on as many occasions as possible? Certainly man has conflicting desires. At times he wishes to be as free and independent as possible; at other times he wishes to be part of some large-scale effort and to be caught up in the web of loyalties and operational goals that make the exercise of unencumbered moral

[84] See T. Nagel, 'Libertarianism Without Foundations', 85 *Yale L.J.* 136, 139 n.4 (1975).

choice difficult. It is not clear that either aspect of man's nature is to be despised.[84a]

In this section we have been examining the arguments for the moral preferability of either anarchy or the minimal state in order to see what, if any consequences, follow for the concept of authority. At most, if one accepts these arguments *in toto*, they support the conclusion that people should not allow others to have authority over them and that we should decry the all too evident fact that people do permit authority to arise. We have also seen that, if we are unprepared to opt for anarchy—either because like Lisa Perkins we feel that anarchy restricts rather than expands human moral autonomy or because we find that it leads to too cramped a view of human existence—any notion like that of the minimal state requires the existence of a fairly extensive authority to maintain it. Unless the minimal state is to degenerate into being merely a coercive order, the moral basis for the organisation of the enforcement staff must be considered. As we have seen, providing such a base is not without its difficulties. The very existence of the minimal state seems to require the presence of a class of helots who have renounced part of the individual moral autonomy that Nozick asserts is the very essence of being a man in the fullest sense. To assert that the subjugation of some is a necessary evil in order to preserve the moral autonomy of others is to make some men a means to other men's ends; and this is ruled out by the concept of individual moral autonomy, the very concept that the theory of the minimal state is designed to fulful.

11. *What does it mean to 'accept' the right of others to issue authoritative pronouncements?*

We have been examining what it is to *have authority*. Under our working definition, which seems widely accepted, a person has authority if he has the ability to issue authoritative pronouncements to others under a claim of right that is accepted by those others to

---

[84a] Some recent scholarship supports the conclusion that, within the evolutionary ladder in which man has developed, relationships based on dominance are the 'natural condition. See F. Willhoite, Jr., 'Primates and Political Authority', 70 *Am. Pol. Sci. Rev.* 1110 (1976).

whom his pronouncements are issued. Although it involves some redundancy at best, people sometimes describe a situation where one person has authority as one where that person's authority is accepted. If this person's 'authority' is not accepted these same people might be tempted to call his 'authority' illegitimate, but, as we have seen,[85] this is inaccurate. If his 'authority' is not accepted he, by definition, does not have any authority at all. He may have power, of course. People out of fear or for some other motive may very well be prepared to accept his pronouncements as authoritative, that is, as dispositive of the matter in question. But, getting people to do what one wants is not identical to having authority; it is only part of the inquiry. For authority to exist, the people to whom the authoritative pronouncements are addressed must not only accept them as authoritative, they must also accept a claim of right on the part of the issuer to issue these pronouncements. All this is straightforward enough and has been explored at length above. The questions still to be examined concern what it is to accept pronouncements as authoritative and to accept someone's claim of right to issue them.

As a preliminary matter, we have proceeded under the assumption that to accept a pronouncement as authoritative is to treat the pronouncement as resolving the matter in issue. In the case of a command a pronouncement which is accepted as authoritative answers the question, 'What should I do?' In the case of resolving a dispute such pronouncements can answer the question 'What should I believe?' as well as the question 'What should I do?' Accepting the claim of right involves interpreting the 'should' in expressions of the form 'What should I do?' or 'What should I believe?', as referring to what it is *right* that I should do (or believe), as opposed to what is the prudential thing to do if I wish to avoid sanctions or some other immediate unpleasant consequences. The problem is, nobody ever does everything he should do. Nor does anybody, if he is pushed hard enough, ever agree that it is right that he should do everything that he is told to do by those whom he accepts as having authority over him.

We have seen this problem before,[86] when we were examining H. L. A. Hart's criteria for the existence of a legal system. These criteria ultimately boil down to the acceptance by the officials of that

---

[85] See the discussion at the beginning of §9, supra (pp. 99 ff., supra).

[86] See §2, supra (pp. 83ff.).

legal system of the system's rule of recognition and the rules generated from that rule of recognition. Leaving aside the difficulty that actually stating the rule of recognition in any reasonably concrete form would be a herculean task—a task further complicated by the circumstance that the rule supposedly describes a matter of fact, namely the psychological frame of mind of these officials and what it is they are prepared to accept—it still remains true that almost nobody, even in his official capacity, always does what he might be prepared to accept he ought, from a legal point of view, to do. And this is not because officials are inescapably venal or lazy or fearful. A highly moral person might be more inclined to depart from the supposed legal norm than a person who is comparatively morally unprincipled. There are many dimensions of ought. Thus, whether the question concerns the acceptance of a rule of recognition or the question with which we are concerned, the acceptance of a claim of right to issue authoritative pronouncements, any interpretation of 'accept' that presupposes *always* is unrealistic. If to 'accept' means that one always does or believes what one is told to do or to believe, than no one ever accepts the pronouncements of others as authoritative and no one ever has any authority. There will always be occasions when authority is ignored. A possible fall-back position is to assert that accept means 'most of the time', but this is too simple. In addition to frequency, the importance of the pronouncements involved is also a factor, as are other considerations. The fall-back position, even if in a sense true, is thus too subjective. Is it possible to establish any more meaningful tests of acceptance that both accord with common sense and yet are not as subjective? I believe it is possible. In the discussion which follows I shall attempt to provide the required explication of the term 'acceptance' and its linguistic variations.

It has been frequently recognised that an obligation to obey what one conceives to be the rules of an institution to which one belongs is a logical consequence of the nature of institutions.[87] Institutions are, after all, constituted by their rules. At the same time it is generally

---

[87] See A. Gewirth, 'Obligation: Political, Legal, Moral', *Nomos XII: Political and Legal Obligation* (1970), at 55, 57 (hereafter *Gewirth*); Winch at 89-100. On the general subject of the constitutive nature of rules, see J. Austin, *How to Do Things with Words* (1962); J. Rawls, 'Two Concepts of Rules', 64 *Phil. Rev.* 3 (1955). For a good and somewhat critical review of this position, see H. Schwyzer, 'Rules and Practices', 78 *Phil. Rev.* 451 (1969).

recognised that, from a moral point of view, this obligation is only a tentative one.[88] For this tentative moral obligation to mature into a determinative moral obligation it is customary to assert that both the institution itself and the particular rules in question must be morally justified. The justifications will typically involve considerations of human welfare, of 'justice', and of human freedom or autonomy. Nevertheless, while our moral obligation to obey the rules of most of the institutions to which we belong is only tentative, the nature of our moral obligation to obey the rules of our legal institutions (i.e., the law of our political society) is often said to be of a higher order. Our moral obligation to obey the law is not fully determinative but it is said to be *prima facie* determinative.[89] This is so because, unlike other institutions, law, in some form at least, is essential if civil society is to be possible. Most other types of institutions are not so clearly essential, and hence we must, presumably, examine whether institutions of that type are morally desirable before we proceed to determine whether the particular institution under examination is morally justifiable. With respect to law, however, we know that, as a general proposition, the institution of law is morally justifiable and indeed necessary. Our only task, therefore, is to examine the morality of individual legal systems and the particular rules we are asked to obey.

I wish to assert, however, that while this conventional analysis makes some very valid distinctions between the legal order and other institutions, it fails to take fully into account all the implications of these differences. Not only is law, and the civil society constituted by it, more essential to human well-being than most other institutions, it is also the most difficult institution to escape from. Renouncing allegiance to one's nation-state is always inconvenient. From a procedural or formal point of view, it is often difficult, as well; and, sometimes, it is impossible, for some nation-states refuse to recognise any attempted renunciations of allegiance. Furthermore, even if one can renounce allegiance to his nation-state, he cannot thereby escape liability for acts committed before his renunciation. Nor can he completely escape possible liability for acts performed after his renunciation of allegiance, even if his acts were performed outside of the territorial limits of his former nation-state. All nation-states,

---

[88] See, e.g., *Gewirth* at 61-3.

[89] See, e.g., Id. at 76-9.

including the United States which claims perhaps the smallest amount of extraterritorial jurisdiction, claim the right to punish even foreigners for some acts performed beyond their borders.[90] It is this difficulty of renouncing allegiance, together with the tremendous inconvenience which renunciation entails, that makes it plausible to distinguish between a person who is merely civilly disobedient and the revolutionary. And, it is on the basis of some or all of these considerations that philosophers usually found the distinction between tentative or even *prima facie* moral duties to obey institutional rules and fully determinative moral duties. With respect to most other institutions, however, I submit that these distinctions make less sense. *Qua* member, one always has a moral duty to recognise and fulfil his obligations to these institutions. If he cannot do so, then he must and can leave the institution, in which case these institutional obligations become at most tentative ones. But if he chooses to remain a member, it is hard to find a plausible reason upon which to base a moral right to disobey. Only when complete renunciation of his institutional allegiance becomes very difficult and exceedingly hazardous to his physical security does the question of a moral alternative, such as the partial renunciation of allegiance, arise. It is instructive to note that the controversy within the Roman Catholic Church over the question of birth control has not largely been waged over whether the Church has promulgated a rule against birth control, which one should not in conscience obey, but, rather, over whether what some bishops assert to be the rule established by the Church is in fact a valid rule of the Church. In the modern world at least, it is possible to renounce one's allegiance to the Church without too many untoward practical consequences.

Returning now to a consideration of the modern nation-state and its legal order, two possible types of civil disobedience are readily discernible. We shall confine the discussion to what might be called 'constitutional democracies', because these are the types of states that are generally considered capable of moral justification. Accordingly,

---

[90] See, e.g., 18 U.S.C. §§ 471 and 474 dealing with counterfeit obligations or securities of the United States and the plates or stones from which such counterfeits may be made. On the attempts to apply extraterritorially the United States antitrust laws, see W. Bishop, *International Law* 567-72 (3d ed. 1971). For an instance of the extra-territorial application of state law, see New York Penal Law of 1909, §§ 1930, 1933. These provisions were not contained in the revision of the New York Penal Law that became effective in 1967.

'civil disobedience' will be used here as a term to describe the situation where the actor wishes to remain a member of a given civil society, because he has concluded that the society is morally deserving of allegiance, but at the same time, for moral reasons, he refuses to obey a particular legal provision of that society and is prepared to accept the legal consequences of that refusal. The first type of civil disobedience, which includes most instances of asserted civil disobedience, concerns the situation in which one refuses to obey a purported legal rule on the ground that there is no such rule—cf. the birth control controversy in the Roman Catholic Church—or on the ground that the purported rule is invalid in that it contradicts some more basic 'rule' of the legal system. Usually this is not an instance of civil disobedience at all, at least where such refusal to obey is an accepted or even a recognised method of challenging the validity of the purported rule that is under attack. Much of the earlier civil disobedience concerning matters of civil rights was of this kind. 'Civil disobedience' of this type is an almost invariable consequence of the dual legal systems obtaining in a federal form of government, although, given the complexity and hierarchial structure of the modern nation-state, it can arise with sufficient frequency in unitary states as well.

The second generally recognised type of civil disobedience concerns the situation in which the purported rules which one refuses to obey are considered either to be immoral themselves or to support what one claims is an immoral policy. Much of the civil disobedience connected with the Vietnamese War was of this second type, as was also some of the later activity of what, for want of a better term, might be called civil-rights activists. It should be noted that civil disobedience of the second type often shades into that of the first type. Many of the challenges to the draft and revenue laws during the war in Vietnam, for example, were motivated by a desire to secure, if not a judicial declaration that the War was illegal, at least a judicial ruling on the legality of the War. There is, however, also a third type of civil disobedience which is not as widely discussed in the literature. It arises when one refuses to obey a law not because he thinks it is invalid nor because he thinks that it is immoral or that it furthers an immoral policy, but, rather, because he wants to call attention to some other law or policy that he is unable otherwise to challenge. This third type of civil disobedience comes perilously close to revolution, especially when its purpose is to cause a change of policy by imposing an excessive amount of inconvenience on society. From the tenor of much of the writing on civil disobedience it is obvious that most writers would probably contend that this third type of civil disobedience is illegitimate, and so would I.[91] It clearly contradicts the ethical imperative of respect for the freedom of others to control their own actions.

The second type of civil disobedience is, therefore, for present purposes, the most interesting. It can be analysed from two aspects, the substantive and the procedural. From the substantive aspect, the morality of refusing to obey a law which one believes is morally wrong or which one believes furthers an immoral policy depends on a balancing process. The degree of immorality of the law or policy in question is naturally relevant, as is also the overall morality of the legal system involved. In this regard, the possible effect of one's civil disobedience is also a factor. What harm will it do the civil society and those in it? Will it lead to repression against all dissident groups in a society? Consideration of this last factor, of course, leads to the conclusion that civil disobedience may be less justified against a repressive civil society than against a relatively benign civil society, although the latter has a greater moral claim for obedience on the part of its citizens. And, indeed, experience seems to bear out that civil disobedience is more likely to occur in a benign and tolerant society than in a repressive one.

From the procedural aspect, however, the situation is different. Alan Gewirth, for example, concludes, that from the procedural point of view all violation of law is equally reprehensible.[92] This seems to be a corollary of the fact that, from the logical point of view, to be a member of an institution is to be bound by its rules. The moral force of this conclusion is strengthened by the fact that in a constitutional democracy, the only type of civil society that Gewirth considers worthy of moral allegiance, the procedural rules themselves provide for a

---

[91] This point emerges fairly clearly in Francis Allen's influential treatment of the subject in his Marx Lectures in 1966. See F. Allen 'Civil Disobedience and the Legal Order', 36 *U. Cin. L. Rev.* 1, 11-13, 35-6 (1967). The remainder of his lecture was published in id. at 175. Likewise, Alan Gewirth states that, in a constitutional democracy, 'the civil disobedients' violating of $laws_3$ [(i.e. immoral laws or laws that support immoral policies)] cannot be such as to cause general disrespect and violation of law_2 [(i.e. the specific legal system)].' *Gewirth* at 87.

[92] Id. at 84-5.

means of changing the substantive and procedural rules of that society. Although, as a practical matter, it may be difficult to do so, laws can be repealed; constitutions can be amended. Gewirth, accordingly, leaves us, then, in this impasse. From a substantive point of view, civil disobedience of the second type may on occasion be morally justified.[93] From a procedural point of view, Gewirth concludes it never can be; for, presumably, one who respects the procedural arrangements of a society cannot at the same time choose to disregard them. A society can be said to stand or fall on the institutional arrangements enshrined in its authoritative procedures. The substantive law of a society, however, is not such a unitary web, and the integrity of some aspects of the substantive law will not necessarily be affected by the disregard of other aspects. I think this is an interesting insight although I am not at all sure that the procedural arrangements of a society are always so much more of a unitary web as to be able to bear, in all cases, the full, moral weight that is thus placed on the procedural/substantive distinction.

At any rate, is there any way out of this impasse which arises from looking at civil disobedience from both the substantive and procedural points of view? There is, of course, the obvious move of saying that, since civil disobedience to the particular laws of a society, *of which one generally approves*, can never be justified from the procedural point of view, it is therefore never permissible from the moral point of view and, furthermore, is not compatible with a citizen's claim that he continues to accept the authority of the State. To many people, however, this move is unacceptable. After all no one, including judges acting in their official capacity, always does what he conceives that he is legally supposed to do. I would suggest that there is another way out of the impasse. Although, of course by definition, it is never *legally* permissible, civil disobedience might, subject to the balancing of its long range effects, not only be morally permissible but also compatible with his acceptance of the authority of the State when, despite an individual's acceptance of the overall moral validity of the society in question, the law being opposed, or perhaps even the policy that it neccessarily supports, so operates on him as to direct him to do something that he considers morally reprehensible. Obviously, the degree

[93] See Id. at 85-8. Most writers on the subject have likewise been unwilling completely to rule out the possibility of civil disobedience as a legitimate moral response even in a constitutional democracy.

of moral reprehensibility of the action he is directed to perform will be a relevant consideration for the individual trying to decide what to do. On the other hand, civil disobedience, even when directed against laws or policies deemed morally wrong, will not be compatible with a citizen's claim to accept the authority of the state when the purpose of the disobedience is not to avoid performing an act which the actor thinks is morally wrong but in order to protest against the immorality of the law he is disobeying or of some other law or to focus the attention of his fellow citizens upon such laws. When an individual believes that moral protest of this type is required—because he has no faith in the efficacy of lawful methods of protest or in his ability otherwise to communicate with his fellow citizens—he can no longer still claim to be a loyal member of his civil society by seeking refuge under the comforting label 'civil disobedience'. Rather, he must frankly recognise that he has breached not only his legal but also his moral obligations towards society, moral obligations which flow from his claimed acceptance of the moral validity of society.

If such a person can no longer claim to be a loyal citizen, how then should we categorise him? In refusing to fulfil his moral obligations towards society, his actions, are in a sense, revolutionary, even if, as is usually the case, his actions are so insignificant in either intention or effect that they are not treated by society any differently than are more 'legitimate' instances of civil disobedience. At the very least, even if a free society is willing or obliged to tolerate him for the sake of avoiding the evils that suppression brings, such a person is disloyal and, if he refuses to admit this, he is also dishonest. The honest and moral thing for him to do would be either to honour his obligation of allegiance or to re-examine his conclusions about the moral value of the civil society to which he belongs. This re-examination may lead him to renounce his allegiance—that is, to reject the authority he has previously accepted—and either to move elsewhere, if he is able, or, in extreme cases, to revolt if he has the courage to do so. For such a person, however, what is *more* likely is that withdrawal of his moral commitment to society will lead him only to engage in sporadic acts of guerrilla warfare against society. But, of course, what is *most* likely is that the practical difficulties involved will lead him, as they do most men, either to shut his eyes to the moral implications of his actions, and to the necessity of re-examining his moral commitments, or to learn to live with himself despite his moral imperfections. One thing he cannot do, however, if he persists in claiming to recognise a moral commitment to the civil society in which he lives, is to try to escape the legal consequences of these 'revolutionary' acts. For, in this context, I agree with writers like John Rawls and Francis Allen, as well as many others who have written in a similar vein; it really only makes sense to use terms like civil disobedience or moral commitment in these situations when the individual concerned is prepared to act openly and publicly and to accept willingly the legal consequences of his actions.[94] If he is not so disposed, then he is no different from the ordinary criminal.

I am not at all sure, however, that when people refuse to obey a law not because they wish to challenge the moral basis of society or to force some changes in public policy but rather because they believe it requires them to perform a morally reprehensible act that the same analysis applied. In these latter circumstances I do not believe they either necessarily do—clearly many people do not—accept the legitimacy of legal punishment or that they necessarily should accept the legitimacy of such punishment. In this context I am not persuaded by the traditional analysis. For these later circumstances present the situation in which the failure to accept the authoritative pronouncements of those recognised as having authority is not, as I have argued earlier, necessarily inconsistent with the acceptance of that authority. The actor is thus not required to reaffirm his acceptance of the state's authority by acting publicly or openly or by willingly accepting punishment. All that is necessary is that he be prepared to accept punishment if he is prosecuted and that he not engage in other types of law violation to avoid being caught or prosecuted.[95]

---

[94] See *Theory of Justice* at 364-7; F. Allen, supra note 91, at 9-11.

[95] John Rawls would probably clarify these situations as instances of what he calls conscientious refusal since for him civil disobedience is a public act. Of course, an instance of conscientious refusal can also be an instance of civil disobedience if it is performed with required political motives and in the proper setting. It should be noted, however, that Rawls is prepared to recognise the legitimacy of civil disobedience in circumstances where I claim that, whatever its moral justification, it is incompatible with the claim that one continues to accept the authority of the state. For example, the injustice of the law in question in its application to others will, for Rawls, sometimes justify the political act of civil disobedience. I have maintained that, under these circumstances, it is incompatible with the claim that one recognises the authority of the state regardless of whether one is prepared willingly to accept the legitimacy of legal punishment. For Rawls' argument, see *Theory of Justice* 363-91. For a recent discussion of the question of obedience to political authority, see A. D. Woozley, *Law and Obedience* (1979).

I believe that in the preceding discussion I have sketched out a meaning of what it is to accept the authoritative pronouncements of others in the context of civil society that takes into account the fact that no one accepts every authoritative pronouncement directed towards him even by those whom he recognises having a right to issue such pronouncements to him. At the same time, the discussion fixes criteria for establishing when that refusal to accept these pronouncements as authoritative may be justified in a way that escapes the morass of pure subjectivity. Without a resolution of this sort, it is only the willingness to accept punishment for one's legal transgressions that might permit one to contend that he is accepting the right of others to issue authoritative pronouncements while at the same time refusing to obey. This seems a pretty slim basis upon which to pitch the claim that such a person accepts authority for at least two reasons. First of all, as I have already noted, despite the repeated statements of moral and political philosophers, it is not at all clear that we are in fact always prepared to accept the rightfulness of being punished, even if we have no alternative but to accept our punishment. Secondly, justification of law violation on the basis of a willingness to accept the legitimacy of punishment permits too extensive a scope for the claim that the rejection of the authoritative pronouncements issued by others is nevertheless consistent with a recognition that these others have authority over one. Having authority is having more than the right to punish. I would further contend that the analysis presented above accords with our intuitive moral beliefs and is implied in much of the philosophical discussion of civil disobedience. Such a possible resolution of the question is what gives coherence and plausibility to that discussion.

12. *The relationship between authority and law*

The relationship between authority and law is a difficult question indeed. Authority in the modern nation-state, where it is not based solely on personal charisma, is dependent upon law and law is dependent upon authority. In some ways therefore the question of which is logically anterior resembles the chicken and egg problem and is equally unanswerable. At the same time, there is something to be said about trying to disentangle the concepts of authority and of law. Accepting that, in a large-scale social setting, neither authority nor law could exist in isolation from the other, it seems clear to me that authority is the more basic concept and that law is more dependent upon authority than authority is upon law. Our normal method of speaking would seem to suggest, of course, that this conclusion is incorrect, that, if anything, the dependence runs the other way. Take, for example, expressions like 'the rule of law', especially when applied to the international order. These expressions seem to suggest that law is impersonal, that it can be divorced from human agencies. This is certainly one reason why such expressions have been used as a cloak to disguise domestic repression and the exercise of brute force in the international sphere. But let us ignore the cases of rhetorical abuse and return to the question of the relationship of authority and law. My thesis is that whatever may be the case in the dispute as to whether the Church authenticates the scriptures or scripture authenticates the Church, in modern secular political societies authority is the ultimate source of law rather than law being the source of authority.

As we saw earlier,[96] the attempts to ground a legal system upon some kind of basic norm such as Kelsen's *grundnorm* or Hart's 'rule of recognition' have been ultimately unsuccessful, however much insight they may have given us into the logical structure of a legal system. Showing the derivation of all of the so-called norms or rules of law of a modern state from any such basic norm is a practical impossibility. Moreover, even leaving this problem aside, for Kelsen, at any rate, the basic norm itself logically depends on the presumed authority of those who promulgated it. According to Kelsen, at least, law must ultimately depend on authority and not vice versa.[97]

Ignoring for the moment the question of whether a basic norm—call it a constitution if you will—must itself be founded upon an exercise of authority, as Kelsen contends, there are other problems. There is, for example, as we have frequently pointed out, an irreducible lack of specificity in any such basic norm. Hart, as we have already noted, quite candidly recognises this feature of his rule of recognition. The open-endedness of his rule of recognition has to be resolved periodically by exercises of power which come to be accepted by the members of the society in question. Nor can the

---

[96] See pp. 83-6 (Pt. III, §2), supra.

[97] Cf. the discussion at 106-13 (Pt. III, §9(ii)), supra.

resolution of such conflicts as to the content of the rule of recognition be accommodated to a model in which law is prior to authority by including within the rule of recognition 'norms' of competence which prescribe who should resolve disputes as to the content of the rule of recognition. For the norms of competence themselves need to be interpreted. Indeed, the question of whether any interpretation is necessary is itself a question dependent on interpretation by human agencies. Thus, the content and scope of the rule of recognition seem, for Hart also, to be the result of successful exercises of authority which must, necessarily, precede the existence of law.

Since, as a practical matter, the mystique surrounding the Supreme Court has come closest to suggesting the primacy of law over authority, it may be instructive to study the development of the Court as the arbiter of fundamental questions under the American Constitution. We may note in the first place that, while the Supreme Court is, of course, specifically provided for in the Constitution and while the practice of judicial review of the actions of the legislature and the executive may not be against the express intent of the framers of the Constitution, its establishment certainly was the result of the exercise of power by the Court that in time came to be accepted.[98] So, the institution of judicial review, although intertwined with notions of law, is itself based on the successful exercise of authority. But what about the situation now that judicial review of the action of other branches of government is an established reality? The problem is no different. Questions as to the scope of the power of judicial review do arise from time to time even in circumstances where it is not clear beforehand that the Supreme Court has the legal competence to resolve these questions. If any modern illustration of this fact is required, the recent case of *United States* v. *Nixon*[99] amply supports my assertion. That the Constitution gave the Court the power to resolve this dispute, over the presidential tapes, between the President and the special prosecutor was not at all clear beforehand. Nor was it clear beforehand that, if the Court so ruled, its decision would be accepted. Fortunately, it was. Finally, if one reads the Court's opinion one will see many such similar questions wisely

---

[98] See, e.g., A. Bickel, *The Least Dangerous Branch* (1962).
[99] 418 U.S. 683 (1974).

unresolved.[100]

It is, of course, possible to create a model of a political society in which law is more basic than authority. The dilemma facing anyone wishing to construct such a model is this, however: For law to be more basic than authority, law must be assumed to pre-exist human society *and* this law must furthermore be beyond the ability of human beings to change by conscious means. In addition, there must be no human institution, such as the United States Supreme Court, with the authority to resolve disputes as to the content of this law. Primitive systems of customary law indeed have some of these features. Custom, of course, does arise as a result of human activity but it is not created consciously nor can it be consciously modified or changed by any single act or any discreet series of acts. At some point actual practice and 'accepted' custom may diverge so greatly that we would be obliged to say that the custom had been changed, but what that point might be is difficult to describe in advance.

In the context of a more advanced type of society, John Locke, in his *Second Treatise of Government*, has also described a model of a political community in which law is more basic than authority. It is a model with much instinctive appeal and with which most people are familiar. That Locke's model influenced the American Declaration of Independence cannot be denied. Nevertheless, the reason why Locke's model was eventually rejected in the evolution of the American constitutional framework is that it ultimately rests on the right of each individual to 'appeal . . . to Heaven'[101] if he disagrees with the construction of the basic law adopted either by the political authority of his society or even by his fellow citizens. A modern society finds this open invitation to revolution difficult to live with. It is not surprising, therefore, that American society evolved the notion of judicial review which is premised on the assumption that there must be an ultimate arbiter, within the framework of government, of what is or is not constitutional. The Jeffersonian position that each branch of government must itself decide the constitutional questions concerning its powers is, of course, more in tune with Locke's views.

---

[100] For some commentators' views, see P. Mishkin, 'Great Cases and Soft Law: A Comment on United States v. Nixon', 22 *U.C.L.A.L.Rev.* 76 (1974); W. Van Alstyne, 'A Political and Constitutional Review of United States v. Nixon', id. at 116.

[101] J. Locke, *The Second Treatise of Government* § 242 (Library of Liberal Arts ed. 1952) at 139. Cf. id. at §§ 211-43 (pp. 119-39).

But one must recognise that the power of constitutional amendment prescribed in the Constitution itself and the acceptance of the concept of judicial review have together made the system of government in the United States much more like the Austinean Model—in which law is based upon authority which has the final say about what is law and what is not law—than the Lockeian model to which, at first glance, our system of government might seem more akin.

We might close this section of the book by noting that the attempt, however laudably motivated it might be, to make law more basic than authority ultimately leads to anarchy. This point can be clearly and succinctly established by examining the conflicting views on civil disobedience of Ronald Dworkin and St. Thomas Aquinas. Dworkin, as we have several times had occasion to note, has insisted throughout his many writings that there are right answers in judicial decision-making. As a necessary corollary of this view, he has insisted that litigants approach the legal process because they have legal rights which the courts must take seriously and enforce. Indeed, his recent book, which includes much of his earlier work, is actually entitled *Taking Rights Seriously.*[102] How can Dworkin then reconcile a position premised upon the existence of legal rights, and concomitant duties, not only with the notion of civil disobedience but also with the position that such disobedience is not necessarily inconsistent with the legal obligations of citizens? After all, if there are right answers in legal decision-making and if the Supreme Court has decided a question, how can the individual claim a 'lawful' right to disobey? Would not that be a classic instance of not taking someone else's rights seriously? Is Dworkin saying that, although he is maintaining that there are right answers to legal decision-making, the courts are not the ultimate arbiter of what is the right answer? But if the courts are not the ultimate arbiter, who is? The only alternative arbiter is each individual, who must decide for himself what the right answer is. But, how can each individual claim to have the competence to decide the right answer to legal questions?

The way Dworkin purports to resolve these difficult problems is as follows. Most instances of civil disobedience in the United States involve, at least initially, claims that some sort of activity is constitutionally protected. Furthermore, the Constitution of the United

[102] R. Dworkin, *Taking Rights Seriously* (1977). For references and cross references to Dworkin's earlier work and our discussion of his work, see Part I, *supra*, pp. 38 ff.

States is shot through with moral references. This is not only true of vague notions like 'due process of law', and of derivative constitutional rights like the right of privacy or the freedom of association, but also of many of the more specific rights to some extent specifically mentioned in the Constitution, like the freedom of speech and of religious belief. Because the law contains this moral reference, it is quite possible, Dworkin claims, even after the Supreme Court has decided a point in a particular way, for an individual to claim in good faith that the Court is just plain wrong.[103] How that approach is consistent with the view that it is meaningful to talk about legal rights that others must take seriously is another matter. After all, one man's right is another man's duty. Certainly, if enough people seriously believed Dworkin's assertion that each individual is the ultimate arbiter of what is the correct legal conclusion, the end result would be anarchy.

St. Thomas Aquinas' views are in sharp contrast. He recognises that one has no moral duty to obey unjust laws.[104] Indeed, one may sometimes even be under a moral duty to disobey unjust laws. For him, unjust laws are not laws. Nevertheless he recognises that obedience to authority is itself a good. He, therefore, distinguishes between laws which are contrary to human good and those which are contrary to divine good. The former are laws that are burdensome and not conducive to human good or laws that exceed the law-makers authority or laws that impose unequal burdens upon the community. These laws do not bind in conscience but a person might nevertheless be advised to obey them 'to avoid scandal or disturbance'.[105] With respect to laws that are opposed to divine law, the situation is different. Here the individual has a moral duty to disobey. The one concrete example he gives are laws prescribing idolatry. Related to Aquinas' discussion of laws that may not bind the individual in conscience is his discussion of the notion of *epikeia* derived from Aristotle. Because laws must be framed in general terms, they do not always apply suitably to particular circumstances. Therefore, those with the authority to interpret and apply the law should do so with the

---

[103] Dworkin presents this argument in *Taking Rights Seriously* at ch.8. particularly at pp. 206-16.

[104] St. Thomas Aquinas, *Summa theologiae*, Part One of the Second Part, Q. 96(4).

[105] Ibid.

view of avoiding these inconveniences.[106] In cases of emergency, private individuals are also authorised to deviate from the written law. But St. Thomas is adamant that this power only exists when there is no time to apply to political authority for dispensation. He declares: ' . . . if the observation of the law according to the letter does not involve any sudden risk needing instant remedy, it is not competent for everyone to expound what is useful and what is not useful to the state: those alone can do this who are in authority, and who on account of suchlike cases, have the power to dispense from the laws . . .'[107]

The implications of Aquinas' discussion are clear. If the matter involves questions within the competence of political authority, the decisions of that authority are final and binding. Even if there is a question of whether the actual political authority is competent in the matter at hand, considerations of respect for authority counsel obedience. Only when the question relates to matters clearly beyond the competence of political authority—ie., matters concerning divine good—is the individual clearly entitled, and even obliged, to disobey. St. Thomas' views on the primacy of political authority on questions of legal interpretation parallel, of course, his views on the role of the Church. On questions concerned with divine good—namely, questions of faith and morals—the Church, as the ultimate moral authority, is the final arbiter. Whether this is a necessary consequence of having an institutional church is another matter, a matter upon which I see no need to comment in this book.

It is not, of course, surprising that law, particularly in the modern state, should ultimately rest upon authority. It is not only that authority can rest partly or even wholly upon charismatic qualities and thus be totally independent of any necessary relationship to law. The more fundamental fact is that law does not exist in the abstract. Law is created by human beings for the governance of other human beings. It depends on authority because only authority—whose very existence carries with it the acceptance of a right to issue commands—insures the voluntary acceptance of legal directives, and of the solutions to social problems that they embody, by those to whom law is addressed. Without authority behind it, law can only be

[106] Id. at Q. 97(4).
[107] Id. at Q.96(6).

effective if acquiescence is secured by the sheer exercise of power.

This conclusion should not be surprising to anyone who has witnessed recent events even in societies most committed to the rule of law; yet many people seem to be continually surprised at rediscovering this simple truth. There is, for example, a nationwide strike of coal miners in violation of a collective bargaining agreement and ostensibly against the wishes of the union leadership. The Government goes to court to secure the enforcement of the Taft-Hartley law and, since the law is clearly on the Government's side, an injunction is quickly issued. But, most of the workers do not go back to work and those that do are threatened with violence. To the amazement of naive observers the shibboleth 'rule of law' becomes meaningless. Here is a prime example where law does not legitimate authority; on the contrary the fact that the miners do not recognise the authority of the judge to order them back to work deprives the legal process of all effectiveness.[108]

The point is that the rule of law is not some abstraction but rather it is ultimately, indeed in the modern world *necessarily*, the rule of one man over another by consent. The state of nature, where men are ruled by the natural law *simpliciter* without arbiter or leaders of any sort, is a philosopher's myth. If there ever were anything like such a social arrangement, one would imagine that it described a situation in which people co-existed with a minimum of interaction, a situation in which whatever coordination was necessary was accomplished by each person acting as much as possible in his enlightened self-interest and accommodating himself as much as possible to the perceived self-interest of others. It would be a travesty, however, to describe this

[108] I am of course describing the coal strike of early 1978. The events described in the text are reported in the *New York Times* for the period, March 7-25, 1978. The Government's seeking an injunction did, however, have the practical effect of encouraging the parties to engage in serious negotiations which eventually led to the ratification of a new contract in late March 1978. The collapse over the years of the utility of injunctions as a means of enforcing laws forbidding strikes by public employees is of course a well-known fact that should have prepared people for the 1978 fiasco in the coal fields. See B. Clemow and T. Mooney, 'Impasse Resolution in Local Government Labor Relations': The Connecticut Approach', 9 *Conn. L. Rev.* 579, 582 (1977): 'There is one major weakness, however, in the general ban on public employee strikes: such prohibitions simply do not work. From 1958 to 1974 the number of annual public employee strikes in the United States increased from fifteen (involving 1,700 employees) to 384 (involving at least 160,700 employees) and the numbers are still rising. Of these, most involved local governmental units and the vast majority were illegal . . .'

condition of human co-existence as a social arrangement *founded* upon
law, that is as a social arrangement founded on a set of prescriptions,
however specific, rational, and internally consistent they may be, that
somehow by virtue of their mere existence justify the application of
sanctions by one individual against another. The application of
purported sanctions under such circumstances is merely rule by force,
whatever the verbal trappings with which it is disguised.

As Richard Hooker long ago said:

Laws they are not therefore which public approbation have not made so.[109]

The theory of norms with its tendency to make the question of the
binding quality of law one of logic helps to obscure this truism. This is
another reason, in addition to the fact that it does not accurately
describe any modern legal system, for rejecting the attempt to make
that theory the focus of the philosophical study of the law. The
modern nation-state, in the Western world, can be considered as a
legitimate legal order because in it some men trust others to act in
accordance with a shared perception of the public or common good;
and those who are trusted generally seek to justify and increase the
trust reposed in them by behaving *consistently* in trying to work out the
shared perception of what the public good requires. That is what the
rule of law is.

---

[109] R. Hooker, *Works*, Bk. I, c. X, 58 (J. Keble, 7th rev. ed. by R. Church and
F. Paget, (1888)).

Part IV

Some Additional Observations

1. *Introduction*

I have presented my main theses: first, that there is very little about the law that can accurately be described as normative; secondly, that if any features of the law can usefully be described as normative it is such basic postulates as the requirement of consistency in judicial decision-making; thirdly, that the relationship between law and authority is complex but that authority is the more basic concept. All authority is ultimately *de facto* and the question of whether authority is 'legitimate' or not is a meaningless question. In this part, I wish to make some additional remarks about the relationship between law and authority. While this discussion will not alter my principal conclusions, it will serve to emphasise the importance of law and legal institutions to the establishment of authority.

2. *The authority of individuals to disobey the law—the notion of legally sanctioned disobedience to law*

At the close of Part III we observed that to elevate law over all authority ultimately leads to anarchy. In discussing Dworkin's suggestion that civil disobedience cannot only be morally justified but also sometimes legally justified, we saw that this position led Dworkin to conclude that the ostensibly civilly disobedient individual can justify his actions by the good-faith claim that his interpretation of the law is correct and the interpretation of the courts is incorrect. Dworkin's position bears some superficial resemblance to the argument advanced by Kadish and Kadish that, under some circumstances, the individual citizen has a 'lawful' discretion to disobey the law.[1] Unlike Dworkin, however, Kadish and Kadish do not reach this position by stressing that law is more basic than authority and that the individual is the ultimate arbiter of the law. On the contrary, they, correctly in my view, recognise that authority is the more basic concept. Rather, their argument is that, in some circumstances, the legal system can and does delegate to the individual the authority to decide what the law requires in some particular circumstances even if this should result in his deviating from some generally accepted 'rule' of law. This is an intriguing suggestion. Although it will require an extensive argument to show why, I believe the Kadishes, thesis is also ultimately, unsatisfactory. While preserving the logical priority of authority, their thesis fails because it undermines the notion of law. Although law must ultimately depend upon authority, authority without law can also quickly degenerate into the chaos of anarchy if it has not previously hardened into tyranny. I shall attempt to support these conclusions by first presenting and then commenting upon the Kadishes' thesis.

Central to the Kadishes' entire argument is the notion of 'recourse roles', which are defined as 'roles that enable their agents to take action in situations where the role's prescribed ends conflict with its prescribed means, including grants of discretion broad or narrow'.[2] All of us have certain roles in the complex set of activities regulated by the legal system. In these roles we are confronted with sets of legal directives prescribing what we may or may not do. We have a recourse role when, in the event we are confronted with a legal directive requiring us to do something or refrain from doing something, we nevertheless may be justified in refusing to follow that directive because to do so would conflict with some more basic end of the legal and political order. It is their central argument that, in the United States at any rate, both officials and private citizens sometimes have recourse roles.

That both officials and private citizens do on occasion refuse to obey legal directives is undisputable. That they are legally justified in so doing is another matter. The Kadishes argue that they sometimes are. In this regard, they of course distinguish the normal cases of civil

---

[1] M. R. Kadish & S. H. Kadish, *Discretion to Disobey: A Study of Lawful Departures from Legal Rules* (1973) (hereafter cited as *Discretion to Disobey*).

[2] *Discretion to Disobey* at 35.

disobedience from the rule departures they are talking about.[3] In the paradigm case of civil disobedience, the actor refuses to obey a legal norm because of overriding moral considerations. In the cases in which they are interested, the actor's refusal to follow a legal norm may or may not be justified by moral considerations.[4] His refusal is, however, legally justified or, to use their term, it is 'legitimated'.

The Kadishes divide the universe of justified or legitimated rule departures into two basic categories, those by officials and those by private citizens. They wish to distinguish those instances where the rule departed from provides a direct sanction for disobedience, such as a fine or imprisonment, from those where it does not. In the typical case of a rule departure by a private citizen, the rule that is 'departed from' provides a direct sanction for noncompliance. Officials, of course, can be confronted with this type of legal directive not only in their capacity as private citizens but also in their official capacity. Officials, however, are often confronted with legal directives which are in a sense legally 'binding' upon them but which do not carry any direct sanction for noncompliance. Prosecutors, for example, arguably may be under a legal obligation to enforce the criminal law against all known violators, but of course they usually choose not to. Or, a jury may be under a legal obligation to convict a defendant if it finds, beyond a reasonable doubt, that he has committed certain criminal acts, but nevertheless it can decide to acquit the defendant even when it has no reasonable doubt that the defendant committed the acts charged. These rule departures by officials, when legally justified, the Kadishes call instances of 'legitimated interposition'.[5] Justified rule departures from legal norms, carrying direct sanctions, whether by private citizens or by officials, are called instances of 'legitimated disobedience'.[6] Because the considerations underlying legitimated interposition are somewhat different from those under-

---

[3] Id. at 181-2; see id. at 8-9.

[4] Normally, of course, an actor who is deciding whether to appeal to a notion of legitimised or lawful disobedience has already decided that his reasons for refusing to obey are morally meritorious. In deciding to act on those reasons, he makes the further decision that he properly may disobey the applicable legal imperatives, even though he accepts the legitimacy of the legal system.

[5] *Discretion to Disobey* at 67.

[6] Id. at 97-8.

lying legitimated disobedience, it is best to consider each of them separately, as do the Kadishes.

(i) *Lawful disobedience by officials—legitimated interposition*

The notion of rule departures by officials resembles the notion of official discretion—the resemblance is often very close—but the notions must be kept separate even when admittedly it is hard to do so. The functioning of final courts of appeal provides an example. The complexity and unpredictability of life, coupled with the inevitable vagueness and even ambiguity of the language used in constitutions and statutes, requires that courts exercise an interpretive role that always involves at least some discretion. In performing this role of applying the 'written law' to the factual setting of concrete legal controversies, courts normally are not engaging in rule departures even if, in the course of interpretation, the law 'changes'. In the administrative process, the evolutionary development of the law in the course of application is even more apparent. But sometimes the development of the law is marked by abrupt changes of direction, as, for instance, when the United States Supreme Court overrules one or more of its past decisions and enunciates new constitutional doctrine. Courts, of course, also occasionally change their minds about the proper construction of a statute. Finally, courts have even been known to change directions rather abruptly in the development of the common law. All these are instances of what the Kadishes call rule departures and not the discretionary application of existing rules.[7]

The distinction between discretion in applying the law and rule departures is easily grasped in the abstract, although it is not always easy to see in practice. This is because as we have already seen in Part I, the law is really not a set of precise rules. Instances of legitimated rule departures by courts are philosophically interesting, however, only if we are prepared to postulate a higher law; otherwise, we lack a basis for judging whether the rule departure was legitimate in the sense of being authorised, or, given the abstractness of the concept, at least justified, by the basic ends of the higher law. One such instance might arise in fundamental constitutional disputes about the relationship between Congress and the President that the Kadishes give as

[7] See id. at 89-91.

the type of conflict that might raise such questions. They suggest that the legitimacy of rule departures in ordinary constitutional adjudication and in nonconstitutional adjudication might be judged against another, higher law encapsuled in something like the notion of the 'proper function of a court'.[8] They quote, for example, Cardozo's statement;

Judges have, of course, the power though not the right, to ignore the mandate of a statute, and render judgment in despite of it. They have the power, though not the right, to travel beyond the walls of the interstices, the bounds set to judicial innovation by precedent and custom. Nonetheless, by that abuse of power, they violate the law.[9]

For what it is worth, I agree that there are ill-defined limits to what judges can do in ordinary litigation and that, if they continually transgressed those limits, perhaps, to use Llewellyn's words, 'we should have to get rid of the guilty judges; we might in the process and for a while get rid even of the courts'.[10] Whether these limits can be profitably said to constitute a higher law is another matter. At any rate, whatever may be true in the exceptional case, in the ordinary case it is impossible to speak meaningfully of a higher law that restrains the courts. For this reason, the notion of legitimated rule departures by final appellate courts is not, from a theoretical point of view, particularly interesting. This is not to say that a judge's perception of the limits upon what he can do is not an important determinant of what he in fact does. The more strongly these limits are felt, the greater the justification—or 'surcharge', to use the Kadishes' term[11]—needed by the judge to persuade himself of the rightness of transgressing these limits. In the operation of a legal system, this is obviously an important factor. Indeed, we have noted this already in the concluding pages of Part I of this book. It is time now, however, to turn to instances of rule departures by officials that are more philosophically challenging.

The Kadishes discuss at some length three basic instances of justified rules departures by subordinate officials; namely, jurors,

---

[8] The role of judges is discussed in id. at 85-91.

[9] B. Cardozo, *The Nature of the Judicial Process* 129 (1921), quoted in *Discretion to Disobey* at 87-8.

[10] K. Llewellyn, *The Common Law Tradition: Deciding Appeals* 220 (1960).

[11] *Discretion to Disobey* at 27-8.

police, and prosecutors. In all these instances, the authority to engage
in rule departures seems to be accepted as an integral part of each
official role. This seems particularly clear for the prosecutorial role.[12]
Indeed, the propriety and desirability of rule departures by
prosecutors seems to be so generally accepted in our legal system that
prosecutors may now have more than authority to depart from the
legal rules that seemingly require prosecution of all known criminals;
their role may have become sufficiently discretionary so that their
failure to prosecute a particular case should not be considered a rule
departure at all.[13]

As we have seen, the Kadishes find the possibility of justified rule
departures by officials in what they call a 'recourse role'. When an
official has a recourse role, the possibility arises of justified rule
departures, of which legitimated interposition is one type. For circumstances to give rise to an instance of legitimated interposition, it is
further necessary that the rule departed from not be constitutive, that
is that departure from the rule should not deprive an official's action
of either legal or practical effect.[14] They also impose the requirement
that the system provide no means for holding the official himself
accountable for disregarding the rule.[15] This lack of accountability is
what makes the concept of justified rule departures by officials
interesting. The official must make his own decision whether he
ought to depart from the rule in question. As might be expected, the
instances which the Kadishes discuss are also instances in which, for
all practical purposes, the official's rule departure finally disposes of
the case before him. Rule departures where the official's decision is
not final are much less interesting because the legal system itself
provides the means for judging the legitimacy of the particular rule
departure, namely some kind of appeal to a higher official.

The Kadishes are quick to point out, however, that these
conditions—departure from a rule that is not constitutive, lack of
accountability, and final disposition—are not sufficient to mark a rule

---

[12] Id. at 81-5.

[13] As the Kadishes state, '[i]n our terms. deviational discretion in the prosecutor's role
has been substantially converted into delegated discretion'. Id. at 82. They note that
the policeman's role likewise has evolved in that direction. Id. at 78-80.

[14] Id. at 67; see id. at 37-8.

[15] Id. at 67.

departure as a case of legitimated interposition.[16] Two more conditions are necessary. First, it must be accepted that it is a legitimate part of the official's role to engage in rule departures; and second, there must be 'role ends', or what we might call ultimate ends and policies of the legal system, to which the official can appeal to justify his decision and which others can use to criticise it.[17] In the case of final courts of appeal, which have the last word in the interpretation of the law, we saw that this last requirement imposes a need for something like a higher law against which the supposed rule departures by these final appellate courts can be judged. In the case of officials who do not have ultimate authority for the proper interpretation of the law, no such higher law is needed; the ultimate ends and policies can and should be found in the existing legal structure.

But how do officials get this authority to depart from rules—and authority which, if exercised often enough, can have the effect of making their roles discretionary? The Kadishes suggest that in the instances which they emphasise—jurors, police, and prosecuting authorities—the authority comes after the event. Because officials have departed from legal rules in the past and will probably continue to do so on occasion in the future the behaviour comes to be socially accepted. That a subordinate official's action is insulated from effective review, as in the case of jurors and prosecutors, may thus suggest that it might be appropriate for these officials to exercise a recourse role which includes rule departures. But this is not enough, however, to legitimate those rule departures. They must be accepted as actions proper to the legal roles performed by those officials. Since our legal system does not seem to contain a means for conferring this sense of legitimacy before the first rule departures occur, it follows that the notion of justified rule departures has its genesis in the exercise of naked power that gradually comes to be publicly accepted or, to use the Kadishes' term, 'institutionalised'.[18] This indeed is accepted by them as the usual historical explanation of the evolution of these interpositional roles.

For me this is one of the difficulties with the Kadishes' concept of justified or legitimated rule departures by officials. The notion seems

---

[16] Id. at 67-9, 86-8.

[17] Id. at 61-2; see id. at 67-9.

[18] Id. at 66-7.

to require illegitimate conduct (or rule departures) by officials before possibility of legitimated rule departures can arise. For this reason, we might be tempted to ask whether or not the function performed by justified rule departures might not be performed in other ways, such as by making the roles of these officials more openly discretionary while, at the same time, trying to prevent the abuse of this discretion. For example, juries might be told expressly when they might acquit a defendant whom they otherwise thought was guilty, and prosecutors might be told by the legislature when they might be justified in not prosecuting known criminals.[19] Of course, in actual practice we could not foresee every situation in which an official might be tempted to engage in rule departures and thus, where it seems desirable to accommodate this impulse, enlarge and guide in advance officials' discretion. But we could certainly cut down the number of situations in which we would be tempted to recognise the possibility of justified rule departures by officials.

The instance of justified rule departures by officials to which the Kadishes devote the greatest attention is that of rule departures by juries, or what is now more commonly called 'jury nullification'. The lack of accountability of jurors for their verdicts in English and American law is generally considered to date at least from the decision in *Bushell's Case*[20] in 1670. It is this lack of accountability together with the right of a jury in a criminal case to bring in a general verdict[21] that makes the jury's role a particularly good candidate for designation as a recourse role. But for the Kadishes the notion of justified rule departures, of which legitimated interposition is one instance, requires more than that the official's action is final or that he cannot as a practical or legal matter be held legally accountable for his action. The authority of the official to engage in rule departures must be widely accepted and the exercise of that authority

---

[19] Professor Kenneth Culp Davis argues that prosecutorial discretion must be reduced, although he emphasises the need for rule-making by the prosecutorial authorities themselves. See K. Davis, *Discretionary Justice* 188-214 (1969). On similar suggestions for confining the 'discretion' of the police, see id. at 90-6. Professor Davis' suggestions deserve careful consideration, although the degree of clarity that he apparently seeks may be neither obtainable nor desirable.

[20] 124 Eng.Rep. 1006 (C.P. 1670).

[21] This right has been reaffirmed in United States v. Spock, 416 F.2d. 163, 180-3 (1st Cir. 1969).

must be guided by principles and standards, lest its exercise be arbitrary. For the Kadishes these principles and standards are the ultimate ends of the legal and political order. The authority of the jury to engage in justified rule departures is said by the Kadishes, who here present the traditional explanation, to follow from the frequent and recurring judicial statements that the jury exists to temper the rigour of the criminal law and to interpose the common sense of the community between the individual and the state.[22] And unquestionably the jury has served in the past as a check upon what we would now agree was arbitrary government or arbitrary enforcement of the law. The jury has also been said to be the 'conscience of the community'. That, of course, is not the same thing as saying that it exists to hear appeals to conscience,[23] particularly appeals by the defendant to be judged according to the standards of his own consicence. Exactly what authority the jury is supposed to have, however, it not at all clear from these statements by the courts. When a jury trial is waived in a criminal case, the judge as the trier of fact has the power to acquit the defendant in the face of the evidence; his action is final and, as a practical matter, he is not accountable for his action. The standard learning on the subject takes it for granted, however, that the judge has no authority to do this.[24] What is the basis and nature of the authority that the jury possesses but the trial judge acting without a jury does not?[25]

This is not the place to discuss the extensive recent literature on the controversial question of jury nullification. Suffice it to say that, historically, much of the support for what we now call jury nullification rested on the notion that the jury had the ultimate

---

[22] *Discretion to Disobey* at 50-5.

[23] With respect, I cannot agree with the Kadishes' suggestion that Duncan v. Louisiana, 391 U.S. 145, 153 (1968), supports the assertion that the jury has the power 'to displace law by appeal to conscience'. *Discretion to Disobey* at 53 & n. 51.

[24] For a discussion of the differences (and similarities) between a judge acting as the trier of fact and a jury, see United States v. Maybury, 274 F.2d. 899, 901-3 (2d Cir. 1960) (Friendly, J.); Curtis, 'The Trial Judge and the Jury', 5 *Vand. L. Rev.* 150, 157-66 (1952).

[25] The Kadishes suggests that a judge who consistently ignored mandatory sentencing provisions might come to be recognised as possessing authority to engage in legitimate interposition. *Discretion to Disobey* at 85-6. Under this view, there is no theoretical barrier to keep the authority of the trial judge from approaching that of the jury.

responsibility for determining the law applicable in a criminal prosecution.[26] The trial judge was entitled to give the jury his view of the applicable law, but his statement was only his opinion. It was assumed that lay jurors had some knowledge of the law and, in some cases, it was even recognised that some of the jurors might have better knowledge of the relevant legal rules than the trial judge.[27] No doubt the prevalence of the belief in the declaratory theory of law made it easier to accept this rationale for a more active intervention by the jury in criminal trials. The comparative simplicity of the criminal law at that time was certainly another important factor,[28] as was the reaction, in post-Revolutionary America, to the heavy-handed efforts of Royal judges to dominate colonial juries, and the fact that many of the judges at the time were not very learned in the law.[29] This willingness of the courts to allow lay jurors to determine the law was qualified, however, in several important respects. First, some courts refused to recognise any such independent role for the jury when a matter of constitutional law was involved.[30] Secondly, and most important, the trial judge had the sole voice on questions involving the admissibility of evidence and the various procedural aspects of a trial.[31] This seeming inconsistency was the basis of some

[26] For a brief review of the legal history of 'jury nullification' as well as citation to some of the recent literature on the subject, see G. Christie, 'Lawful Departures from the Legal Rules: "Jury Nullification" and Legitimated Disobedience', 62 *Calif. L. Rev.* 1289, 1297-8 (1974). Much of the discussion contained in this section of my book has been adopted from that article.

[27] Fisher v. People, 23 Ill. 218, 230-1, (1860).

[28] Consider, for instance, the following statement from Justice Gray's dissent in Sparf v. United States, 156 U.S. 51, 173 (1895): 'The rules and principles of the criminal law are, for the most part, elementary and simple, and easily understood by jurors taken from the body of the people. As every citizen or subject is conclusivley presumed to know the law, and cannot set up his ignorance of it to excuse him from criminal responsibility for offending against it, a jury of his peers must be presumed to have equal knowledge, and, especially after being aided by the explanation and exposition of the law by counsel and court, to be capable of applying it to the facts as proved by the evidence before them'.

[29] See Howe, 'Justice as Judges of Criminal Law', 52 *Harv. L. Rev.* 582, 602-3, 615 (1939) (hereafter cited as Howe).

[30] Sparf v. United States, 156 U.S. 51, 164 (1895) (Gray, J., dissenting); cf. Howe, supra note 29, at 602-3, 615.

[31] Sparf v. United States 156, U.S. 51, 165-6, 171 (1895) (Gray, J., dissenting). In the first of these two references Justice Gray cites Chief Justice Marshall's statements in the Aaron Burr trial.

of the arguments used in the effort—ultimately largely successful—to restrict the scope of the jury's announced authority.[32]

Modern arguments for jury nullification, on the other hand, are not primarily based upon a feeling that the jury should be permitted to find the law. Indeed, to guard against the possibility that a jury expressly instructed on nullification might convict in the face of the law, it is generally argued by proponents of jury nullification that certain constitutional provisions—those concerning the procedural rights of the accused—are beyond the jury's power either to construe or to ignore.[33] Rather, the proponents of jury nullification are concerned with the right of the jury 'to refuse to apply the law, as it is given to them by the judge . . . if in good conscience they believe the defendant should be acquitted'.[34] The grounds for its refusal are openly recognised as being 'moral reasons'[35] and not a different view of the law. While the modern doctrine of jury nullification might in practice operate in much the same way as the older notion that the jury is the final arbiter of the law as well as the facts—a doctrine still ostensibly the law in three states[36]—it rests on a completely different conceptual basis. It thus receives only indirect support from the now largely overruled older cases. If the modern doctrine of jury nullification is to be adopted, it must be adopted on its own merits and not because it is required by the weight of ancient legal learning.

[32] Montee v. Commonwealth, 26 Ky. 132, 149-51 (1830); Commonwealth v. Anthes, 71 Mass. (5 Gray) 185, 220-1 (1957).

[33] Should the jury convict under these circumstances it 'ceases to act as the conscience of the community because it violates commitments to legal procedures and protections upheld as normative values by that community' and 'makes a mockery of the social commitment to a government of laws and not men'. Scheflin, 'Jury Nullification; The Right to Say No'. 45 *S. Cal. L. Rev.* 168, 214-15 (1972) (hereafter cited as Scheflin). See also id. at 210-11; Van Dyke, 'The Jury as a Political Institution', 16 *Catholic Lawyer* 224, 226-7 (1970) (first published in an abridged version under the same title in *The Center Magazine*, vol. 3, no. 2. Mar. 1970, at 174).

[34] Scheflin, supra note 33, at 169.

[35] Id. at 213.

[36] *Ga. Const* art. 1, § 2-201; *Ind. Const.* art 1, §19; *Md. Declaration of Rights*, art. 23, previously *Md. Const.* art. XV, §5. One must use the qualifying word 'ostensibly' because in Indiana it has been held *not* to be error to refuse to instruct the jury that it might 'disregard [the judge's instructions] altogether if you desire and to determine what the law of this case is for yourselves'. Beavers v. State, 236 Ind. 549, 554, 141 N.E.2d 118, 120 (1957). See also id. at 554-65, 141 N.E.2d at 120-5. In Georgia, the courts have gone further and actually instruct the jury that it is bound by the judge's instructions on the law. Hopkins v. State, 190 Ga. 180, 8 S.E.2d 633 (1940); Myers v.

If, as the Kadishes claim, the jury has the right to engage in justified rule departures, which is the nub of the jury nullification doctrine, what authority does the jury have and what authority should it have? The jury certainly has the power to acquit whom it will, and occasionally to convict as well. But is its authority that extensive? And what criteria should the jury use in excercising its admitted power? For the Kadishes, these criteria are found in the ultimate ends of our legal and political order. In this regard, as well as in others, they are departing from the line of argument advanced by most supporters of the doctrine of jury nullification, who urge that the jury be told that it may resort to purely moral considerations. For them, moral considerations are only relevant insofar as they are reflected in the ultimate ends of our legal and political order.[37] Their thesis is reminiscent of the old notion of the jury as the final judge of the law but with, of course, a profound difference. The jurors must accept the judge's interpretation of the *ordinary law*. The jurors' function, if they are to act legitimately when they acquit in the face of the judge's instructions, is to resort to a higher law—the 'deeper structure', of our law, to use the argot of structuralism—of which they are ultimately the interpreters. But it is difficult to identify these ultimate ends of our legal and political order, and even more difficult to decide what they might require in a particular case. Moreover, why should the articulation and ordering of these ends be the function of private citizens who are randomly selected and largely unable to assess the importance of consistency in applying the law in question? Should not this function be left to a popularly elected legislature?

The process of enunciating and applying these criteria seems fairly subjective. It might be helpful, therefore, to see how the jury might perform its interpositional role in some concrete cases, so that we can understand when it may be said to be acting legitimately and when illegitimately.

State, 151 Ga. 826, 108 S.E. 369 (1921); Edwards v. State, 53 Ga. 429, 433 (1874). In Maryland, where the jury is instructed that it may disagree with the trial judge, that freedom has long been restricted by refusing to let questions of constitutionality be argued to the jury *and* by making the trial judge the sole arbiter of questions of admissibility of evidence and competency of witnesses. For a recent reaffirmation see Hamilton v. State, 12 Md.App. 91, 97-8, 277 A.2d 460, 464 (1971), *aff'd*, 265 Md. 256, 288 A.2d 885 (1972).

[37] For a discussion as to how officials and others are to proceed when they perceive a conflict between the needs of the legal and social order and some particular legal provision, see *Discretion to Disobey* at 189-94.

The Kadishes discuss several types of recent cases where a jury legitimately might wish to exercise its interpositional role. They indicate that prosecutions of 'Vietnam War resisters and protesters' might be an appropriate occasion.[38] Another such occasion, albeit one in which they would not so act if they were jurors, would be 'a Southern jury that acquits a white segregationist of killing a civil rights worker, on the grounds that in the public interest carpetbag trouble-makers must be discouraged from venturing into their community, and that in any event the defendant's act was a political act that should not be punished as a common crime'.[39] A somewhat different case easily comes to mind, and I wonder how the Kadishes would have treated it. Defendant is being prosecuted for armed robbery and assault with a deadly weapon. On cross-examination, in an attempt to impeach the defendant's testimony, his prior convictions of serious crimes of violence are brought out. The case is a very close one. The judge lets the case go to the jury with proper instructions, because a reasonable jury could find the defendant guilty beyond a reasonable doubt. Several jurors, although believing that the defendant is guilty, are not convinced of his guilt beyond a reasonable doubt. Nevertheless they vote to convict because they believe it is in the public interest to remove defendant from society, and because they believe that, with the rise of crimes of violence in American society, conviction is necessary in order to deter others. Moreover, as already noted, these jurors are pretty sure that defendant is in fact guilty of the crime charged. Is this legitimate? If not, why not? Protecting society from violence is surely one of the ultimate ends of the legal system.

It might be argued, however, that the case I have posed should be distinguished from the two posed by the Kadishes, because the judge in my case would vacate the verdict if the facts were revealed to him. I am not sure the fact that the lack of absolute finality for the jury's determination is such a crucial point of distinction. After all, absolute finality of decision is not required before an official is said to have a recourse role. A prosecutor who refuses to prosecute can change his mind, and of course, if the statute of limitations has not run, his successor could decide to prosecute. Moreover, as a practical matter,

---

[38] Id. at 64; cf. id. at 8.
[39] Id. at 68.

proving the state of mind of the jurors would be extremely difficult, particularly since normally it is not considered proper to inquire into their mental processes; as a practical matter, their finding of guilty would be very nearly as final as a jury's finding of not guilty in the Vietnam War and Southern civil rights cases posed by the Kadishes. Accordingly, if the slight difference in finality is not enough to account for the conclusion that the jury is functioning 'illegitimately' in the case I have posed, what is? The fact that the jury has ignored the judge's instructions cannot be the distinguishing factor, because this has happened in all three cases. Indeed, that is why they are classed by the Kadishes as rule departures. The remaining possibility is that some ultimate end or rule of our legal order legitimates rule departures when they result in acquittal but not when they result in conviction. But how does the jury know this? The jury is never told about the legitimacy of rule departures, even in the few jurisdictions where it is supposedly the 'judge of the law'.

The Kadishes do examine the arguments for instructing the jury on its power to acquit a defendant in the face of the facts and the law, but they are too diffident of their own judgment to make any definite recommendations. While they have some sympathy for the argument that logic requires that the jury be told what it can do, they nonetheless are not prepared to urge that the present practice of not instructing the jury be changed.[40] They recognise the validity of the oft-expressed fear that if juries are expressly told that they can acquit in the face of the law and the facts, they will do it too often. To use their terminology, the 'surcharge' upon the juror's interpositional role might become too small. This notion of 'surcharge' is crucial to their argument;[41] it is the means they use to prevent their argument for justified rule departures from becoming a defence of anarchy. Roughly speaking, the essence of surcharge is that an official (or anyone else, for that matter) should behave in the manner in which the legal rules ostensibly prescribe unless, to use the Kadishes' term,

[40] Id. at 64-6; see id. at 59-63. In discussing this issue the Kadishes take note of the conclusion of the most exhaustive study ever undertaken of the jury system in the United States: 'Perhaps one reason why the jury exercises its very real power so sparingly is because it is officially told it has none.' H. Kalven & H. Zeisel, *The American Jury* 498 (1966), quoted in *Discretion to Disobey* at 65.

[41] See *Discretion to Disobey* at 65.

he has a 'damn good reason' not to.[42] The surcharge will be higher, they presume, and I am not prepared to disagree, if the jury is not expressly told it may acquit 'if it has a damn good reason'. The jury's sense of doing something arguably improper, by disregarding the judge's express instructions, will increase the surcharge.

I agree that the jury should not be told specifically that it may ignore the judge's instructions and acquit in the face of the law and the facts, but only because I do not agree that it is proper to speak of the jury's role as one that permits justified rule departures. I am not saying that if the jury does acquit against the law and the evidence it necessarily is acting illegitimately, I am saying merely that it is not engaging in legitimated interposition. It should be remembered that what the Kadishes term justified rule departures, of which legitimated interposition is one type, are those rule departures not merely permitted, but in a very real sense authorised by the legal system. It seems to me that if the legal system really does recognise justified rule departures by juries, then a defendant is entitled to have the jury instructed on that subject.[43] Otherwise, his fate depends upon whether the jury chosen to hear his case happens to be sufficiently cantankerous or tough-minded or imaginative to disregard what the judge tells them and look instead to the deeper structure of the legal system. I do not see how anything so chancy can be called legitimate; the stakes are too high to resort to a lottery.

But if the jury's acquittal in the face of the judge's instructions is not legitimate, what is it? Must it not then always be illegitimate? My own answer is, not necessarily. The legal order is not a closed system. The law need not command nor even authorise what it permits. If it did, every act done by an individual would have to be traced back to some precept or 'rule' of law; everything done by an individual would

---

[42] For a discussion of this point as it applies to the jury's role, see id. at 62.

[43] This is what makes me uncomfortable with Judge Leventhal's opinion for the court in United States v. Dougherty, 473 F.2d 1113 (D.C.Cir. 1972). Relying in part upon an earlier, law-review version of the Kadishes' theory of rule departures by juries, Judge Leventhal accepted the legitimacy of rule departures by juries but was apprehensive about 'the danger of removing the constraint provided by the announced rules'. Id. at 1135. This apparent inconsistency was powerfully exploited in Judge Bazelon's dissent. Id. at 1138. Judge Sobeloff's opinion for the court in United States v. Moylan, 417 F.2d 1002 (4th Cir. 1969). *cert. denied*, 397 U.S. 910 (1969), seems to provide a more satisfactory basis for refusing to instruct the jury on nullification. All Judge Sobeloff was prepared to do was to recognise the power of juries to bring in a general verdict of acquittal contrary to the law and the evidence. Id. at 1006.

become state action.[44] The power that juries have to ignore the judge's instructions is the price we pay, and I think should pay, to insulate the jury as much as we can from official pressure. It is like academic freedom. Under that principle, instructors cannot be prevented from teaching nonsense. Is this because it is legitimate to teach nonsense? Of course not. It is the price we pay to free teachers from the control of authority. If an instructor 'seeking truth' is in fact propagating nonsense, is he acting illegitimately? Again the answer is, not necessarily. The legal and moral universes are not always two-valued.

The question may be posed, however, why not legitimate the jury's interpositional role? That is, why not instruct the jurors that the law expressly authorises them to depart from the rules enunciated by the judge, but only if they have a 'damn good reason', or, to reinforce the point, a 'goddamn good reason'. A quick answer to this question and one consistent with the thesis of this book is that the potential variation in the application of the law would undermine the postulate of consistency which I have argued is the most important factor in legal decision-making. My reason for opposing such legitimation is, however, only partially dependent on a fear that juries might exercise their power too freely if it became an accepted part of the folklore. I also object to legitimation of the role because I believe it erodes the jury's sense of responsibility. To legitimate the jury's interpositional role is to declare that the law authorises, even requires, a jury to acquit if the jurors feel strongly enough about the matter. By acquitting, they are performing their civic function. I am against instructing the jury on its power to acquit in the face of the evidence and the judge's instructions because I believe that the jurors alone bear responsibility for acquitting in these circumstances, not the law which permits them to get away with doing so.[45] To ask whether they

---

[44] The underlying issue here illustrates one of the basic differences between the legal philosophies of Jeremy Bentham and his disciple, John Austin. For both men, laws were commands. The question arose: What happens when the legal system enforces the commands created by private power-holders, such as property owners? For Bentham, the sovereign not only *enforced* but by that very action *adopted* the commands of private power-holders. For Austin, the sovereign merely enforced the commands of private power-holders; it did not adopt them. His notion of a legal power was accordingly much less complex. I find Austin's view much more in accord with common experience. See G. Christie, *Jurisprudence* 598 & n. 222 (1973).

[45] Justice Baldwin's charge to a jury that it could disagree with his rulings on questions

have acted legitimately is to ask basically a moral question. The answer depends on your moral principles. It does not shock me that a legal system, by insulating an official from legal accountability, permits him to exercise his moral judgment in certain cases. But instructing the jury that it may acquit for good reason not only erodes its moral responsibility if it acquits—the point that has just been made—but also, without paradox, increases its moral responsibility if it convicts. For, if jurors have legal authority to engage in rule departures, they can no longer completely disavow responsibility for convictions by relying on a lack of authority to do otherwise; they are responsible as moral agents not only for the exercise of their authority to acquit for good reason, but also for their failure to exercise that authority. That is why the jurors must be told expressly what their authority is. I am opposed both to eroding their heavy moral responsibility for acquittals in the face of the evidence and the law and to increasing their moral responsibility for convictions. The appropriateness of conviction has already been passed upon by the legislature subject to the safeguard of proof beyond a reasonable doubt.[46]

If my argument is unpersuasive, however, if jury nullification must be considered 'legitimate', first, because it does occur and, secondly, because people are not prepared to say it should not occur—and I accept both premises although not the conclusion—then I submit that the only course is to try to articulate criteria the jury can use in disregarding the evidence and the judge's instructions. There must be some serious attempt to achieve consistency in the application of

---

of law, has not lost its significance, even though such instructions are no longer given in most jurisdictions; '[W]hen the law is settled by a court, there is more certainty than when done by a jury, it will be better known and more respected in public opinion. But if you are prepared to say that the law is different from what you have heard from us, you are in the exercise of a constitutional right to do so. We have only one other remark to make on this subject—by taking the law as given by the court you incur no moral responsibility; in making a rule of your own there may be some danger of a mistake.' United States v. Wilson 28 F.Cas. 699, 708 (No. 16,730) (C.C.E.D.Pa. 1830). Under the modern theory, the point is not so much that the jury may be mistaken in acquitting in the face of the judge's instructions, but that it has incurred the moral responsibility for its choice, for better or worse.

[46] Judge Bazelon has recognised that proponents of jury nullificatioon must indeed deal with the fact that the legislature has already expressed the conscience of the community. United States v. Doughterty, 473 F.2d 1113, 1140 n.5 (D.C.Cir. 1972) (Bazelon, J., dissenting).

the criminal law. Moreover the jurors must be told what their power is. 'Damn good reason' they must have, but more is required before the jury's exercise of its power is to be considered legitimate or legally authorised.

(ii) *Legitimated disobedience by private individuals*

I now turn to the question of justified rule departures by private citizens,[47] a phenomenon the Kadishes call 'legitimated disobedience'.[48] They point out that the notion of legitimated disobedience is required by the normal operation of the American legal system. In our federal system, how else can one explain the individual's undoubted right to refuse to obey state law that he claims to be contrary to paramount federal law. Many of the same considerations apply when the asserted conflict is between federal law and the provisions of the Constitution. Moreover, in the early days of the Republic, we retained the English practice of requiring an individual to violate a criminal statute in order to gain standing not only to challenge its validity but also to ascertain its scope. While there are now other ways to challenge criminal statutes, they are not always available and, at any rate, it is still usually possible to challenge the validity of a law by violating it. If the challenge is upheld, the violator is not punished—his disobedience is legitimated. If the challenge is not upheld, he loses his gamble and suffers the prescribed penalty. The severity of the penalty and the likelihood that his challenge will succeed are factors that determine the 'surcharge' an individual must pay in order to exercise his right to engage in justified rule departures.

But the most interesting instances of justified rule departures, or, if you will, legitimated disobedience by private citizens, involve the

[47] For the Kadishes' detailed discussion of this subject, see *Discretion to Disobey* at 95-140.

[48] Id. at 97-100. As will appear in the discussion in the text, the necessary conditions for legitimated disobedience are: 'First, the legal system must recognize what we shall call a legitimating norm, the applicability of which falls within the final authority of a legal official, usually but not necessarily a court of law, to determine. Second, the norm must have the effect, when found to apply, of relieving the citizen of the usual liability to punishment for disobedience. Third, the norm must function not as a qualification of the rule but as a justification for the citizen's disobeying the rule. And fourth, the citizen must make a colorable appeal to the norm as the justification for departing from the rule.' Id. at 99.

application of what the Kadishes call the 'norm of the lesser evil'.[49] The Kadishes use of this notion depends in large part on their earlier distinction between judicial discretion in the application of supposedly pre-existing rules of law and judicial power to depart from these rules.[50] Suppose, for example, that a statute makes it a crime to wound a person with a firearm. In a criminal prosecution, defendant argues that he should be exonerated because he was acting in self-defence. Is his appeal to the court directed at the process of applying the statute or is he asking the court to depart from the statute just as he himself apparently has departed from it? The Kadishes suggest that although many exceptions are read into statutes in the process of applying existing norms, some exceptions are created by departing from existing norms. This latter position requires the assumption that the meaning of a statute, or of a common-law 'rule', can be stated with sufficient clarity so that one may be fairly confident of exactly what is and is not encompassed within it. I have previously in this book and elsewhere argued that this assumption normally is not warranted.[51] The instances often cited to support the contention simply do not withstand detailed analysis.[52] Upon such analysis the prior rule normally appears less clearly defined and the asserted judicial modification less abrupt and certainly less unexpected than it appeared at first glance. But if and when, in circumstances like those in the hypothetical case, an accused appeals to a court to 'depart' from an established rule so as to legitimate his own departure from the rule, he is appealing to what the Kadishes call 'the norm of the lesser evil'. That is, he is claiming that it is a lesser evil to depart from the rule in the given circumstances than to enforce it. As in all instances of what the Kadishes call legitimated disobedience by private citizens, there are four requirements: (1) the legitimating norm, such as the norm of the lesser evil or the norm that constitutional law supersedes ordinary law, lies within the province of a judge or other official to apply; (2) it is asserted that the norm relieves the citizen of the obligations and punishments imposed by the rule

---

[49] Id. at 120.

[50] For the Kadishes' restatement of this point as it applies to legitimated disobedience, see id. at 97-100.

[51] See the discussion in Part 1, §§ 3 and 4, and Part II, §2, supra.

[52] See G. Christie, *The Model of Principles*, 1968 *Duke L.J.* 649, 660-7.

departed from; (3) the norm functions not as a qualification of the rule but as a justification for departing from the rule; and (4) the citizen is in fact appealing to the norm as the justification for his departure from the rule.[53]

The surcharge that the individual must pay in order to appeal to the norm of the lesser evil is determined again by the severity of the statutory penalty discounted by the likelihood of success.[54] The surcharge is the same whether the accused is appealing to the norm of the lesser evil or to the court's discretion in applying existing law or, for that matter, to the constitutional invalidity of a statute. What difference does it make, then, how the defendant's challenge is characterised? I suggest that the difference is this; If, in a significant number of decisions, defendants have succeeded in persuading the courts to depart from an existing 'rule' of criminal law by resort to the norm of the lesser evil, then this fact itself would be a strong argument in favour of institutionalising the defendant's right to present this defence. For example, the Model Penal Code permits the defence where 'the harm or evil [to himself or another] sought to be avoided by such conduct is greater than that sought to be prevented by the law defining the offense charged'.[55]

As the Kadishes point out, however, New York's recently enacted version of the lesser evil defence highlights some of its difficulties.[56] First, in order to confine the defence within narrow limits, it is made available to justify only 'conduct which would otherwise constitute an offence when . . . [s]uch conduct is necessary as an emergency measure to avoid an imminent public or private injury which is about to occur . . . through no fault of the actor . . .' Secondly, the injury sought to be avoided must be of 'such gravity that according to ordinary standards of intelligence and morality, the desirability and urgency of avoiding such injury clearly outweigh the desirability of avoiding the injury to be prevented . . .'. Thirdly, the necessity and justifiability of such conduct may not rest on considerations

---

[53] See note 48, supra.

[54] The situation is actually a little more complicated: the defendant's assessment of his chances of success will affect his decision to plead to a lesser offence. Hence, it becomes even more unfair to encourage the defendants to assert the defence when in reality they have little chance of success.

[55] *Model Penal Code* § 3.02(1) (a) (Proposed Official Draft, 1962).

[56] *N.Y. Penal Law* § 35.05 (McKinney 1967).

pertaining only to the morality or advisability of the statute, either in its general application or with respect to its application to a particular class of cases arising thereunder? The emphasis on emergency situations and the attempt to prevent or at least restrict appeals to purely moral principles obviously reflects a fear—in my opinion justified—that the lesser evil defence has certain anarchic tendencies which will be accentuated by permitting appeals to considerations that might be considered relatively subjective. Nevertheless this restrictive approach presents certain difficulties. By recognising the defence, the statute may encourage people to resort to it but at the same time its actual wording greatly diminishes the chances that a citizen's appeal to the defence will be successful. In this regard the broader provisions of the Model Penal Code or the following Illinois statute seem preferable:

Conduct which would otherwise be an offense is justifiable by reason of necessity if the accused was without blame in occasioning or developing the situation and reasonably believed such conduct was necessary to avoid a public or private injury greater than the injury which might reasonably result from his own conduct.[57]

But the vagueness of terminology in these provisions—even in the Model Penal Code version—can again make the defence a trap for the unwary. One might note that in one New York case an attempt was made to utilise the 'lesser evil' defence in a prosecution for crime committed during a prison riot. The defendant unsuccessfully argued that the conditions in 'The Tombs' were so appalling that only in this way could they be brought to the public's attention.[58]

The Kadishes argue that recognising the possibility of legitimated rule departures, of which the successful appeal to the norm of the lesser evil is one instance, provides a certain flexibility which enables the legal system to respond to the disparity between the rule's

---

[57] *Ill.Stat.Ann* ch. 38, § 7-13 (1961). In People v. Dalton, 7 Ill.App.3d 442, 287 N.E.2d 548 (1972), the court declared: 'It is the opinion of the court that the type of necessity contemplated as a defense to a crime under ˄this statute] is not the emergency repair of a water heater on a Sunday afternoon at a Nike site where some 40 other employees are employed.' id. at 444, 287 N.E.2d at 550-1. The offence charged was driving with a revoked licence. The defendant was also convicted of driving while intoxicated.

[58] People v. Brown, 70 Misc.2d 224, 333 N.Y.S.2d 342 (1972).

demand and the demand of the moment'.[59] In this way, '[r]ule
departures become not simply extralegal actions of individuals that
compensate for the inadequacy of law, but sometimes, when
legitimated, a part of the legal framework itself by which rule
ordering is made adaptive to unforeseen circumstances, change, and
conflict'.[60] These are admirable goals but I wonder if the courts can
achieve them through the technique of legitimisation. For instance,
the device of prosecutorial discretion can achieve some of the same
results as appeal to the norm of lesser evil, although perhaps on a
more ad hoc basis. If, however, the courts are to be permitted to hear
appeals to the norm of the lesser evil, I think that fairness to the
defendant requires that the vagueness of the norm be taken into
account in assessing the penalty to be imposed on him if he is
unsuccessful, even though a reduced penalty will itself encourage
more rule departures by private citizens. The various ways in which
the burden of the surcharge for unsuccessful defendants can be eased
are discussed by the Kadishes and need not be entered into here.[61]
Whether society should recognise openly and encourage resort to the
norm of the lesser evil depends in part on how much energy society
can afford to devote to conceptual challenges to the legal structure. It
also depends in part on the competence of the courts to determine the
'evils' that should be avoided and to compate them with the evils
sought to be prevented by the criminal law, in areas so diverse as lit-
tering, speeding, and smoking marijuana. Would the courts be forced
to construct some common morality for our society in order to assess
and compare these evils? That prospect makes me somewhat
uncomfortable. Finally, if for some the norm of the lesser evil seems
desirable because of dissatisfaction with government policy towards
Vietnam, does it still seem as desirable after Watergate?[62] Is a Daniel
Ellsberg more justified in resorting to it than an Egil Krogh and,
more to the point, is this for a court to determine?

---

[59] *Discretion to Disobey* at 146.

[60] Id.

[61] Id. at 153-83.

[62] Cf. A Bickel, 'Watergate and the Legal Order', *Commentary*, vol. 57, no. 1, Jan.
1974, at 19.

(iii) *Conclusion*

While I believe I have shown why law ultimately depends on authority, claims of authority, if they are to be accepted, must be based upon law to the fullest extent possible. Furthermore, the actual exercise of authority must likewise, and for the same reasons, be based upon law as much as it possibly can. To the extent that authority must exercise a discretion that is not legally circumscribed, common sense dictates that authority be politically accountable. For, if law ultimately rests upon authority, authority itself, in the long run, rests upon consent. The danger incurred from granting a large number of people, whether they be officials or private citizens, substantial authority to disregard the law is thus twofold: first, it destroys the consistency in legal decision-making that is central to the core notion of law; and secondly, it grants this power to a whole host of people, bureaucrats and nameless private citizens, such as jurors or criminal defendants raising the lesser-evil defence, who are not politically accountable. The likely result of such a course of action is to destroy much of the social cement that accounts for the common feeling that law is somehow binding; the common feeling that authority is authority because it is more than just power but, rather, that authority is authority because it is based upon the claim of a right to command that is recognised by those to whom the commands are addressed.

3. *On the binding nature of law and the origins of authority*

Why is it that some people trust others to issue them authoritative pronouncements that will preserve and enhance the public good? This is a complex question of human psychology to which no one can claim to be able to give a complete answer. The question is another way of asking, how can one account for the 'binding' quality of law? Certainly, the majority of people in most modern western societies do not obey the law because of any conscious immediate fear of the sanctions that might be imposed upon them by those exercising political authority in the society or because of any specific calculation of self interest. Most people generally obey the law because they feel it is right for them to do so. Why do they have this feeling? How does it originate?

Perhaps no group of legal philosophers has given as much thought to these questions as has the group of scholars known as the 'Scandinavian legal realists'. The germinal figure among this group of thinkers was Axel Hagerstrom. In much of nineteenth-century German philosophy, the binding nature of law was founded on the will of the legislator. This, of course, was similar to the view taken by many of the writers in the natural-law tradition. The only difference, in this respect, was a shift in the nature of the legislator. Under these so-called 'will theories', law was binding because it expressed the will of someone who ought to be obeyed. This someone, in turn ought to be obeyed because he was God and created us, or because God delegated authority to him, or because we agreed to obey him, or etc. Hagerstrom set out with a passion to destroy the will theories of the binding nature of law.[63] At least in modern Europe, it was impossible to identify anyone whose will the law was supposed to express. Moreover, he pointed out, certain collective bodies like parliaments have no wills. At the same time to talk about an enactment of a parliament as an expression of the wills of the invidual legislators was specious. Leaving aside the question of those legislators who voted against the legislation in question, how does one deal with the problem that most of the legislators voting on a bill may never have read it? And, even if they had read it, they might not all have ascribed the same meaning to what they had read. Notions like the will of the state he dismissed as meaningless. Only individuals have wills and therefore, if the will of the state is to be anything but a figurative abstraction, it can only refer to the wills of certain power-holders. We are accordingly back where we started, as in the example about parliaments. How do the 'wills' of these power-holders find expression in what we call the law? Finally, even if we lived in a society with an absolute monarch we would be confronted with difficulties in ascribing the binding nature of law to the will of the sovereign. Hagerstrom explains these difficulties and summarises his general conclusions about the unsatisfactory nature of the 'will-theories', as follows:

If the will-theory concerning positive law regards the latter as a system of imperatives or declarations of intention on the part of the *legal* power, it is involved in a circle. If a 'general will' is assumed, that will must be supposed to be either the will of all or a superindividual will. On the former alternative

---

[63] A. Hagerstrom, *Inquiries into the Nature of Law and Morals* 1-55, 74-105 (C. Broad transl. 1953) (hereafter *Inquiries*). See also id. at 56-74, 105-26.

the theory comes into conflict with facts; on the latter it leads to absurdities. If the basis of the theory is alleged to be *the will of the holder or holders of de facto power* in a society, the difficulty arises that the law itself is the foundation and the limit of that *de facto* power. If, finally, the *power actually enforcing the law* (the 'state-will') is taken as starting-point, we are faced with the impossibility of assigning this to an actual will. But this exhausts the possible forms of the theory.[64]

If the binding quality of law cannot be explained by stating that law is the expression of the will—the command—of someone who ought to be obeyed, neither can it be explained, asserts Hagerstrom, '(a) by any valuation of the action from the point of view of its being necessary in order to avoid unpleasantness, or (b) by reference to objective values which stand over and above the individual'.[65] He therefore concludes 'it must be explained in some other way', and, in this light goes on to assert:

It would seem that there remains only one possible form of explanation, viz., that we are here concerned with an impulse towards a certain action, which is felt as compulsive just because what is here determinative is not the subject's free valuation, but something which is, in that respect, external to him. The impulse imposes itself on us, no matter what evaluatory attitude we may take towards the action. That is to say, the feeling of duty is a conative feeling, and, to put it more definitely, a feeling of being driven to act in a certain way. Undoubtedly a free valuation of the action is not the determining factor in this feeling.[66]

The conative impulse, as this quotation suggests, is the impulse to obedience engendered by a directive, such as a command, merely by the imperative form of expression. 'Duck!' and 'Look out!' are perhaps the clearest examples of expressions which create in the hearer a conative impulse. Hagerstrom recognises that the conative impulse is not enough to explain the binding quality of law which requires the notion of 'duty'. The problem is how do we move from the 'I must' of the recipient of a command to the 'I am under an obligation to' of the person subject to a duty? In other words, how does what we 'must do' become a 'duty'?[67] Hagerstrom suggests that the answer lies in the hierarchical and structured form of the legal

[64] *Inquiries* at 55.

[65] *Inquiries* at 130.

[66] Ibid.

[67] *Inquiries* at 132ff.

system with its aggregate of individual imperatives and which, with its monopolisation of organised force, completely overwhelms the individual.[68] He suggests that 'conscience' is similarly created in the individual.[69] In both cases the force of custom and habit are important conditioning factors, particularly in primitive societies.

These are themes upon which Karl Olivecrona has elaborated. Olivecrona's main discussion revolves around law considered as a system of 'independent imperatives'. In the first edition of *Law as Fact* Olivecrona described law as chiefly consisting of rules about force.[70] But the influence of force on the individual is largely indirect; so is the role of fear.[71] Olivecrona suggested that the self-binding nature of law arises from the individual's internalising a system of norms as a means of making it possible for himself to live in society without fear.[72] As a small child he confronts his family environment and adjusts to it in this way. As he grows up, the larger society seems as overwhelming, as structured, and as all powerful as his family milieu and the power of his parents seemed to be when he was a child. He adjusts to the situation in the same way. As a mature adult he would, of course, reject indignantly the notion that he obeys the law because of a fear of the sanction. He obeys because he ought to. But Olivecrona suggests that if law enforcement continually broke down before his eyes, the individual would gradually cease to internalise the norms of the legal system.[73] H. L. A. Hart makes the same sort of suggestion about the indispensability of force in an analysis of the legal system.[74] Without it, the internalisation of the legal system would not receive the periodic reinforcement that it needs in order to

[68] Id. at 143-70, 192-8. See also id. at 127-43, 170-92.

[69] *Inquiries* at 157-8.

[70] K. Olivecrona, *Law as Fact* 134-6 (1939) (hereafter LF(I).

[71] LF(I) 140-50.

[72] LF(I) at 143-50. For a more extended discussion of the thesis that a sense of justice and an awareness of legal institutions arises out of childhood anxieties, see Bienenfeld, 'Prolegomena to a Psychoanalysis of Law and Justice', 53 *Calif. L. Rev.* 957 (Pt. I), 1254 (Pt. II) (1965). Bienenfeld suggests that the primordial anxiety from which the individual's sense of obligation arises is the child's fear of being abandoned. Id. at 1254. There is a bibliography at the end of this lengthy—indeed book-length—study. Id. at 1332-6. For an important study of the general subject of 'law and psychology', see A. Ehrenzweig, *Psychoanalytic Jurisprudence* (1971).

[73] LF(I) at 136-43, 168-86.

[74] *Concept of Law* at 193-5. See also id. 211-15.

survive. And, without that internalisation, law simply becomes force writ large. People would then obey because they must, not because they want to. Olivecrona suggests, contrary to the popular supposition, that, although law must seem reasonable to most people, law probably has a greater influence on morality than morality has on the law.[75]

In the second edition of *Law as Fact*, Olivecrona devotes a substantial amount of space to discussing what he calls the 'imperantum', namely, that part of a legal norm which conveys 'the impression that the behaviour in question shall be observed'.[76] The aspect of a norm that identifies the behaviour in question he calls the 'ideatum'.[77] He elaborates his definition of the *imperantum* as follows:

Rules of enacted law are independent imperatives that have passed through a series of formal acts. The *imperantum* is the whole setting in which the enactment takes place: The working constitution, the organisation functioning according to its rules, the familiar designations of parliamentary bodies and state officials, etc. Once a constitution has been firmly established, the people respond automatically by accepting as binding the texts proclaimed as laws through the act of promulgation. Thanks to this attitude among the addressees the *imperantum* becomes effective.[78]

The *imperantum* 'is aimed at the volitional side of the recipient's mind, not at the intellectual side'.[79] Ritual and language can be very important, especially among primitive peoples. Olivecrona refers to the Scandinavian experience:

In my own country it is recorded in the oldest sources that the law was authoritatively preserved in the memory of wise men ('men of young memory') before the time that it was written down. The 'lawman' (*lagman*) had to recite the law at the *ting*, the assembly of free men. The text was rhythmical and alliterative, which made it impressive (the language was beautiful) and easily remembered. Probably the men acclaimed the recitation by the clang of arms. This procedure corresponded to the modern act of promulgation, though it had often to be repeated.[80]

---

[75] LF(I) at 150-68.

[76] K. Olivecrona, *Law as Fact* 126-7 (2d ed. 1971) (hereafer LF(II). Despite the common name these are really two different books.

[77] LF(II) at 126.

[78] LF(II) at 130.

[79] LF(II) at 128.

[80] LF(II) at 131.

Since the language in which legal directives are couched and promulgated are an important part of the *imperantum*, Olivecrona is particularly concerned with the ritual use of words even in modern law.

The work of the Scandinavian legal realists is rich with possibilities. Hagerstrom's notion of the 'conative impulse' as underlying the sense of legal obligation is intriguing. It is, however, a difficult concept because most of the law is neither imperative in form nor, in the modern welfare state with its emphasis on the organisation of large-scale social activity, predominantly imperative in effect. Nevertheless, building upon the work of the Scandinavian legal realists we can certainly conclude that the perceived consistency of the authoritative pronouncements issued by those who actually have authority will be a major factor in inculcating a sense of security and trust and in strengthening authority. Consistency in the application of the enormous force available to the public authority of the modern nation state will help individuals to internalise the standards set forth by public officials. Such internalisation of the standards promulgated and enforced by public authority permits the individual to escape from the anxiety which he might otherwise feel as some minute and weak individual in the vast sea of humanity. Acceptance of the publicly proclaimed standards, however, also provides the individual with the means of engaging in purposive activity that can satisfy his wants and aspirations. It makes authority more beneficial to him.

Furthermore, while law, and particularly the vast coercive machinery at the disposal of legal authorities, only serves to accentuate the pathetic weakness of the lone individual, its vast and complex structure seems to give the individual something to which he can cling with certainty and assurance. In an increasingly mobile and secular society, in which other social institutions such as the family and the Church have seen their authority seriously eroded, the legal order has become the principal means for satisfying our emotional need for order. The law and its machinery provide the living embodiment of tradition. By professing allegiance to the law and particularly its institutions people are enabled to reaffirm their belief that the social universe can be comprehended in a rational manner. However iconoclastic an individual may perceive himself to be, the fact that his father found security and comfort in certain institutional arrangements will make those arrangements a source of security to him too, even if ultimately he feels he must reject those arrangements. The solemnity and the ritual assciated with the law and its machinery will enhance this aura of structural security.[81] Although I have only been able briefly to touch on these complex and difficult matters, I believe that these are the factors that ultimately account for the human willingness to accept the right of others to issue authoritative pronouncements to them. It is on all these phenomena, rather than on the 'logic of the law', that the study of how the sense of the appropriateness of authority is inculcated in people must focus.

4. *A summary statement of the argument of this book*

(i) The theory of norms presupposes a degree of unity, of completeness, of purposiveness and central direction to law that is incompatible with the complexity of society and its legal system. Our law, rather, has largely grown haphazardly and by accretion. As Hayek has pointed out,[82] modern society is largely a spontaneous order. It was not generated from any one source like a social contract or the will of some identifiable person or persons. Our present social structure was generated by the often conflicting actions of countless individual attempts to adjust to the circumstances of human existence. There is no mind that can comprehend it in its entirety and impose a conceptual unity upon it. Our law mirrors our society.

(ii) The notion of normative consistency now espoused by Dworkin as the unifying force to legal decision-making is likewise chimerical. The values underlying modern society are too diverse, often inconsistent and incomplete, to permit any such theory to be capable of application in the real world.

(iii) To organise our experiences we obviously engage in a process of abstraction and organise our experiences in the form of simplified propositions or so-called 'rules of law'. But the intellectual tools we use to organise our experiences are not the equivalent of the real world with its inordinate complexity and mass of particulars. Thinking about law is one thing—it can be organised and rationalised and reorganised—the law as a concrete phenomenon is another thing.

[81] I have discussed the thought pursued in this paragraph at greater length in G. Christie, 'Rhetoric, Consistency, and Human Progress, Legal or Otherwise', 26 *Cath. U.L. Rev.* 73 (1976).

[82] F. Hayek, *Law, Legislation and Liberty: Vol. 1, Rules and Order* (1973).

(iv) The fact that law does not really consist of a set of norms in any rigorous sense does not mean that law does not have normative force, or that it is not capable of being the focus of emotional attachment and of guiding human activity.

(v) The mass of legal materials—which are accepted as authoritative bases of legal decision-making—together with our commitment to consistency normally provide a good measure of predictability to legal decision-making. They help generate the social expectations which no governmental decision-making procedure can ignore.

(vi) The essence of law is that it provides a system of authoritative decision-making to resolve social disputes. It ultimately depends on our acceptance of the authority of certain people to serve in the role of decision-makers. The establishment and organisation of this authoritative decision-making machinery is complex and depends greatly on historic and psychological factors.

Table of Cases

Index